Restoring the Balance

Restoring the Balance:

Using the Qur'an and the Sunnah to Guide a Return to the Prophet's Islam

By

John Andrew Morrow

Foreword by Barbara Castleton

Cambridge
Scholars
Publishing

Restoring the Balance:
Using the Qur'an and the Sunnah to Guide a Return to the Prophet's Islam

By John Andrew Morrow

This book first published 2016

Cambridge Scholars Publishing

Lady Stephenson Library, Newcastle upon Tyne, NE6 2PA, UK

British Library Cataloguing in Publication Data
A catalogue record for this book is available from the British Library

Copyright © 2016 by John Andrew Morrow

All rights for this book reserved. No part of this book may be reproduced, stored in a retrieval system, or transmitted, in any form or by any means, electronic, mechanical, photocopying, recording or otherwise, without the prior permission of the copyright owner.

ISBN (10): 1-4438-9014-6
ISBN (13): 978-1-4438-9014-4

I am a stranger in Your country
And lonely among Your worshippers:
This is the substance of my complaint.

—Rabi'ah al-Adawiyyah

TABLE OF CONTENTS

Foreword xi
Barbara Castleton

Preface xvi

Chapter One 1
Islam and Extraterrestrials

Chapter Two 5
Racism in the Shiite Seminary

Chapter Three 7
Concerning the Color of Adam, the Prophets, and the Imams

Chapter Four 26
Selecting a Source of Emulation

Chapter Five 30
The Barbarity of Blood-Letting

Chapter Six 47
You da Bomb! The Sheer Stupidity of Suicide Bombing

Chapter Seven 48
The Obligation of English

Chapter Eight 51
Sell-Out Scholars: The Uncle Tom Ulama

Chapter Nine 53
Shiism in China

Chapter Ten 57
Syrian-Lebanese Settlers in the Dakotas

Chapter Eleven 62
Stylistic Analysis of Prophetic Arabic

Chapter Twelve 64
Advances in Arabic Pedagogy

Chapter Thirteen 66
Bye, Bye Burstad and *Ahlan* Abboud!

Chapter Fourteen 67
Who Speaks Arabic?

Chapter Fifteen 68
Monotheistic Indians of the Americas

Chapter Sixteen 69
The Path of Precaution: *Fiqh* for the 21st Century

Chapter Seventeen 71
Will the Real Sunnis Please Stand Up?

Chapter Eighteen 74
Terrible Translations: Weakening Islam from Within

Chapter Nineteen 75
Universal Islam: The Faith of the Future

Chapter Twenty 77
The Nation of Islam is not Islamic

Chapter Twenty-One 82
Talk to the People in the Language of the People

Chapter Twenty-Two 86
Tahrif: The Problem of Pious Lies

Chapter Twenty-Three 88
Where Work Needs to be Done

Chapter Twenty-Four 92
Freedom of Expression in Islam

Chapter Twenty-Five 95
To Reform or to Deform?

Chapter Twenty-Six 97
The Misguided and the Madrasa

Chapter Twenty-Seven 100
The Muhammadan Covenants: A Revolutionary Revelation

Chapter Twenty-Eight 102
How Has a Religion of Beauty Been Presented as Ugly by ISIL?

Chapter Twenty-Nine 104
The State of Our Ummah

Chapter Thirty 114
The Roots of Takfirism: How to Confront the *Fitnah* of Takfirism

Chapter Thirty-One 117
Muhammad's Legacy: The Covenants of the Messenger of Allah

Chapter Thirty-Two 122
ISIS versus Islam: What would the Prophet Muhammad Do?

Chapter Thirty-Three 136
Early Christian-Muslim Encounters

Chapter Thirty-Four 145
Can We Truly Know Muhammad?

Chapter Thirty-Five 151
The Covenants of the Holy Prophet

Chapter Thirty-Six 155
Nightmares in Takfiristan: A Cautionary Tale

Chapter Thirty-Seven 190
Hope?

Appendix 1: The Covenants Initiative 195

Appendix 2: The Genocide Initiative 197

Appendix 3: Edict against ISIS 199

Appendix 4: What Should Muslims Say to Donald Trump? 203

Permissions 216

Index 217

Foreword

By Barbara Castleton

While this volume is certainly intended for an audience of scholars and Muslims of both Shiite and Sunni persuasions, it has topics that will inform the curious readers' general understanding of Islam. It is successful in this last motivation in that the short informative articles consist of subjects close to Muslim experience and concerns. Perhaps Dr. Morrow was channeling a weekly "Everything You Wanted to Know…" column as he constructed this body of opinion, advice, and scholarly rebuttal.

A greater call here, though, is for Muslims to look mindfully at their belief system, observe how the intent of Qur'anic instruction, the wisdom of the hadith literature, and the preaching of early religious and spiritual leaders may have been bent, distorted, or diametrically altered to suit a political or other agenda. Included, as well, are logical and well-documented statements on how modern life and scientific advances are in accord with the basic teachings of Islam.

It was not whimsy, I think, that led Morrow to begin this volume with a discussion of extraterrestrials. Whether prodded by recent advances in astronomy, astrophysics, or the waning years of NASA, religions with ages-old doctrines are trying to pick their way through the seeming mine field of the divine versus Dr. Who. This doctor, using quotes from the Qur'an and an elegantly decipherable analysis, attempts to dispel the paradox and pave the way, perhaps, for a revival of science in the broader Islamic Ummah or Community.

Of riveting interest further on is the monograph on the topic of race in relation to Jesus, Muhammad, and a variety of other towers of religious focus. The issue of Allah himself is not widely bruited about given that those who have read the Qur'an carefully realize that if you are seeking a form for Allah, that is not Allah; if you are trying to ascribe a coloration or shape to Allah, that is not Allah either; and if you are attempting to identify, quantify, or design Him, you will miss the mark because Allah is beyond the scope of human language, perception, or conception. That being the case, some clerics, out of their zeal to enhance their own membership in a certain racial group, are trying to recruit as equal members, Jesus, Adam, and others.

The irony of this campaign is touched by a regrettable poignancy as well since an essential aspect of Islam, one lauded by even its critics, is the undeniable diversity and equality among believers. America's own Malcolm X was transformed during his pilgrimage to Mecca, where he ate, slept, befriended and was befriended by people of every color, national background, political affiliation, and ethnicity. Dr. Morrow reiterates that color or race is a non-issue for Muslims and to attempt to introduce it by assigning race to revered historical figures is to taint its very precepts.

Having lived in Kuwait for many years, I took for granted that the extreme expressions of devotion, such as self-flagellation, were, if not obligatory on the occasion of Ashura, at least a legitimate declaration of piety. Morrow dispels that notion, as he does with many other widely accepted ideas about the roots and practice of Islam, in an essay provocatively called "The Barbarity of Blood-Letting." Just as WMDs somehow wormed their way into our standard of "what is true" before the war in Iraq, so too has the habit of causing injury to self when honoring Imam Husayn taken on a legitimacy that has no grounding in Islam whatsoever, according to Morrow and respected experts, as well as Qur'anic sources. The discussion makes very clear how problematic it is to dissuade a vested population from retaining a false, but long held belief, or from performing a customary practice, however contraindicated it may be by the facts or doctrines. It is notable that, when explaining the background or current status of such issues, Dr. Morrow details respected religious clerics, listing the Ayatullahs like a mantra of veracity. As a non-Muslim, and one who practices a laity-based religion, this repertoire of expert commentators is fascinating.

In the section on "Shiism in China" we learn that 20-100 million people in that nation are Muslim. Yet, there is an unknown factor of 80 million people in between the two statistics. Can 80 million people be lost or unaccounted for? Not in America to be sure. We are driven here by numbers and verifiable data. And although we all know that they can lie, demographic statistics here have yet to lose 80 million people. To be sure, in a country of nearly 2 billion people, 80 million is a relatively small number, but I was interested to read Morrow's account of their background and current situation. He does not offer a solution to the distinction between the two possible population levels of Muslims in China, but his explanation of the history and recent circumstances hints at a level of suppression that could be reflected in that numerical gap.

In the chapter on "Syrian-Lebanese Settlers in the Dakotas," we trace the immigration patterns, contributions, and influence of Arabs, generally from the Levant, on the history of North and South Dakota. The refrain of ignorance--"why doesn't anyone know this?"--is one which rings a familiar, and, as Morrow says, ethnocentric chime. The concept of forefathers, of ancestors who laid a path we continue to follow, orbits almost exclusively around the English and western Europeans. Yet, the fact that these settlers from Syria and Lebanon are not well remembered says something for both their ability to "blend in" and the local community's acceptance of them over time.

The discussion of veracity and authentication in "The Stylistic Analysis of Prophetic Arabic" deals with the "was told to" tradition in relation to the teachings of the Prophet Muhammad. The Christian Bible, in Matthew, Genesis, the Chronicles, and others, contains a variety of "begat" chains as a demonstration of continuity and blood heritage. The words of the Prophet Muhammad, in order to be considered reliable, must likewise have a traceable lineage. Although the Qur'an is the ultimate source of information on Islam, the hadith, or teachings of the Prophet, are powerful sources for understanding as well. Thus, their legitimacy needs to be verified. The new field of forensic linguistics, which can analyze phrases and passages based on a person's unique idiolect, is just one of the strategies Islamic scholars can use.

Further on, in Chapter 17--"Will the Real Sunnis Please Stand Up?" -- Dr. Morrow points to legitimacy of another kind, but one with threads throughout the book. "Real," meaning genuine, authentic, and true, among other synonyms, is at the heart of every argument about this versus that in the realm of religion. When a person chooses a religion--his or her connection to the infinite, the divine, or merely the connection between humans and everything else--it is natural to want that ideology to be verifiable; namely, to be an accurate expression of the original teachings.

Attracted to Islam for reasons both personal and intellectual, Morrow first came to understand the Qur'an and the teachings of the Prophet Muhammad on his own. It was only after that he was well-versed in the primary sources of Islam that he began to look for the group that best expressed those teachings. He describes with some chagrin his early associations with Muslims who claimed to be Sunni but whose attitudes and practices mirrored nothing so much as ignorance and intolerance. In time, he found a more accepting home among traditional Sunni, Shiite and Sufi Muslims, who better reflected the Islam of the Prophet versus, as he would say, the Saudi princes. The so-called Sunnis he encountered early on were in reality Salafi, Wahhabi, and Takfiri extremists and fundamentalists. Ironically, it was the Shiites and the Sufis who taught him the true meaning of the Sunnah. In fact, it would take him years to actually come across bona fide Sunnis, namely, true, traditional Muslims who rejected extremism, essentialism, radical Islamism, sectarianism, and Takfirism. Today, as always, Dr. Morrow remains a proponent and practitioner of traditional Islam who accepts the Muslim faith in its totality and who analyzes any issue from a myriad of traditions: Sunni, Shii, and Sufi, among others.

Unfortunately, I fear his paean to rationality with regard to "true teachings" will be lost in a chorus of similar tunes. And yet, it was heartening to read in the chapters that follow how the author observed, analyzed, and reached his own conclusions about the different sects in Islam and how there are those who would classify themselves in one way and take action and practice in another. Perhaps the lesson here is to not only "question authority," but also to hold that authority to the principles it professes to espouse. Morrow's goal seems to be to return Islam to its roots in unification, acceptance, and tolerance by erasing the contrived barriers between sects and the demonization of one group for another within Islam itself.

Through this set of essays, Dr. Morrow moves from the position of castigator, a Dr. No if you will, to that of messenger, a Dr. Know. This second distinction is evident in the study on the Nation of Islam, Chapter 20. In my own experience, I have found many international Muslims seemingly unaware of the exact nature of the Nation of Islam's doctrine. They relate the Nation of Islam to Malcolm X, who was one of its early leaders and teachers, and that is where their knowledge and understanding stops. They do not know that those of the Nation pay tribute to a newly minted prophet, one who appeared in the 20th century, a manifestation in clear violation of the *shahadah*, the testimony of faith, with which every Muslim declares submission and allegiance, "There is no god but God, and Muhammad is His Messenger." From the 1930s on, Elijah Muhammad portrayed himself as the final messenger of Islam and spun a new web of ideology that may have had its roots in Islam, but which diverged so drastically that it raised another in the place of the Prophet Muhammad. Global Muslims seem so overjoyed to hear of the spread of their religion that they do not question the fine print in this nouveau spiritual contract.

In chapter 26, "The Misguided and the Madrasa," Morrow cries out from his teacher/scholar heart in setting the record straight about the function and purpose of madrasas or Islamic schools. In literature easily accessible, we can find ample evidence that one of the reasons for European colonial powers to close or prohibit madrasas was because they were so democratic and because they provided a valuable education to not only aristocratic children but the offspring of the masses as well. They were not the first, nor, alas, the last, to feel that an educated populace was a dangerous thing.

The final chapters are particularly poignant. In "The State of Our Ummah," Morrow provides a sobering analysis of the crisis of Islam while in subsequent chapters he champions the Covenants of the Prophet as an essential tool in intrafaith and interfaith relations. In Chapter 36, "Nightmares in Takfiristan," he relates some of the hilarious but also heart-rending experiences he endured after he embraced Islam. The last chapter recounts Morrow's cautious return to the Muslim community after decades of exile. Although titled "Hope" it ends with a question mark, suggesting that Morrow remains wary and worried about the future of the Muslim Ummah or Community.

Merging the conceptual with the practical, the work concludes with four appendices: The Covenants Initiative, which calls upon Muslims to abide by the Covenants of the Messenger of Allah; the Genocide Initiative, which seeks to hold Takfiri terrorists accountable for the atrocities they commit; and the Edict against ISIS which delegitimizes violent extremists by placing them outside the fold of orthodox Islam. The final appendix, "What Should Muslims Say to Donald Trump?" challenges the propaganda and proposals made by Islamophobes and calls upon all Muslims to renew their pledge of allegiance to the Prophet Muhammad.

In sum, this is a book of passionate pleas to reason, and it raises ideas that are at once unpopular and urgent. Dr. Morrow's own teachers would no doubt be much pleased.

Preface

For many decades, I have devoted myself to the jihad or sacred struggle of the pen in the firm belief that the ink of a scholar is more precious than the blood of a martyr. This does not suggest that I view myself as a living martyr or intellectual warrior: it simply means that I made a conscious choice to pick the pen over the pistol, a decision that I wish more misguided "Muslim" militants would make.

If my journalism is directed towards students and intellectuals, my peer-reviewed articles and books are aimed at scholars and academics. Unlike my previous books, which were written in dialogue with specialists, this work is aimed at a much broader audience that consists of both educators and educated readers. The motto, which I have observed in most instances, has been "short and sweet." As such, I have provided over thirty opinion pieces on a wide range of topics. In order for this book to be more readable, I have kept my style and vocabulary as accessible and concise as possible and limited most entries to two to three pages. For the sake of variety, however, I have included some lengthier and more detailed studies for readers who seek greater depth.

Following standard journalistic conventions, I have excluded specific details concerning citations as well as burdensome bibliographical references. The lay-person does not require detailed references and any expert in the field can easily identify and locate the sources of my citations. The lack of bibliographical information does not mean that I do not acknowledge my sources. I do so indicating sources in brackets after citations. I simply do not include page numbers or a separate bibliography. For Qur'anic citations, I always indicate chapter and verse. For books of prophetic traditions, I merely mention the source, such as Bukhari, Muslim or Majlisi, all of which are easily accessible in digital format.

Besides citing the source of quotations, I also make every attempt to distinguish my voice and opinions from those of others. I treat history and science as facts that do not require references. This should never be construed as an attempt on my part to pass off the ideas and works of others as my own. While authors own their original ideas, findings, and the precise language in which they express them, they do not own information. Knowledge is public property. Whether it was researching race and genetics or the flagellations of Ashura, I drew upon numerous sources, and synthesized the facts they contained. For the latter, I am indebted to the works of Yitzhak Nakash, Volker Adam, and Tatbir.org which are repositories of information on the history and evolution of the sanguinary side of Muharram mourning rituals.

During these hectic times, in which centuries have become decades, decades have become years, years have become months, months have become weeks, weeks have become days, days have become hours, hours have become minutes, and minutes have become seconds, it has become decidedly more difficult for readers to find the time to study scholarly monographs. It is with this realization in mind that I have authored this less formal work which I hope will appeal to youth, of both high school and university age, educated working adults, as well as scholars of the field who seek food for thought before calling it quits for the night.

JAM

Chapter One

Islam and Extraterrestrials

"Praise be to Allah, the Lord of the Worlds," commences the first chapter of the Holy Qur'an. Rather than refer to the world in singular, Almighty Allah refers to "worlds," plural, on 46 different occasions. Although the word in question refers to different physical realms of existence on our planet, applying collectively to the various plant and animal worlds, as well as to various spiritual spheres, the term also refers to the 70 sextillion visible stars found in the universe as well as the planets and satellites which orbit around a myriad of them. Thus, besides confirming the existence of other worlds, the Qur'an acknowledges the existence of other earth-like planets. As we read in the Muslim Scripture, "Allah is He who has created seven heavens and of the Earth a similar number" (65:12). Although the existence of other worlds and other planets is not evidence of life, the Qur'an specifies that Almighty Allah has indeed created life on other planets. As we read in the Muslim Scripture, "Among His Signs is the creation of the heavens and the Earth, and the living creatures that He has scattered through them" (42:29). According to the Qur'an, everything in existence worships Almighty Allah: "And to Allah doth obeisance all that is in the heavens and Earth, whether living creatures or the angels" (16:49). In Arabic, the word *dabbatun* or "living creatures" denotes sentient, corporeal beings which are capable of movement in contrast to incorporeal, spiritual beings, like the angels and the jinn, which are interdimensional beings. When asked whether life existed on other planets, Imam Ja'far al-Sadiq responded:

> Each star is a small universe within the great universe. It is a collection of heavenly bodies. They are in perpetual motion so that they may not fall down and break up. If their movement stops, the universe will come to an end. It is perpetual motion which creates life. In other words, perpetual motion itself is life. If the motion stops, life would cease to exist. (qtd. Yazdi)

Manifestly, the existence of life on other planets does not prove the presence of intelligent, rational, beings. According to the Qur'an, however, we are not the only humans to have been created by Allah. As we read in the Muslim Scripture:

> Behold, thy Lord said to the angels: 'I will create a vice-regent on Earth.' They said: 'Wilt thou place therein one who will make mischief therein and shed blood whilst we do celebrate Thy praises and glorify Thy Name?' He said: 'I know what ye know not.' (2:30)

In all evidence, Adam was not the first conscious, soul-bearing, being created by Allah. As the angels implicitly attested, other beings had existed prior to Adam. They spread corruption on Earth and, for all intents and purposes, were destroyed by their Creator. Since angels do not know the future, how could they have known that the sons of Adam would spread mischief throughout the land and shed blood? They could only have based their judgment on past experience.

As the Imams from *Ahl al-Bayt*, the Household of the Prophet, have explained, there have been many Adams, the Adam referred to in the Bible and the Qur'an being the most recent of them all. When asked who came before Adam, Imam 'Ali replied: "Adam." When asked who came before that Adam, he replied, "Adam." When asked who came before that Adam, he responded: "Thousands of Adams" (Ibn Babawayh). In other words, different species of humans have existed before us in this world as well as other worlds, the exact number of which is only known to Allah. As Imam Ja'far al-Sadiq has explained, "Perhaps you think that Allah has not created humans other than you. No! I swear to Allah that He has created thousands upon thousands of human species and that you are the last among them" (Majlisi). As Imam Muhammad al-Baqir has elucidated,

> Since this world was created, Allah, the Exalted, has created seven human species none of which were of the race of Adam. He created them from the surface of the Earth, and set each species of beings, one after another, with its kind upon the Earth. Then he created Adam, the father of humankind, and brought his children into being from him. (Majlisi)

It should be stressed that the number 7 has the symbolic meaning of "many" or a "multitude" in Semitic languages. Hence, when the Imam says that seven species of humans were created, he is simply expressing that a vast number of human species existed prior to *Homo sapiens*. Based on the Qur'an, there does not appear to be a missing link between *Homo sapiens* and other human species which preceded them. They all appear to have been separate creations and not part of a single evolutionary process. Otherwise, we would have to face the possibility of polygenesis as opposed to monogenesis.

If Almighty Allah created various waves of humans on Earth, there is no reason why He would have failed to create other beings, both similar and different, on other planets which are capable of sustaining life. As Ayatullah Pooya Yazdi has explained in *The Essence of the Holy Qur'an*, Imam 'Ali believed that the luminous heavenly bodies that we see in the sky contained cities connected with columns of light. These cities, according to the Imam, were populated by conscious beings who worshipped the Creator, and who had never heard about our Adam and his progeny (244).

When Ibn 'Abbas, the cousin and companion of the Prophet Muhammad, was asked to interpret the Qur'anic verse regarding the seven earths (65:12), he explained that "In each of those earths there is a Prophet like your Prophet, an Adam like your Adam, a Noah like your Noah, an Abraham like your Abraham, and a Jesus like your Jesus" (Ibn Jarir, Ibn Abi Hatim, Hakim, Bayhaqi, Ibn Hajar, Ibn Kathir, and Dhahabi). Great scholars, like Imam al-Ghazali, also believed that there were people on other planets, that they had learned how to travel through space, and that they had the technology to communicate with other celestial civilizations.

When asked whether there were human beings on other planets, Imam Ja'far al-Sadiq was more cautious, responding that: "I cannot say that there are human beings in other worlds, but I can say that there are living beings that we cannot see because of the great distance between us" (*Maghz-e Mutafakker Jehan Shi'ah*). While the Imam could not confirm that *Homo sapiens* existed on other planets, he did believe in the existence of extraterrestrial beings which, instead of having a science-fiction overtone, merely means "off planet Earth."

Far from being Earth-centered, the Holy Qur'an encourages human beings to explore the universe. As Almighty Allah says,

> O ye assembly of Jinn and men! If it be you can pass beyond the regions of the heavens and the Earth, pass ye! Not without authority will ye be able to pass! Then which of the favors of your Lord will ye deny? (55:33-34).

As the Holy Qur'an and the Sunnah have established, we are not alone in the universe, nor are we unique. We are the most recent in a long line of beings created by the Creator. As Imam Ja'far al-Sadiq has eloquently expressed,

> Do not think that after the passing away of the affair of this world and the Day of Judgment and the placing of the virtuous in heaven and the

evil in hell there will no longer be anyone to worship God. No, never! Rather, again God will create servants without the marriage of the male and the female to know His Oneness and to worship Him. (Majlisi)

Chapter Two

Racism in the Shiite Seminary

Claims that the Shiite seminary in Iraq, Iran, and Syria, discriminate against non-Persians have been circulating for several decades. Although this allegation is often made by Orientalists and outsiders, it is also spread by a small cohort of disgruntled Arabs and non-Arabs who appear to be embittered because Persians have dominated Shiite Islam for centuries, often eclipsing others in scholarly, academic, and spiritual eminence. That Persians are at the center of Shiism, there can be no question. The claim that Persian scholars discriminate against non-Persian scholars, however, is unfounded and can be disproven by a simple survey of current, and recent, Grand Ayatullahs.

Grand Ayatullah Muhammad Shahroudi and Grand Ayatullah Muhammad Taqi Modarresi are both Arabs as were Grand Ayatullah Sadiq al-Sadr, Grand Ayatullah Muhammad Husayn Fadlullah, and Grand Ayatullah Muhammad Baqir al-Sadr. Grand Ayatullah Muhammad Husayn Najafi and Grand Ayatullah Bashir Najafi are both of Indo-Pakistani origin, as was Sayyid 'Ali Naqi Naqvi. Grand Ayatullah Asif Muhsini, an ethnic Tajik, Grand Ayatullah Muhammad Ishaq Fayyad, an ethnic Hazara, and Grand Ayatullah Qorban Ali Kabuli, are all Afghanis. Grand Ayatullah 'Ali Khamene'i, Grand Ayatullah Musavi Ardabili, Grand Ayatullah Musa Shubayr Zanjani, Grand Ayatullah Javad Gharavi Aliari, Grand Ayatullah Moslem Malakouti, and Grand Ayatullah Husayn Musavi Tabrizi are all ethnic Azeris, as were Grand Ayatullah Kazem Shariatmadari, Grand Ayatullah Abu al-Qasim al-Khu'i, 'Allamah Tatababai, and Grand Ayatullah Fazel Lankarani, as well as Grand Ayatullah Javad Tabrizi, and Ayatullah 'Ali Meshkini.

While many Ayatullahs and Sources of Emulation are ethnic Persians, the upper hierarchy of the *hawzah* is a body well-represented by Arabs, Indians, Pakistanis, Tajiks, Hazaras, and Azeris, while the middle to lower echelons include individuals from every imaginable global ethnicity. Scores of students from around the globe have been trained in the Shiite seminary in Qum since the triumph of the Islamic Revolution of Iran. Some have reached the level of *muballaghun* or missionaries. Some have reached the level of ulama or scholars. Some have reached the intermediate level of *Hujjat al-Islam* or Proof of Islam. And some have even reached the level of *ijtihad*, independent interpretation of Islamic sources, becoming Ayatullahs or Signs of Allah in their own right. Considering that there are thousands of advanced students completing *dars al-kharij* or graduate studies in the *hawzah*, including individuals originating from Africa, Europe, the Americas, and Asia, the Shiite scholarly establishment has the potential of soon producing and nominating its first European, African, or Latin American Source of Emulation.

While tribalism, nationalism, and ethnic chauvinism exist to some extent among the lower echelons of the Shiite seminary, there is little to no evidence that such considerations have tainted the process of professional promotion in the clerical hierarchy. Clearly, if an individual has risen to the rank of *'alim*, *mujtahid* or *marja*, scholar, jurist or Source of Emulation, it has not been on the basis of race, ethnicity or nationality. In the best of cases, it has been exclusively on the basis of academic aptitude and piety. In the worst of cases, it has been the product of ego, agenda, and ambition. Still, race does not appear to play a prominent role in the process. As the Prophet Muhammad said in his "Final Sermon," "An Arab is not superior to a non-Arab nor is a non-Arab superior to an Arab. A black is not superior to a white nor is a white superior to a black." Such is the standard to which the Shiite seminary aspires.

CHAPTER THREE

CONCERNING THE COLOR OF ADAM, THE PROPHETS, AND THE IMAMS

According to Eurocentrists, Adam was white. According to Afrocentrists, Adam was black. While such ideas are understandable among anthropomorphists, who believe that God literally created human beings in His Corporeal Image, they have no place within the monotheistic mindset of Islam. It is therefore regrettable that some black Muslims from the West remain obsessed about racial matters, echoing the racial doctrines of Marcus Garvey, Noble Drew Ali, Wallace Dodd Fard, Elijah Muhammad, and Louis Farrakhan. While nobody enters the Shiite seminary in a state of ideological purity, it is disturbing to see some black Shiite scholars spread such racist ideas after having spent ten, fifteen or twenty years studying in the *hawzah*. With their scholarly robes and turbans, some of these newly trained Shiite scholars give credence to racist ideas that are rejected by Islam.

For the overwhelming majority of Muslims, the color of Adam, the Prophets, and the Imams, is not an issue. As believers who embrace the brotherhood and sisterhood of humankind, Muslims view themselves as the children of Adam and consider any differences in color, language, or culture, to be blessings from Almighty Allah, and a means to bring them together, as oppose to divide them. In short, they embrace the words of Almighty Allah which state,

> O humankind! We created you from a single (pair) of a male and a female, and made you into nations and tribes, that ye may know each other (not that ye may despise (each other). Verily the most honored of you in the sight of Allah is (he who is) the most righteous of you. And Allah has full knowledge and is well acquainted (with all things). (49:13)

In a misguided effort to fortify their self-esteem, which was shattered and soiled through centuries of slavery, segregation, and discrimination, some believers of African origin or ancestry insist that Adam was black. In reality, they are merely responding to centuries of European Christian indoctrination which insisted that Adam was white, Abraham was white, Moses was white, Jesus was white, and Almighty God, the Father, in Heaven, was white. In Islam, however, we do not fight fire with fire. We fight fire with water. Though counter-intuitive, the most appropriate response to Christian claims that Adam was white is not to affirm that Adam was black. The appropriate response to Christian claims that God is white is not to affirm that God is black. Instead, the appropriate response is the Islamic response. God does not have a body. As such, God does not have a color. We are all the children of Adam and Adam's color is irrelevant. After all, as the Bible teaches, God "made of one blood all nations of men" (Acts 17:26). This is a fact that Malcolm X came to realize as a result of his pilgrimage to Mecca. As he expressed in a letter dated April 20th, 1964:

> Never have I witnessed such sincere hospitality and overwhelming spirit of true brotherhood as is practiced by people *of all colors and races* here in this ancient holy land, the home of Abraham, Muhammad, and all the other Prophets of the holy scriptures. For the past week, I have been utterly speechless and spellbound by the graciousness I see displayed all around me by people *of all colors...*
>
> There were tens of thousands of pilgrims, from all over the world. They were *of all colors*, from blue-eyed blondes to black-skinned Africans. But we were all participating in the same ritual, displaying a spirit of unity and brotherhood that my experiences in America had led me to believe never could exist between the white and non-white.
>
> America needs to understand Islam, because this is the one religion that erases from its society the race problem. Throughout my travels in the Muslim world, I have met, talked to, and even eaten with people who in America would have been considered white--but the white attitude was removed from their minds by the religion of Islam. I have never before seen sincere and true brotherhood practiced by all colors together, irrespective of their color.
>
> You may be shocked by these words coming from me. But on this pilgrimage, what I have seen, and experienced, has forced me to rearrange much of my thought-patterns previously held, and to toss aside some of my previous conclusions. This was not too difficult for me. Despite my firm convictions, I have always been a man who tries to face facts, and to accept the reality of life as new experience and new knowledge unfolds it. I have always kept an open mind, which is necessary to the flexibility that must go hand in hand with every form of intelligent search for truth.

During the past eleven days here in the Muslim world, I have eaten from the same plate, drunk from the same glass, and slept on the same rug--while praying to the same God--with fellow Muslims, whose eyes were the bluest of blue, whose hair was the blondest of blond, and whose skin was the whitest of white. And in the words and in the deeds of the white Muslims, I felt the same sincerity that I felt among the black African Muslims of Nigeria, Sudan, and Ghana.

We were truly all the same (brothers)--because their belief in one God had removed the white from their minds, the white from their behavior, and the white from their attitude...

All praise is due to Allah, the Lord of all the worlds.

As Malcolm X makes patently clear, the vast majority of Muslims could not care less whether Adam was white, black, brown, red or green. The issue does not even occur to them. The only Muslims who insist on Adam's color tend to be racially insecure black converts from the Western world, the very same individuals who insist that Moses was black, Jesus was black, Muhammad was black, the Imams were black, and that the "real" Arabs and Berbers were black. Despite the pseudo-scholarly arguments that they advance to defend their claims, the only thing they demonstrate is their ignorance of Islam and their own poorly-veiled prejudices. Since when have Muslims asserted that Adam, the Prophets, and the Imams were white, brown or yellow? On the contrary, Muslims of all colors have been comforted by the fact that prophets and messengers were sent to all tribes and nations. As Almighty Allah says, "To every people (was sent) a messenger" (10:47). And again, "We assuredly sent amongst every people a messenger" (16:36). As far as Muslims are concerned, the color of any prophet is irrelevant. As the Qur'an teaches, "We make no distinction between one another of his apostles" (2:285).

In reality, the racial doctrine that Adam was black is as ridiculous as the racial doctrine that Adam was white. The belief that the "original man" was black is as fallacious as the belief that the "original man" was white. While many blacks have attempted to Africanize Adam, the Prophets, and the Imams, no such attempt has ever been made by white Muslims. No white Muslim has ever presented Allah, Adam, the Prophet, and the Imams as white. It was W.D. Fard, the mysterious man who appeared in Detroit on July 4th, 1930, and his follower, Elijah Muhammad, who disseminated the belief that Allah, the Prophets, and the Imams were black. The fact that W.D. Fard was actually a white man who associated with white supremacists is reason enough to seriously question any assertions that he made. His teachings, namely, that the black man is God and the white man is the devil, have had a profound impact on certain groups in the African American community. Imagine, instead, the outrage that would arise if a white Muslim claimed what is presented in the following hypothetical quote which is an inversion of Black Muslim doctrine:

> Almighty Allah is a white man. He appeared to the oppressed white working class of Detroit on July 4th, 1930 in the form of W.D. Fard, a Caucasian man from Greece. The white Wallace Fard Muhammad founded the Aryan Nation of Islam. He taught that Adam, the Prophet, and the Imams, all belonged to the white master race. He taught that whites were gods and that blacks were devils. As the Master instructed us, Jewish, Christian, and Muslim teachings all confirm that Ham was punished by God for having sexual intercourse in the sanctuary of the Ark of the Covenant. As Ibn Qutaybah, Ibn 'Abd al-Hakam, al-Ya'qubi, and al-Tabari explain, Ham's complexion was changed to black by the curse of God. In fact, he was smitten in his semen, assuring the perpetuity of his curse among his descendants. As Master Fard said, "Once you go black, you don't come back! You a nigga for life!" Rather than evolve from apes, the Aryan Allah explained that degenerate black people devolved into primates through a genetic mutation triggered by Yakub, a mad scientist.
>
> To demonstrate the demonic nature of blacks, Fard, the White Deity, quoted the Prophet Muhammad who said that "There is no good in black people; when they are hungry, they steal, and when their stomachs are full, they fornicate and commit adultery" (Tabarani). He also taught us that when Allah created Adam, he tapped him on the right shoulder, and out came the white race, and he tapped him on the left shoulder, and out came the black race. Allah then told the white race, "To heaven for all of you," and told the black race, "To hell with all of you" (Ahmad). As the Qur'an confirms, the people of Hell have darkened faces (10:27). As the Prophet pointed out, however, the skin of the women of Paradise is so fair that it is transparent (Tirmidhi).
>
> To demonstrate that blacks can never be true Muslims, the white incarnation of Allah cited Imam Ja'far al-Sadiq who said that black Muslims were hypocrites. As W.D. Fard taught us, it was a black man who killed Hamzah, the Lion of the White Race, and it was another black man who martyred Imam Husayn, the Lord of Whiteness. The murderer of Hamzah, of course, was Wahshi, an Ethiopian, who was appropriately named "The Animal." The murderer of Husayn, of course, was Shimr, the "House Nigger of the Umayyads."
>
> W.D. Fard, the white savior, shared with us the true nature of blacks or

Zinjis through the writings of Muqaddasi, Ibn Khaldun, Jahiz, Mas'udi, Biruni, Hamadani, Nasir al-Din al-Tusi, and Ibn Qutaybah. Most importantly, W.D. Fard, the White Allah, preached the supremacy of the Original White Asiatic Man, the Caucasian, who was made from the quintessence of clay (23:12). Since porcelain, which is the purest of clay, is white and even translucent, Wallace Fard Muhammad proved that Adam was the whitest of white men, as were his progeny, the Prophets, and the Imams. Since Adam was white, only white people can go to heaven, for as the Prophet said, "Any person who will enter Paradise will resemble Adam" (Bukhari).

In order to protect the racial pride of the Prophet, the White Savior reiterated the edict of Ahmad ibn Abi Sulayman, the companion of Sahnun ibn Sa'id ibn Habib al-Tanukhi, the great Maliki jurist from Qayrawan, which states that "Anyone who says that the Prophet was black should be killed."

The authenticity of the *ahadith* or traditions in question, and the inappropriate interpretations of the Qur'an which are cited, are all categorically rejected. The purpose of this piece is to give blacks with racial issues a mirror in which to view their own contentions. While there are some racist sayings attributed to the Prophet Muhammad and the Imams, they have always been rejected by Muslim scholars as they contradict the Qur'an, authentic narrations, and the very spirit of Islam.

If we cast Christian sources and their biases aside, and focus on Jewish sources, we find that the word "Adam" derives from the Hebrew root for "red." Hence, according to Judaism, Adam was a red man. He was made of red clay. When the Bible says that "the Lord God formed man of the dust of the ground" (Genesis 2:7), and Job says that "I also am formed out of clay" (Job 33:6), Jewish commentators describe that clay as having been red. If Adam was indeed red, as his name indicates, then all other skin tones manifested themselves later among his descendants. From a Jewish perspective, whether we are white, black, brown or yellow, we are all descendants of the original red man. However, this does this mean that Adam was a Native American. The color red may simply symbolize the common red blood that unites all humanity. It can also represent the ruddy color of Adam's skin. In the Book of Genesis, Esau, also known as Edom (a name meaning "red" and derived, like "Adam," from the root *'dm*), is described as "hairy" when compared to his brother Jacob. As such, he is the emblem of the primordial and primitive man who resists the further spiritual development of the patriarchal line represented by Jacob, his sons and his descendants, those who will eventually include the Patriarchs of the Twelve Tribes of Israel, as well as the Prophet Moses.

If we rely exclusively on Islamic sources, the foremost of which is the Qur'an, we find that Allah made Adam out of clay. As we read in the Muslim Scripture, "He it is Who has created you from clay" (6:2); "We created man from sounding clay, from mud molded into shape" (15:26); "I am about to create man, from sounding clay, from mud molded into shape" (15:28); "Thou didst create from sounding clay" (15:33); "Thou didst create from clay" (17:61); "Man We did create from a quintessence (of clay)" (23:12); "He began the creation of man with (nothing but) clay" (32:7); "Them have We created out of a sticky clay" (37:11); "I am about to create man from clay" (38:71); "Thou didst create me from fire; and him from clay" (38:76); and finally, "He created man from sounding clay like unto pottery" (55:14).

In a clear indication of academic and linguistic dishonesty, some scholars and translators insist that the Qur'an speaks of "black mud" and "black clay." The words used in the Qur'an include *tin*, which simply means "clay," as has been accurately conveyed by Yusuf 'Ali, Arberry, Hamidullah, Cortés, Vernet, Sarwar, and 'Ali, among others, and which has been confirmed by *Hans Wehr*, *Ibn Misr*, and *Mawrid*, as well Spiro Socrates' *Arabic English Vocabulary*, and John Penrice's *Dictionary and Glossary of the Koran*, among others.

The other word employed in the Qur'an in relation to the creation of humankind is *salsal*, which also means "clay," and which has been correctly translated by Yusuf 'Ali, Hamidullah, Cortés, Vernet, 'Ali, Sarwar, Khalifa, and Qaribullah, but mistranslated as "black mud" or "black slime" by Asad, Pickthall, Sale, Rodwell, Shakir, Hilali/Khan, and Malik, among others, because the word is qualified by the adjective *hama'in* which they rendered as "black." Rather than rely on authoritative dictionaries, these translators turned to the *Arabic-English Lexicon* compiled by Edward William Lane, an Orientalist whose proficiency in Classical Arabic has been diligently and repeatedly proven to be sub-par, and whose translations were mechanical and devoid of subtlety.

As any scholar with a veritable mastery of Classical Arabic can confirm the words *salsal* means "clay," "dry clay," "argil," or "argillaceous earth," the word *hama'* means "mud," "mire," "sludge" or "slime," and the word *hama'in* means "dredged," "cleaned out," or "purified." If we base ourselves on *Hans Wehr*, *Mawrid*, and the *Dictionary and Glossary of the Koran*, when Allah says that He made human beings out of *salsalin min hama'in masnunin*, it means, out of "pure clay" or out of "purified mud."

While it is true that the *Lisan al-'Arab* and *al-Muhit* describe *hama'* as "black clay," Ibn Manzur (d. 1312) explains that the word has different meanings in different contexts. As he explains in *Lisan al-'Arab*, the word *hama'* means *mutaghayyir* or "altered" in the Qur'anic context. If we follow the opinion of the greatest authority on the classical Arabic language, *salsalin min hama'in masnunin* means "from clay of altered mud." Those who have the most elementary knowledge of Arabic will confirm that the word *salsal* or "clay" is not qualified by an adjective of color such as *aswad* or "black." The word *salsal* is qualified by the word *hama'in* which means "altered," "pure," or "clarified." In this context, the word "black" is actually the opposite of the word *hama'in*.

Even if the Qur'an said that Adam had been made of "black mud," that does not mean that he was a black man, as the word "black" would refer to the richness of the soil. Even if he had been literally molded from black clay does not mean that Adam was a black man. For example, when black corn is popped, it becomes the brightest of white. "Black clay," however, is a contradiction in terms. Depending on the content of the soil, raw clay varies from white to deep orange-red to umber. In short, there is no such thing as naturally black clay. Any clay which is darker than light brown acquired its color through the application of a glaze.

Although some misguided mullahs may seek to manipulate the Word of Allah and impose their retrograde concepts of color upon the Qur'an, the Muslim Scripture does not use the words "clay" or "mud" in order to convey color. As the following tradition from the Prophet makes clear, dust, clay, and sounding-clay represent different stages of creation. As the Messenger of Allah explained, "Allah created Adam from dust after He mixed the clay, left him for some time until it became sticky mud, after which Allah shaped him. After that Allah left him till it became like potter's clay" (Bukhari). As both Qur'anic and hadith commentaries explain, Allah took some clay, mixed it with water in order to make sticky mud, and created the figure of Adam. He then laid him out to dry until he became like potter's clay or sounding clay, namely, dry to the point that hitting the statuette made a sound. It was then that Allah breathed life into Adam. Unless one is a literalist, it is evident that this story is allegorical.

Second only to the Qur'an, in terms of veracity, is the authenticated Sunnah, which also stipulates that Adam was made of earth. According to the Prophet Muhammad,

> Allah created Adam from a handful that He gathered from the entire Earth, so the sons of Adam come like the Earth. Some of them are red, some are white, some are black, and some are in between. Some of them are easy, some of them are difficult, some of them are evil, and some of them are good. (Abu Dawud and Ahmad)

As the Messenger of Allah explained, Adam was not made of black mud nor was he made of white clay. He was made from a variety of earth tones. Both al-Tabari and al-Mas'udi explained that Allah created Adam out of black, red, and light earth, which explains the various complexions of his progeny. As such, the descendants of Adam vary in their skin color in the same fashion that the soil differs in color. As Imam 'Ali further elaborates in *Nahj al-Balaghah*,

> Allah collected from hard, soft, sweet and sour earth, clay which He dripped in water till it got pure, and kneaded it with moisture till it became gluey. From it He carved an image with curves, joints, limbs and segments. He solidified it till it dried up for a fixed time and a known duration. Then He blew into it out of His Spirit whereupon it took the pattern of a human being with mind that governs him, intelligence which he makes use of, limbs that serve him, organs that change his position, sagacity that differentiates between truth and untruth, tastes and smells, colors and species. He is a mixture of clays of different colors, cohesive materials, divergent contradictories and differing properties like heat, cold, softness and hardness.

If Adam contained every skin color, he must have been black, argue some Afrocentrists, claiming that white people cannot produce black children while black people can produce white children. Evidently, this reference is to albinos. Albinos, however, are not white in the northern European sense. They are not white-skinned: they suffer from a genetic disorder which prevents tyrosine from being converted into melanin. Caucasians, however, do not suffer from a lack of pigmentation: they are simply pale-skinned. In reality, white people can produce black offspring, just as black people can produce white offspring, since the variation in skin color is triggered by independent genetic mutations and sexual selection, something which has nothing at all to do with recessive genes.

According to some religious scholars, all the skin colors in the world derived from two medium skinned parents over the course of a single generation, a genetic change that occurred during the time of Adam or the time of Noah. According to various traditions, Noah's son, Shem, was the eponymous ancestor of the Semites; his son, Japheth, the ancestor of the Caucasians--since according to Josephus and Isidore of Seville, his descendants populated Europe--and his son, Ham, was the ancestor of the Africanoid branch, though the etymology of "Ham" as meaning "black, burnt" has been disputed. Still, other religious scholars have determined that early human beings were medium skinned, as are the majority of human beings today.

Very dark skin and very pale skin are simply two extremes at each side of the skin spectrum. This view is supported by recent research which holds that light brown skin is the likely ancestral skin color of modern human beings. In fact, if we look at the San people of southern Africa, the oldest and most genetically diverse human population on Earth, we find that their skin is neither black nor white, but beige. The original man was neither black nor white but light brown. In truth, there is no such thing as white skin, just as there is no such thing as black skin. In reality, all human beings are varying shades of brown, ranging from very light to very dark. As Katie Kissinger explains in *All the Colors We Are: The Story of How We Get Our Skin Color*:

> All of us have skin color that is a shade of brown. Asians do not have yellow skin. Their skin is a shade of brown because it contains melanin. White people are not really white. Their skin also contains melanin. Black people are not really black. Their skin contains melanin to create a shade of brown. American Indians do not have red skin. It is a shade of brown because it contains melanin. (28)

According to evolutionary scientists, the first hominids were pale skinned, as the skin under the hair of primates is light colored. Without hair, however, pale skin was a disadvantage in the African heat. As a result of natural selection, claim evolutionists, hominids with darker pigmentation had an adaptive advantage. Thus, dark skin was probably not the original skin color of early human beings: it was something that supposedly evolved to prevent low folate levels in sun-drenched Africa. From 1.2 million years ago to 1.35 million years ago, the ancestors of modern humans were brown. When human beings migrated to northern regions where there was less sunlight, low vitamin D^3 posed a problem. As a result, a lighter skin color reportedly re-emerged to help facilitate vitamin D production. Further skin variations are arguably the result of genetic mutations and selective reproduction. In Africa, black skin is described as a relatively recent development in genetic terms, tracing its beginnings back to more recent migrations. As a point of evidence for this argument, the most ancient of African populations, like the San or Bushmen of the Kalahari, have light brown skin. Such is the stance taken by modern science whether one accepts it or not.

The problem with many Jews, Christians, and Muslims, is that they take creation stories literally. According to the *Popul Vuh* or Mayan Bible, the gods created human beings out of corn. Not a single Mayan Indian would assert that the first Mayans were yellow, red, purple or black, the colors of Indian corn. If the *Popul Vuh* says that humans were made of corn, it simply symbolizes that corn was the staple food for the Mayan Indians, and that it represented life itself. If the Bible and the Qur'an assert that human beings were made from mud, it refers to the physical fact that they share the same chemical constituents as the earth and it refers to the spiritual fact that they are "earthy" or "worldly" in nature. In reality, all human beings are made of star dust, as all essential elements originate from distant stellar nurseries. As such, we are very much sons and daughters of the stars.

If Adam was not black, then neither was Abraham, Moses, Jesus, Muhammad or the Twelve Imams. As has been demonstrated by modern DNA analysis of Jewish people from throughout the world, there has been a low level of admixture into the Jewish gene pool. In many cases, today's descendants of Abraham, Moses, and the other Hebrew prophets were of Jewish Semitic stock. As DNA analysis has shown, the Semites originated in southwestern Asia, settled in the Fertile Crescent in the Near East, and spread into Arabia and Africa. Claims that the "real" Arabs were black Africans is as preposterous as the claims that the "real" Jews, the "real" Egyptians, and the "real" Berbers were also black Africans, something which is simply not supported by linguistic, literary, archeological, cultural, and genetic evidence.

According to genetic analysis, Egyptians have an average of 67.6% of Eurasian genes, as opposed to 30.9% of sub-Saharan African genes. While it may be argued that modern-day Egyptians have been subject to centuries of genetic influx, studies conducted on Ramses II demonstrated that he was a white-skinned, red-headed man. As Dr. Zahi Hawass, the Secretary General of the Supreme Council of Antiquities of Egypt, has categorically confirmed, the Pharaohs and the ancient Egyptians were not black Africans, although the members of the Nubian Dynasty most certainly were. As this eminent expert has explained, "Tutankhamen was not black, and the portrayal of ancient Egyptian civilization as black has no element of truth to it." Genetically-speaking, most Egyptians are not closely related to black Africans. In fact, Egyptians are most closely related to other North Africans, and to a lesser extent to southern European, Mediterranean, and Middle Eastern populations.

The Berbers of Morocco and other parts of North Africa are a complex mosaic of European, Sub-Saharan African, and West Asian influences. A Caucasian people by origin, they have mixed, to varying degrees, with blacks, Arabs, and Europeans. The percentage of black genes among the Berbers varies from a mere 3% to an overwhelming 84%. Some Berbers, like the Tuareg, are predominantly black, with 84% of sub-Saharan African genes, as opposed to 7.7% of Eurasian genes. The Souss

Berbers, in contrast, are 68% Eurasian and 26% black African. North Central Moroccan Berbers, who are the purest representative of Amazigh ancestry, are 88.4% Eurasian, 8.3% North African, and only 3.3% black African. Overall, the Berber gene pool is predominantly Western Eurasian, with a lower frequency of sub-Saharan lineages. Contrary to claims made by Afrocentrists, the Berbers are not of black African origin. As recent research has shown, they are of Near Eastern origin, and are genetically related to European populations, particularly the Celts and the Scandinavians. Sixty percent of Riffian Berbers have blond hair. In fact, their percentage of red-heads is comparable to that of the Irish. Black African DNA entered the Berber and Arab gene pool as a result of Berber and Arab men having children with their black bondmaids.

As DNA analysis has demonstrated, even the Nubians are a predominantly Caucasian people, containing an average of 59.5% of Eurasian genes, as opposed to 40.5% of sub-Saharan genes. Among African Americans, the percentage of Caucasian genes varies from 2 to 50% with most African Americans averaging 25%. On average, the Nubian people have twice as many Caucasian genes than African Americans. Even Ethiopians, who come from the "cradle of the black race," contain 62% of white genes, 40% of which are Caucasian.

Other DNA research indicates that only 24% of Ethiopians share the same genetic profile as the Bantu and Afro-Caribbean populations. Africanoid Ethiopians, such as the Oromo, only established themselves in Ethiopia in the 1500s. The most ancient Ethiopians, like the Aksumites, are a Semitic people with Sabaean ancestry. Since most Ethiopians are Amharic speakers or speakers of other Semitic languages such as Trigray-Tigrinya, many of them are of Semitic ancestry. In fact, the first Jewish emperor of Ethiopia, Menelik I, is said to have been the son of King Solomon of Israel, and Queen Sheba of the Yemen, both of whom were Eurasian in ancestry. Although many Ethiopians have dark skin, their facial features are more Eurasian than Africoid. Like many Arabs and Berbers, Ethiopians have become increasingly Africanized through intermarriage with black African women.

Research studies establish that Ethiopians fall into the same genetic cluster as Jews, Norwegians, and Armenians. Ethiopians are more closely related to Mediterranean Caucasian groups like Berbers and Arabs than they are to West Africans. As such, placing Ethiopians into a "black" cluster is an inaccurate reflection of their genetic structure. Interestingly, the flow of Caucasian genes into the Ethiopian gene pool has occurred predominantly through the male lineage. If Ethiopians are predominantly composed of Caucasian DNA, then Ethiopia can be rightfully considered the mother of both the black and white races. The Somalis have an even smaller percentage of black African genes: a mere 5% from sub-Saharan Africa as compared to 15% from Eurasia. The vast majority of their genes are shared with Ethiopians, Eritreans, Berbers, North African Arabs, as well as Mediterranean and Balkan Europeans.

Like the Berbers, the Arabs are a heterogeneous population. Moroccan Arabs, for example, are a predominantly Caucasian people. On average, their genes are 71.8% Eurasian, 21.9% sub-Saharan, and 6.5% North African. According to recent DNA analysis, the Arabs of Saudi Arabia have 85% Eurasian genes, 7% sub-Saharan African genes, 7% North African genes, and 3% of Indian genes. The genetic makeup of other Arabian Peninsula populations, from the Bedouins of the Negev Desert to the Yemeni and Levantine populations, is remarkably similar to that of the Saudi population, conclusively overriding the claim that the Lebanese and Syrians are not "real" Arabs. If some Omani Arabs are quite dark, it is because they have a larger influx of East Indian genes. If some Yemeni Arabs are quite dark, it is because they have been mixing with black African women for centuries. Whether they are found in Morocco, Saudi Arabia, or Palestine, "black" Arabs are invariably the descendants of black African slaves. As recent research has confirmed, the Ethiopian genes circulating in the South Arabian gene pool trace back to maternal lineages from East Africa.

Like all Semitic peoples, the original Arabs were Caucasians as the overwhelming majority of Arabs continue to be. According to all accounts, the Prophet Muhammad had very fair skin. Imam 'Ali described him as "white with a reddish tinge." The earliest, authentic, accounts, passed down by eye-witnesses state that his skin would turn red when exposed to the sun while that which was covered by clothing was white. His companion, Abu Bakr, was a red-head, as was his daughter, 'A'ishah, to cite but a few examples. As Bernard Lewis has confirmed in *Race and Color in Islam*, the ancient Arabs applied the term "black" to the natives of sub-Saharan Africa and their offspring. They applied the term "white" and occasionally "red" to Arabs, Persians, Greeks, Turks, and Slavs, as well as to other peoples who lived to the North and east of Black Africa. At times, in order to distinguish them from the white Arabs and Persians, they designated northern Europeans as "dead white," "pale blue," and various shades of red in order to describe their pinkish complexion and their freckles. Although East Indians are Caucasians, the ancient Arabs sometimes described them as "blacks" due to their dark skin.

Since the spread of Islam in the 7th century, and the expansion of the Arabic language and culture throughout the Middle East, Africa, North

Africa, and al-Andalus, the Arabs ceased being a racial or ethnic group and converted themselves into a linguistic and cultural family. The early Islamized Arabs eagerly intermarried with the populations they conquered, integrating and absorbing them into Arabic culture. These Arabs, who were white or light-skinned, unfortunately continued to associate blackness with derogatory physical and personal traits. The sons of white Arab men and black slave women, known as *hajin* or "half-breeds," were subjected to a great deal of discrimination. As Sudanese scholar Abduh Badawi explains, Arab men were reluctant to recognize the sons of black mothers because of their color as "they despised the black color as much as they loved the white color." In fact, like other whites, the Arabs used "white" as a positive descriptive adjective, applied to beauty and nobility, and used "black" as a negative descriptive adjective, applied to all things ugly and evil. As evidence that Arabs were white, and slaves were black, the Arabic term *'abd* or "slave" was applied to African slaves during the High Middle Ages. If the white Arabs were really the descendants of Slavic slaves, then the term *'abd* should have been applied to whites, as opposed to blacks, which is not the case. Even today, the Arabic term *'abd* is applied as a racial slur to blacks and is very much the unfortunate equivalent of the anathematic American English term "nigger."

Although Afrocentrists argue that white Arabs descend from the white concubines that belonged to black Arabs, DNA analysis has demonstrated that the Africoid genes found among Arabs and Berbers belongs to the maternal line while their Caucasoid genes belong to the paternal line. In other words, the black genes found among Arabs and Berbers trace back to black slave girls who belonged to white Arabs and Berbers. In fact, the largest influx of black genes into the Arab and Berber gene pool traces back to the Islamic period during which nine million black slaves were brought from sub-Saharan Africa to North Africa to serve in the households of their Caucasoid masters, a cultural cataclysm on a par with the Trans-Atlantic slave trade.

As a result of 1400 years of racial mixing, Arabs can be white, olive-colored, brown, and even jet black. Yet, despite their motley genetic origin, Arabs do not identify themselves on the basis of skin color. Rather, they identify themselves on the basis of a shared language, history, and culture. Even the darkest Arab, with the tightest Afro-textured hair, would be insulted if he were identified as a "black" person. He would rightfully protest that he was an Arab, and that he was proud of it. In this regard, Arabs are very similar to Latinos. Regardless of whether they are of European, Native American, African, Arab, or Oriental ancestry, they all identify themselves as Latinos. When Western converts to Islam of

African ancestry attempt to label Arabs as white Arabs and black Arabs, they are attempting to impose an entirely Western framework upon the Arab people.

Rather than rely on the hadith literature, which describes Jesus as having been a freckled red-head, some black Muslims prefer to point to the Book of Revelations as alleged evidence that the Messiah was a black man. Since Jesus was described as having hair "like wool" (1:14) and "feet like brass" (1:15), they insist that he was an African. They conveniently ignore that he was also described as having a white head (1:16). These arguments are as foolish as they are futile since the source purports to describe the heavenly form of Jesus, and not his original earthly one. Although many black Muslims insist that Moses was black because his hair "was like wool," Moses was a Jew, and Jewish people are overwhelmingly Eurasian in ancestry. While most Jewish people have predominantly Jewish genes, with various mixtures of northwestern European genes, Georgian genes, Arab genes, Berber genes, and Indian genes, the Ethiopian Jews are almost exclusively Ethiopian, with little or no Jewish genetic trace. Ethiopian Jews are not the "real" Jews: they are the descendants of black African converts to Judaism.

As a result of time poorly spent in the Shiite seminary in Qum, some black scholars have come back claiming that Imam Musa al-Kazim, Imam 'Ali al-Rida, Imam Muhammad al-Taqi, and Imam Muhammad al-Mahdi were all black men. These subjective and subversive scholars insist that the color of the Imams has been "de-emphasized." In reality, the color of the Imams has never been de-emphasized by Shiite scholars. On the contrary, it is this small segment of black Shiite scholars from the West who seek to stress it and to make an issue out of a non-issue. Instead of having a racial agenda, Shiite scholars from all ages have objectively presented the facts, pointing out the possibility that some of the wives of the Imams were black bondmaids. In the case of Imam Mahdi, for example, all of our scholars have presented the various perspectives, namely, that the mother of Muhammad al-Mahdi may have been either a white slave or a black slave.

Unlike some Afro-Caribbean, African American, and African Canadian Shiite scholars, the great Shiite luminaries attempted to determine the truth on the basis of empirical evidence as opposed to racial bias. Concerned more about racial pride than academic integrity, some black Shiite scholars seek to Africanize the Prophets and the Imams at all cost. According to the scholars in question, Imam Musa al-Kazim was black because his mother, Hamidah, was supposedly a slave from Nubia. Although she was a slave, Hamidah is reported to have been a Berber from the Maghreb or a white woman from al-Andalus. As a result of the conquest of the Maghreb and al-Andalus, many Berbers and Andalusians were taken as captives by the Muslims and sold throughout the Islamic world. One such slave was Hamidah al-Barbariyyah, the daughter of a nobleman named Sa'id, who was nicknamed Lu'lu'ah or Pearl because of her beauty.

If Hamidah was a Berber, she may have been a Muslim, a Christian, a Jew or a pagan. Although Muslims are not allowed to take other Muslims as slaves, it was, nevertheless, common practice among the Umayyads, a dynasty which actually demanded that conquered and converted Berbers pay part of their taxation by means of the delivery of slaves. If Pearl was a Berber, she was most likely a Kharijite, a Shiite or a Sunni, in order of likelihood. If she was a *rumi* or a Roman, the Arabic term for a white person or a European, she was either an indigenous Andalusian of Christian origin or from a family which had recently converted to Islam.

Regardless of whether she was from the Maghreb or al-Andalus, and regardless of whether she was of Berber or European extraction, Hamidah found herself in the slave market in Medina where she was purchased by the fifth Shiite Imam, Muhammad al-Baqir, who presented her to his son, Imam Ja'far al-Sadiq, for marriage. Not only did the sixth Imam marry Hamidah, he paid close attention to her education. As a result of his training, his wife Hamidah became a leading jurist. Imam Ja'far al-Sadiq assigned her to work with women whom she educated about Islam's traditional beliefs and practices. Besides being a great scholar, Hamidah was the mother of Musa al-Kazim, the seventh Shiite Imam.

Considering that the fifth, sixth, and seventh Imams all had family ties to the Maghreb and al-Andalus, it seems quite natural that they would have sent missionaries to Hamidah's people whether they were found in the Maghreb, al-Andalus or both. If Hamidah was, in fact, a Berber from the Maghreb or al-Andalus, she most certainly had tribal kin in both regions, as most of the Berber tribes had a presence in both Northern Africa and the Iberian Peninsula. It makes perfect sense, then, that Hamidah al-Barbariyyah would have purchased Najmah al-Barbariyyah, another fellow Berber, when she appeared on the slave market in Medina.

Today's black nationalists disguised in black abayas or clerical cloaks also claim that Imam 'Ali al-Rida was a black man because his mother, Umm al-Banin Najmah, was allegedly black. Since Najmah was a former slave of African origin, these scholars immediately assume that she was black. They seem to be oblivious to the fact that Arabs have long lived in Africa. They also appear ignorant of the fact that the Amazigh or Berbers are indigenous white Africans native to North Africa. Najmah Khatun, also known by the titles of Tuktam, Umm al-Banin, and Tahirah was from North Africa, not black Africa. This is not an uncommon error on the part of those who are not well-versed in the history, peoples, languages, or cultures of the region. Najmah was not a black African; she was a Berber. She was purchased by Hamidah al-Barbariyyah, the mother of Imam Musa al-Kazim, who, as her name indicates, was also a Berber. It is quite possible that both Hamidah and Najmah belonged to the same Berber tribe and spoke the same Berber language. Taught and trained by Lady Hamidah, who had been educated to be an *'alimah* or religious scholar by Imam Ja'far al-Sadiq, Lady Najmah attained an impressive level of intellectual and spiritual expertise. According to Lady Hamidah, the Prophet appeared to her in a dream, and told her, "Make Najmah the wife of your son, Musa ibn Ja'far, so that soon the best of people in the world [namely, Imam 'Ali al-Rida], will be born to her." Lady Hamidah acted upon this order. Najmah married Imam Musa al-Kazim and later became the mother of Imam 'Ali al-Rida and Lady Fatimah Ma'sumah. Regardless of Imam 'Ali al-Rida's complexion, he was not a black man in the Western sense of the term: he was an Arab in paternal Semitic lineage. The Berbers, however, traced their genealogy through their maternal line. Hence, from an Amazigh perspective, any Imam with a Berber mother was invariably a Berber.

Besides claiming that Imam 'Ali al-Rida was black, these ethnocentric and racially obsessed Shiite scholars assert that Imam Muhammad al-Taqi was also black. In fact, they boast that black students and scholars at the Shiite seminary refer to him as "the black one." While there is no doubt that Sabikah or Khayzaran, the mother of 'Ali al-Naqi, was from Nubia, this does not necessarily mean that she was a black African. On the contrary, the historical literature specifies that Sabikah belonged to the same tribe as Maryah al-Qibtiyyah or Mary the Copt, the wife of the Prophet. However, it was only in 719 that the Church of Nubia transferred its allegiance from the Greek Orthodox to the Coptic Church. If Sabikah was indeed a Muslim convert of Coptic Christian origin, then it is unlikely that she was an ethnic Nubian. She was probably an ethnic Egyptian. And, as DNA analysis has demonstrated, the Copts are a predominantly Caucasian population, regardless of their varying complexions.

According to the hadith literature, Imam al-Taqi did not have the fair complexion that the Arabs admired. As a result, his enemies used to spitefully call him *al-Aswad* or "the black one." The insult, of course, was not so much directed at the Imam as it was to his mother, who came from the African continent. The uncles and brothers of Imam al-Rida complained that "there has never been a dark-complexioned Imam among us," demonstrating that the previous Imams had all been fair-skinned. The relatives of Imam 'Ali al-Rida even went to the extreme of bringing in physiognomists to determine if he was really the father of the child. Although rooted in pre-Islamic pagan practice, the Imam did not prevent them from seeking outside confirmation. After examining the child's facial features, the experts all confirmed that Imam 'Ali al-Rida was the father of Imam Muhammad al-Taqi. Another Imam that Afrocentric Shiite scholar claim was black was 'Ali al-Naqi. Once again, since his mother was a former slave, these scholars assume that she was a black African. Known as Samanah, Susan, Hadithah and Umm al-Fadl, the mother of Imam 'Ali al-Naqi was a slave girl from Morocco, in North Africa, where she had been taken captive. As her name, Samanah al-Maghribiyyah, clearly indicates, the mother of the eleventh Imam was a Berber from the Maghreb.

Even if one of the Imams had a black mother that would not make him "black" in the global sense of the word. Unfortunately, as a result of five hundred years of racial indoctrination, blacks from the West have come to accept that anyone with a drop of black blood is black by definition, an idea which is viewed with ridicule throughout the rest of the world. If a person is half black, and half white, that does not make them black: that makes them 50% black and 50% white. They are bi-racial. Among the Arabs, as it is among the Hispanics, one's ethnicity is based upon a cultural and linguistic identity. A non-Arab black may be viewed by Arabs as black. A non-Arab white may be viewed by Arabs as white. However, if these individuals identify themselves as Arabs by language and culture they are simply accepted as Arabs, and they will never be categorized as either "black" or "white." Even if one of the Twelve Imams was half black African genetically, he would never have identified himself as black. He would have identified himself unequivocally as an Arab from the tribe of Quraysh.

The last Imam considered to have been black by some Shiite racial chauvinists is Muhammad al-Mahdi. Although there are three theories concerning the identity of the mother of the twelfth Imam, Black Nationalist scholars and sympathizers cast aside all objective considerations and embrace the version which serves an overzealous self-interest, asserting that his mother was a black slave-girl from al-Naqbah, the northern province of Sudan. According to one theory, however, the mother of the twelfth Imam was a Byzantine princess and a direct descendant of Peter. According to another set of traditions, she was a black-slave girl. By yet another conjecture, she was a Berber from Morocco. While this is neither the time nor the place to engage in a comparative study of the various theories regarding her background, it suffices to say that scholarly research generally supports the claim that the mother of the twelfth Imam was European, namely, a Byzantine princess known as Narjis. That the Awaited Imam was light-skinned is further supported by a wide body of traditions describing his radiant countenance. Since prophets and messengers were sent to all tribes and nations (10:47) and saints come in every color, there is no need to Africanize the Prophet or the Imams. History is filled with distinguished African and African American Muslim scholars, saints, and activists, including Bilal, Usman dan Fodio, and Malcolm X, among many others.

In reality, debating the color of Adam, the Prophets, and the Imams, is an ill-conceived matter on its face. A true Muslim should not care about the skin color of a Prophet or an Imam. The only reason I am compelled to address this unfortunate racialist obsession is to debunk the deviant beliefs being spread. One sad result of this campaign is that it provides laypeople with arguments they can use to assert the presence of racist ideas in what has always been a racially neutral environment: the mosque. If Muslims of all colors are attracted to the mosque, it is because of the brotherhood and sisterhood which reigns within. It is a place where people cease being "white," "black," or "brown," and become human beings, plain and simple. Instead of creating a space where all are welcome, some are spreading racial animosity and ethnic discord, alienating non-blacks, and creating a hostile worship environment. If the racist ideas of W.D. Fard, Elijah Muhammad, and Louis Farrakhan merely remained among those attached to the aberrant Nation of Islam, there would be no cause for concern among Muslims. Those racially divisive and separatist ideas, however, have spread, to a certain extent, into the mainstream Muslim community through some African-Caribbean, African American, and African Canadian converts from the West. So long as these nationalist, supremacist, and separatist concepts are circulated among common believers, they pose a problem of contagion. When they are spread by some black Shiite scholars from Qum, however, they are given greater credibility.

Rather than representing the authentic teachings of Islam, which came to abolish racism, and conveying the spirit of Muslim brotherhood, these misguided mullahs regurgitate racist doctrines from far beyond the teachings of Islam, doctrines which naturally alienate non-blacks as much as they offend pious black believers. If race, which is not even a scientific concept, has become their religion, these black Muslim scholars who suffer from a racial complex would be well advised to cast off their abayas and their *amamahs*, namely, their cloaks and turbans, put on a tuxedo and bow-tie, return to the Nation of Islam, where they can join their like-minded friend, Louis Farrakhan, and start selling bean pies and peddling *Muhammad Speaks* or rather *The Final Call*. As far as bona fide believers are concerned, we should respond to racist discourse with the words of Almighty Allah, "(We take our) color from Allah, and who is better than Allah at coloring. We are His worshippers" (2:138).

Chapter Four

Selecting a Source of Emulation

Selecting a Source of Emulation is an important decision for a Shiite Muslim. That source, or person, is the one the Shiite believer will use as a religious and spiritual model. In the recent past, when there were only one or two Sources of Emulation in the Shiite world, the decision was relatively simple. In the late twentieth century, Shiites could select from Grand Ayatullah al-Khu'i or Grand Ayatullah Khomeini. In the mid-twentieth century, the sole Source of Emulation was Grand Ayatullah Muhsin al-Hakim. With the exponential growth of the Shiite seminary, however, an unprecedented number of Sources of Emulation have surfaced through the scholarly ranks, and the decision has become much more difficult to make. Instead of selecting the sole Source of Emulation, or picking between two leading figures, Shiites in the early twenty-first century can select from approximately fifty Grand Ayatullahs.

Although there is no shortage of Sources of Emulation at the moment of writing, they are not all prominent. In fact, most of them have only a handful of followers. Currently, as of 2016, the leading Sources of Emulation include Grand Ayatullah 'Ali al-Sistani, Grand Ayatullah 'Ali Khamene'i, Grand Ayatullah Ishaq Fayyaz, Grand Ayatullah Bashir Husayn Najafi, Grand Ayatullah Luftullah Safi Gulpayghani, Grand Ayatullah Husayn Vahid Khorasani, Grand Ayatullah Yusuf Saanei, and Grand Ayatullah Nasir Makarim Shirazi.

Although all of these Grand Ayatullahs are learned, Shiite jurisprudence specifies that the most learned and most pious jurist is the one who should be followed. These qualities, however, are hardly measurable by legal or academic standards. Traditionally, the "most learned" jurist was the one who had the most students in his *dars al-kharij* or graduate class. Following this standard, the most learned Shiite jurist is currently Grand Ayatullah Vahid Khorasani who has several thousand advanced students studying the highest level of jurisprudence under his direction. After Grand Ayatullah Khorasani, the most prominent supervisors of *buhuth al-kharij* or independent research in Qum are Grand Ayatullah Nasir Makarim Shirazi and Grand Ayatullah Luftullah Safi

Gulpayghani.

Although Grand Ayatullah 'Ali Khamene'i lectures in Qum in order to maintain his status as a Source of Emulation, the individuals who attend his lectures are not traditional students and seekers of knowledge but rather ideologically minded Muslim militants who embrace Political Shiism, a modern re-invention of Shiite Islam. While Grand Ayatullah Saanei has a large number of pupils, his students are overwhelmingly liberal reformists. Despite his prestige, Grand Ayatullah 'Ali al-Sistani has not lectured for decades. Advanced students in Iraq all study at the hands of Grand Ayatullah Bashir Najafi and Grand Ayatullah Ishaq al-Fayyaz, both of whom have several hundred graduate students. Although attempts are being made to revive the *hawzah* or seminary in Najaf, the number of students studying in Iraq pales in comparison with the tens of thousands of students studying in Qum. As for the late Grand Ayatullah Fadlullah, who was an authority in his own right, he was considered by many clerics to be more preacher and politician than senior scholar and teacher. Without advanced students, one has little standing in the religious establishment and no extended network of alliances to rely upon.

If by "most learned," one focuses on scholarly accomplishments, rather than sheer number of advanced students, the quest for the most educated of jurists becomes even more complicated. For starters, it takes knowledge in order to judge knowledge. Unless one is a trained scholar, an individual who is a non-specialist is simply not qualified to judge scholarly knowledge. In such cases, a lay person would have to rely on the advice or recommendation of at least two scholars who can confirm that one particular Source of Emulation is more accomplished and gifted than his peers. Scholars can only be evaluated by their peers.

Academic accomplishments, as opposed to number of students, is certainly a sounder approach to selecting a Source of Emulation, since a good lecturer is not necessarily a good scholar, and a good scholar is not necessarily a skilled administrator with an elaborate network of connections or a wealthy financier able to provide stipends to thousands or even tens of thousands of students. So long as one has sufficient knowledge to judge knowledge, one can compare the contributions that the various Grand Ayatullahs have made to the field of Islamic Studies. Some Sources of Emulation have published very little: perhaps a few books on *fiqh* or jurisprudence while others have published prolifically in a vast array of fields such as Qur'anic commentary, hadith science, philosophy, and mysticism...

Selecting a Source of Emulation on the basis of "piety" is particularly problematic as the only thing individuals can judge is outward behavior.

While perceived piety should not be discarded, as Grand Ayatullah Fadlullah has suggested, it should be a necessary complement to knowledge and wisdom. It should be remembered, however, that Sources of Emulation are the legal authorities of Shiite Islam. They are not necessarily spiritual authorities. Jurists are specialists in Islamic jurisprudence. They are the lawyers who are experts in Islamic law. They are not necessarily spiritual guides and masters. Seeking spiritual guidance from a *faqih* or jurist is like taking spiritual guidance from an attorney. What seekers really need is a *murshid* or spiritual guide. These are most often found among specialists in Islamic Gnosis: *tasawwuf* or *'irfan*. In fact, Grand Ayatullahs, who are both legal and spiritual authorities, are quite rare. Grand Ayatullah Khu'i was a legal as opposed to a spiritual authority, while 'Allamah Tabataba'i was a spiritual figure rather than a legal authority. Exceptions to this rule include Grand Ayatullah Ruhullah Khomeini, Grand Ayatullah Behjat, Grand Ayatullah Abdollah Javadi-Amoli, and Grand Ayatullah Muhammad Sadiq al-Sadr, who were simultaneously legal and spiritual leaders.

In recent decades, an entirely new dimension has been added to the search for a Source of Emulation--that of political proclivity. While many Grand Ayatullahs have traditionally been apolitical quietists, Grand Ayatullahs like Imam Khomeini, Grand Ayatullah Muhammad Baqir al-Sadr, Grand Ayatullah Khamene'i, and Grand Ayatullah Fadlullah assumed a strong political presence. If one is searching for a politically active person to follow in *taqlid* or emulation, then the best choice would be Grand Ayatullah Khamene'i. Since politics and jurisprudence are two entirely different fields, it is possible to follow one Source of Emulation in matters of jurisprudence while following another Source of Emulation in political matters, if that is one's preference.

Since Allah has placed a blessing in diversity, Shiites can search for Sources of Emulation on the basis of different ideological considerations. Increasingly, the Grand Ayatullahs can be divided into neo-fundamentalists, traditionalists, and reformists. The neo-fundamentalists include the likes of Grand Ayatullah Nuri Hamadani, who believes that Sufi Muslims are infidels, Grand Ayatullah Luftullah Safi Gulpaygani, who opposes the participation of women in politics, Grand Ayatullah Makarem Shirazi, who believes that women are prohibited from attending soccer matches, and Grand Ayatullah Ja'far Subhani, who opposes freedom of expression. The traditionalists include the likes of Grand Ayatullah 'Ali al-Sistani, Grand Ayatullah Bashir Najafi, and Grand Ayatullah Ishaq al-Fayyaz. And the reformists include the ranks of Grand Ayatullah Javad Gharavi Aliari, Grand Ayatullah Sayyid 'Ali Muhammad Dastghayb Shirazi, Grand

Ayatullah Asadullah Bayat-Zanjani, and Grand Ayatullah Yusuf Saanei, some of whom believe in religious relativism, right to abortion, and who insist that hijab is not mandatory.

It should be recalled, however, that simply because a Source of Emulation is conservative politically does not necessarily mean that he is conservative jurisprudentially. Similarly, simply because a Source of Emulation is more liberal jurisprudentially does not mean that he is liberal politically. Grand Ayatullah Khamene'i, who is a political conservative, passed an astonishingly liberal edict allowing women to be inseminated with the sperm of men who are not their husbands. It should also be pointed out that some Grand Ayatullahs, like Makarem Shirazi, have attempted to remain relatively neutral when it comes to internal politics.

As can be appreciated, the fifty odd Sources of Emulation represent every degree of the political and social spectrum. More liberal Shiites, particularly young people and women, have been drawn into the orbit of Grand Ayatullah Fadlullah and Grand Ayatullah Saanei. More traditional Shiites tend to follow Grand Ayatullah 'Ali al-Sistani, Grand Ayatullah Bashir Najafi, Grand Ayatullah Ishaq al-Fayaz, or Grand Ayatullah Khorasani. Ideologically driven Shiites tend to follow the line of Grand Ayatullah Khamene'i, while ultra conservative hardline Shiites stick with Grand Ayatullah Nuri-Hamadani. Ultimately, the selection of a Source of Emulation is a highly personal issue. While Shiites are expected to mirror their Source of Emulation, Sources of Emulation are increasingly being selected because they reflect the socio-political and religious attitudes of their followers. Rather than adhering to the views of the "most learned" scholar, Shiites are selecting scholars who happen to share their own views.

Chapter Five

The Barbarity of Blood-Letting

What can be more emotional than a passion play? Such theatrical displays have aroused multitudes to faith and devotion. Yet, what could be more dangerous than a debate regarding the legality or illegality of self-flagellation? Likewise, who on Earth would want to argue with people who beat themselves black and blue with chains, with people who strip the flesh off their backs with whips and blades, with people who split their heads open with swords as an act of self-mortification and who even slice the foreheads of their infant children with razors? I, for one, for I fear none but God, stand for truth, promote the good, and forbid the wrong.

According to arguments advanced by the proponents of blood *matam* or self-flagellation, Allah judges people on the basis of their intentions. They claim that those who engage in blood *matam* have good intentions. Consequently, they will be rewarded, as opposed to punished, for inflicting harm upon themselves. While it is true that Allah judges people according to their intentions, he judges them according to their good intentions. If people intend to deliberately inflict physical harm upon themselves or upon others, then their intentions are bad from the get go, and their actions are reproachable and punishable as opposed to commendable and rewardable.

In the eyes of some scholars, blood *matam* is only prohibited if it causes permanent harm. They argue that the only self-harm outlawed in the Qur'an is the infliction of permanent, life-threatening or mortal injuries. According to this line of reasoning, knocking out one's teeth, ripping out one's hair, chopping off one's nose and amputating one's ear or other "non-essential body parts" is perfectly acceptable.

If human beings were made in the spiritual image of Adam, if the human form was fashioned by Almighty Allah, and if the bodies of the created belong to the Creator, then human beings do not have the right to damage their bodies, regardless of whether the damage is temporary or permanent. As Grand Ayatullahs Khomeini, Khamene'i, and Fadlullah have all established, any practice that causes bodily harm is forbidden, the sin increasing with the severity of the damage inflicted.

As Volker Adam explains in "Why do they Cry? Criticisms of Muharram Celebrations in Tsarist and Socialist Azerbaijan," which appears in *The Twelver Shia in Modern Times: Religious Culture and Political History*, edited by Rainer Brunner and Werner Ende, the opposition to blood *matam* is as old as the practice itself. 'Allamah Ahmad ibn Muhammad Ardabili, who died in 1585, may have been the first Shiite scholar to outlaw excessive expressions of mourning which had no basis in the lives or practice of *Ahl al-Bayt*, namely, Household of the Prophet.

Although we do not have details about the type of *matam* that was practiced, it appears to have involved chains, a ritual popularized by the Safavids and which was adopted from Christian flagellants and penitents. Rather than respect the ruling of 'Allamah Adarbili, Shiite extremists expressed their contempt for this great scholar by intensifying the severity of their self-flagellation. Ardabili himself, acting out of disgust for the practice of these Turkish-born religious deviants, decided to leave Ardabil and settle in a surrounding village.

By 1640, Safavid Shiite extremists were wounding their heads, faces, and bodies with knives during Ashura processions, thereby causing their own blood to flow. As Roy Mottahedeh relates in *The Mantle of the Prophet*, some of these blood smeared flagellants would be paraded around on wheeled platforms as *tableaux vivants*, portraits of living, butchered martyrs. Such practices were encouraged by the Safavids, who thus flamed the fires of religious fanaticism and sectarianism in an attempt to defend their empire from the Sunni Ottomans.

Since most Twelver Shiite scholars were either on the payroll of the Safavids or under their watchful eye, they were not in a position to openly object to these practices. One Shiite scholar, Mirza 'Abd Allah Afandi, who lived during the time of the Safavid Shah, Sultan Husayn (1694-1722), did, however, allude to his opposition to such perversions. There was little he could do, however, since the Safavids were supported by a military force composed of Qizilbash Shiite *Ghulat*, religious extremists who deified the Twelve Imams from the Prophet's Household. Opposing blood *matam* was to oppose the imperial army.

Concurrently with Safavid times, Iranians settled in what is now India and Pakistan, bringing with them the practice of blood *matam*, an act which was similarly held in abhorrence by the early Shiite scholars from India. In 1820, writes Juan Cole in his *Roots of North Indian Shiism*, Sayyid Mohammad Nasirabadi, the chief *mujtahid* or jurist of Lucknow, ruled that wailing, beating one's chest, and self-flagellation were only permissible if one lost control of one's self. In short, it was one thing to be overcome by grief. It was another, altogether, to premeditate a plan to beat oneself black and blue, lash one's back, and slash oneself with razor blades.

In 1907, narrates Volker Adam, the leading Shiite scholars from Baku, Azerbaijan, headed by Axund Mir Mahammad Karim Mircafarzada, finally took a stand against blood *matam*, a practice that actually originated in their midst, and which was not rooted in Iran and the Indian subcontinent. The consensus of the Council of Shiite Scholars was categorically clear: blood *matam* was a major sin which was both *batil* and *haram*, namely, religiously invalid and prohibited. In 1922, Axund Abdulrahman Hadizada, *qadi* or Muslim judge of Baku, ruled that flagellation was forbidden in principle. He pointed out the pagan origin of the practice and objected to the fact that Shiites had readopted rituals that had been outlawed by the Prophet Muhammad. Speaking on behalf of the Shiite scholars of Azerbaijan, he declared blood *matam* to be a *bid'ah* or prohibited innovation in religion. Since the action was a forbidden innovation, he ruled that it could not be meritorious. Not only was blood *matam* a sin, it was a sin for Shiite scholars to fail to put a stop to the practice. If they failed to do so, they themselves would be sinners.

A few days after his *fatwa*, explains Volker Adam, the Shiite scholars of Azerbaijan asserted that the traditional Muharram ceremonies were instigated by pseudo-scholars who sought to enrich themselves from the mourning of Imam Husayn. They insisted that the rituals violated both the sharia and *adab*, namely, Islamic law and good manners. The Shiite ulama or scholars emphasized that they had always objected to the celebrations. They explained that the only reason they had not spoken out earlier was due to the objection of the Tsarist government, and the fact that the advocates of blood *matam* or self-flagellation used to curse the Shiite scholars who opposed the practice. The Shiite scholars of Azerbaijan asked the Soviet government to put an end to blood *matam*, using force if required, and urged them to close the border to prevent ignorant Iranian mullahs or dervishes from entering the region and reinforcing such prohibited practices.

As Volker Adam explains, the *fatwa* or religious edict of the Shiite scholars of Azerbaijan was not limited to Baku. In fact, it was adopted throughout the country. Shiite dignitaries insisted that Muharram commemorations should only be permitted if they were conducted in an appropriate manner. The Shiite ulama of Karabagh, the very region where the practice of self-flagellation commenced, issued a *fatwa* in 1923 against flagellation and against all attempts to portray the practice as authorized by the sharia. In their ruling, they strongly condemned previous generations of Shiite scholars for lacking the fortitude to prohibit the practice, leading to the present miserable state of affairs.

As the debate over blood *matam* reached its peak in Azerbaijan, relates Volker Adam, the same issue boiled to the surface in Syria, Lebanon, and Iraq. In the mid 1920s, Grand Ayatullah Muhsin al-Amin al-Amuli, the leader of the Shiite community in Syria, ruled that,

> Blood *matam* and the likes in mourning sessions of Imam Husayn are forbidden according to religion and rationale. Injuring one's head does not have a worldly benefit nor does it hold reward in the hereafter. It is *idha' nafs* which is forbidden in religion and the Shia of the *Ahl al-Bayt* are ridiculed as a result of this. People call the Shia barbaric. There is no doubt that these actions stem from satanic whispers and will not cause Allah's, the Prophet's, or the pure *Ahl al-Bayt*'s satisfaction. Of course, changing the name of this action will not have any effect on its ruling, which is being forbidden.

Around 1926, reports Yitzak Nakash in *The Shiis of Iraq*, Grand Ayatullah Abu al-Hasan al-Isfahani, in Najaf, and Grand Ayatullah Muhammad Mahdi Qazwini, in Basrah, both issued edicts outlawing this practice. As Grand Ayatullah Isfahani ruled, "The usage of swords, chains, drums, horns, and the likes today, which have become common in mourning ceremonies on Ashura, is definitely forbidden and against religious doctrine."

Grand Ayatullah Qazwini also supported 'Allamah al-Amin's *fatwa*, commenting that the use of metal chains and sharp objects in mourning sessions was introduced a century ago, namely in the 1800s, by people who knew little about Islamic law. Sayyid Mushin was also supported by Shaykh Abdul-Karim Jaza'iri as well as Shaykh 'Ali Qummi and Shaykh Ja'far Badiri, two famous Gnostics.

The rulings of Grand Ayatullahs Isfahani, Qazwini, and al-Amin were strongly opposed by Grand Ayatullah Husayn Na'ini, as well as Ahmad and Muhammad Husayn Kashif al-Ghita who exploited the great strife among the Shiites to improve their own rank within the religious hierarchy. Rather than appeal to reason, they appealed to the emotions of extremists for political and economic gain, a pattern we continue to see to this day, as some scholars have a vested economic interest in maintaining these Muharram rituals. So, although he admitted that blood *matam* was forbidden in *al-Firdaws al-a'la*, Kashif al-Ghita sided with the common people, thus increasing his popularity and position.

The supporters of Muhsin al-Amin came to be known pejoratively as the Ummayis while the supporters of Kashif al-Ghita came to be known as the Alawis. Not only did the Alawis criticize Grand Ayatullahs Muhsin al-

Amin, Qazwini, and Isfahani, those revered religious authorities were slandered and cursed. Some fanatics even collected funds to launch holy war against Sayyid Muhsin. Despite the pressure that was placed upon them by ignorant and violent fanatics, the Ayatullahs never rescinded their rulings. When Sayyid Muhsin finally visited Najaf, he forgave all the laypeople who had opposed him, but he never forgave the scholars who had incited the ignorant against him.

Well-aware of the consequences of opposing blood *matam*, most of the Grand Ayatullahs during the twentieth century found themselves with their hands tied. Grand Ayatullah Burujerdi, who was the sole Source of Emulation of his time, saw for himself the danger of attempting to reform the rituals. When he objected to un-Islamic practices that took place during Muharram, many of his followers opted to drop his *taqlid* during Ashura.

Although Grand Ayatullah al-Hakim is often cited as a supporter of blood *matam*, he commented that "The issue of blood *matam* is like a thorn in our throat." In other words, like many *marjas* or religious authorities, he felt compelled to tolerate the practice for fear of losing his followers. It is well-known that some of the Sources of Emulation were concerned that those who practiced blood *matam* would break away from Twelver Shiism and form their own sect. For these Grand Ayatullahs, it was better to put up with the practice and attempt to eradicate it gradually through education as opposed to edicts. In order to avoid the issue, some scholars attempted to remain neutral, passing "fatwas of convenience" that stated that the practice was neither obligatory nor forbidden.

With the advent of the Islamic Revolution, and the power of the State behind him, Imam Khomeini was able to openly object to blood *matam*. As the Imam ruled,

> Mourning and chest-beating for Imam Husayn is considered a good act. However, it should be noted that no blood should be drawn from the body; otherwise, it will be considered an act of hurting one's body. Since such an act harms the image of the religion, it is unlawful, and should be avoided in all circumstances.

In another edict, he said: "Do not perform blood *matam*." The Imam's courageous stance was supported by such scholars as Grand Ayatullah Muhammad Baqir al-Sadr among many other forward-looking *fuqaha* or jurists. Due to the overwhelming authority of the Imam, few scholars dared to object to his ruling in public, particularly when he was alive and in power.

With the passing of Imam Khomeini, his successor, Imam Khamene'i, reiterated the ruling of his predecessor. According to the *fatwa* of Imam

Khamene'i, "If the use of such chains lead, in the eyes of the public, to damaging the image of our school of thought or inflicting a noticeable harmful effect on the body, it is not permissible." Regarding piercing one's body as an act of mourning, he ruled that "These acts, which are inevitably bound to portray our school of thought in a negative shade, are impermissible." When asked about individuals who cut themselves with swords and who walk on fire during Ashura, the Imam ruled that:

> Any practice that causes bodily harm, or leads to defaming the faith, is *haram*. Accordingly, the believers have to steer clear of it. There is no doubt that many of these practices besmirch the image of the school of *Ahl al-Bayt* which is the worst damage and loss.

When asked whether hitting oneself with swords was universally outlawed, Imam Khamene'i responded that:

> *Qama zani* or *tatbir* is absolutely impermissible. In addition to the fact that it is not held in the common view as manifestations of mourning and grief and it has no precedent at the lifetime of the Imams and even after that, and we have not received any tradition quoted from the Infallibles about any support for this act, be it privately or publicly, this practice would, at the present time, give others a bad image of our school of thought. Therefore, there is no way that it can be considered permissible.

Besides Grand Ayatullah Khomeini and Grand Ayatullah Khamene'i, Grand Ayatullah Fadlullah also outlawed blood *matam*, describing it as a backwards tradition and custom. Blood *matam* has also been banned by Grand Ayatullah Makarem Shirazi, Grand Ayatullah Mahmud Shahrudi, and Ayatullah Ahmadi Miyanji on the basis that it causes physical harm and damages the image of the religion. Blood *matam* is prohibited by Grand Ayatullah Salihi Mazandarani and Ayatullah Muttahari on the grounds as there are no rational or religious arguments to support it. Blood *matam* is outlawed by Ayatullah 'Ali Mishkini because it is a forbidden innovation.

According to the following scholars, blood *matam* is outlawed since it has been forbidden by Imam Khamene'i, the *wali al-'amr* or ruling authority. They include Grand Ayatullah Sayyid Mahmud Shahrudi, Grand Ayatullah Araki, Ayatullah Mazaheri, Ayatullah 'Ali Mishkini, Ayatullah Muhammad Yazdi, Ayatullah Muhammad Mu'min, Ayatullah Ahmadi Miyanji, Ayatullah Husayn Rasti Kashani, Ayatullah Ibrahim Amini, Ayatullah Shar'i, Ayatullah Sayyid Ja'far Karimi, Ayatullah Sayyid Muhsin Kharazi, Ayatullah 'Abbas Mafuzi, Ayatullah Muhsin Haram Pinahi, Ayatullah Hasan Tehrani, Ayatullah Ahmad Adhari Qumi,

Ayatullah Sayyid Muhammad Abtahi, Ayatullah Ustadi, Ayatullah Muhammadi Gilani, Ayatullah Musawi Tabrizi, Ayatullah Muqtada'i, Ayatullah Sayyid Kazim Ha'eri.

According to the following scholars, blood *matam* is forbidden if it harms the image of the Shiite faith. They include Grand Ayatullah Imam Khomeini, Grand Ayatullah Khu'i, Grand Ayatullah Imam Khamene'i, Grand Ayatullah Makarem Shirazi, Grand Ayatullah Jawad Tabrizi, Grand Ayatullah Jawadi Amuli, Grand Ayatullah Mahmud Shahrudi, Ayatullah Ahmadi Mianji, Ayatullah Ibrahim Amini, Ayatullah Malakuti, Ayatullah Muqtada'i, Ayatullah Muhammadi Gilani, Ayatullah Musawi Tabrizi, Ayatullah Rasti Kashani, Ayatullah Husayni Nasab, and Sayyid Abdul-Karim Hashimi-Nejad. Blood *matam* is also outlawed as illogical and unacceptable by Grand Ayatullah Fazel Lankarani, Grand Ayatullah Nuri-Hamadani, and Ayatullah Muhammad Ibrahim Jannati.

While there are many Shiite scholars who believe that blood *matam* is not intrinsically prohibited, the vast majority of them agree that it is forbidden if it causes permanent physical harm or damages the image of the Islamic religion. Although some scholars do not explicitly outlaw blood *matam*, they have ruled that any action that violates the sanctity of the Shiite school of law it forbidden. Grand Ayatullah Gulpayghani, however, stated that blood *matam* should be avoided on the basis of precaution. While Shiite scholars may have different opinions on the subject of blood *matam*, some holding that it is *halal* or permissible and others holding that it is *haram* or prohibited, it is always best to exercise caution regarding such issues. No harm shall come from failing to flay one's flesh. Plus, if such an act is indeed forbidden, then anyone who engages in it will be held accountable for his actions.

The reasons for the prohibition of self-flagellation and self-mutilation are self-evident. These practices are forbidden innovations which were introduced to Twelver Shiites a couple of centuries ago. Muslims are naturally prohibited from imitating the erroneous ways of the Jews and Christians, and the prohibition of following pagan and *Ghulat* practices is even greater. Both the Qur'an and the Sunnah forbid Muslims from blindly following Islamically unacceptable cultural customs. Almighty Allah repeatedly cautions against following the false beliefs of one's ancestors (23:24; 7:70; 11:62; 11:87; 26:74; 12:40; 28:36; 34:43), consistently inviting believers to use reason and intelligence to ascertain the truth (38:29; 47:24; 43:3; 21:10). Not only does the Qur'an provide evidence against the claims of those who maintain this practice (4:174; 6:104), it also demands that they provide proof for their practices (21:24; 27:64; 2:111; 37:157).

When faced with Islamic documentation, the advocates of blood *matam* react as the unbelievers do in the Qur'an: "And when it is said to them: 'Follow what Allah has revealed!' They say: 'Nay! We will follow what we found our fathers following.' What! Even though their fathers were void of wisdom and guidance?" (2:170). Almighty Allah warns that blind submission to cultural beliefs is the work of Satan: "When they are told to follow what Allah has revealed, they say: 'Nay we shall follow the ways that we found our fathers following!' 'What! Even if it is Satan beckoning them to the penalty of the blazing (fire)?" (31:21). Almighty Allah also warns that those who blindly follow their fathers will face severe chastisement (37:68; 37:69; 37:70; 23:104). Almighty Allah will question them as to why they failed to pay heed to the Qur'an (23:104; 23:105; 23:106). Acknowledging the error of their ways, they will respond: "Had we but listened or used our intelligence, we should not (now) be among the companions of the blazing fire!" (67:10). As if the Qur'an did not suffice, the Prophet also warned Muslims not to follow in the footsteps of the Christians, Jews, Zoroastrians, and pagans. As the Messenger of Allah foretold: "You will follow the tradition of those who came before you exactly" (Ahmad and Abu Dawud). For Shiite Muslims, the Qur'an and the Sunnah must suffice, as there is no place for prohibited pre-Islamic practices in the religion of Allah.

As a cultural innovation deeply rooted in superstition, blood *matam* has no place in the intellectual and evidence-based religion of Islam. Besides causing physical and spiritual harm, both of which are outlawed in Islam, blood *matam* incites emotion, rather than intelligence, damaging the *din* or religion by presenting Shiites as violent, bloody fanatics, who have a blatant disregard for the Islamic rules pertaining to ritual purity as they spurt *najasat* or ritual impurity all over themselves, participants, and spectators. The practice of self-flagellation and self-mutilation is also a public health hazard that poses serious biological risks to both participants and spectators. Participating in group blood *matam* is as risky to one's health as participating in an unprotected sexual orgy or sharing dirty needles during intravenous drug use. The ritual provides a perfect medium for the spread of blood-borne pathogens such as malaria, syphilis, brucellosis, viral hemorrhagic fevers, hepatitis B, hepatitis C, and HIV. Furthermore, blood *matam* focuses on past oppression rather than present oppression. The focus falls on the crimes committed against Imam Husayn and his Household in the seventh century to the detriment of current injustices. These Husaynis do not hesitate to shed their blood for Husayn, who died 1400 years ago, but rarely rise up in revolt against the oppressors of the age.

Chapter Five

Although advocates of blood *matam* insist that its opponents are agents of the enemies of Islam, it is actually the enemies of Islam who have insisted on promoting the practice. In Azerbaijan, for example, the Soviets destroyed many vestiges of Islam, with the exception of blood *matam*. In Iran and Iraq, the practice of blood *matam* was promoted by the British embassies in Tehran and Baghdad who used to pay the participants. The CIA has also played an active role in supporting superstitious practices in an attempt to divide and conquer the Shiite community. Rather than view blood *matam* with fear, communist and capitalist imperialists view the practice as risible. Instead of directing their animosity towards their occupiers, Shiites were attacking themselves physically: harming themselves and harming the image of Islam in the process. Let me just repeat that, because it is at the core of how those ignorant of the truth of the Qur'an and Sunnah are manipulated by those who do not have their best interests at heart: they are harming themselves and harming the image of Islam in the process.

Besides being irrational, blood *matam* is not a method of mourning. If one is informed that one's child has died, the logical emotional and spiritual response is not to cut one's head open with a sword. Furthermore, blood *matam* cannot be viewed as mourning when some of the participants are actually joyful and smile as they perform it. Although some scholars have strongly supported it, those same people have rarely, if ever, engaged in blood *matam*. This leads one to wonder what their motive is in upholding a practice that they themselves do not perform. Finally, the sole aim of some of the organizers and participants of the processions is self-enrichment given that they depend on the donations, bequests, and endowments of practitioners for their livelihood. In fact, an entire economy revolves around blood *matam*. The sale of blood *matam* videos, for example, is a thriving business, with people profiting from this sickening spectacle which seems to satiate a sublimated sexual urge through blood lust. As Ramita Navar notes in *City of Lies: Love, Sex, Death and the Search for Truth in Tehran*, "young men self-flagellate at the religious festival of Ashura, purporting that each lash is for Imam Hossein, when really it is a macho show to entice pretty girls, who in turn claim they are there only for God" (xi).

While some scholars may wish to debate the subject self-harm until the Day of Doom, the Qur'an is categorically emphatic on the subject, and for true believers it must stand as the final arbiter: "Do not cast yourself into destruction" (2:195). As the Prophet stated himself, "What is forbidden in small quantities is forbidden in large quantities" (Abu Dawud, Tirmidhi, Ibn Majah, and Bayhaqi). A glass of wine is as *haram* or forbidden as a bottle of wine. A single cigarette is as *haram* as an entire pack of cigarettes. A sip of windshield washer fluid is as *haram* as drinking an entire cup of the poisonous product. As such, causing a temporary, deliberately inflicted, injury is as *haram* as causing a permanent injury. If Islamic law forbids a person from beating, cutting, and whipping another human being; what right does a person have to beat, cut, and whip themselves? If Islamic law bans masturbation because it is a form of pleasurable "self-abuse;" should not other forms of painful self-abuse also be outlawed?

If Islamic law views wailing, tearing one's clothing, casting off one's veil, ripping out one's hair, slapping and hitting oneself, and throwing dust upon oneself over a dearly departed as a major punishable sin which requires expiation; what right does one have to engage in these illicit activities when commemorating the martyrdom of Imam Husayn? If it is *makruh, haram ihtiyat wajib* or *haram* [reprehensible, prohibited as an obligatory precaution or forbidden] for men to parade around shirtless in front of non-*mahram* women, females who are not direct relatives; how can such behavior be tolerated at an Islamic event such as Ashura? If Islam forbids *shirk*, associating partners with God, as well as statues and idolatry, how can Shiites idolize physical replicas or images of Imam Husayn?

If Islamic law imposes a punishment for causing redness, bruising or cutting the skin of another person; should not a person be punished or subjected to psychological treatment for injuring themselves? In 2007, ten participants in blood *matam* ceremonies were hospitalized while two thousand required medical attention with an average of seven to eight stitches per person. In some extreme instances, individuals have even succumbed to their self-inflicted wounds. Are such actions meritorious or self-destructive and suicidal? Furthermore, what right do Shiite parents have to cut open the foreheads of their babies, infants, and small children? As Grand Ayatullah Fadlullah has rightly ruled,

> If tormenting one's self is religiously forbidden since it is forbidden to inflict damage on the self, how do you think the situation would be if someone is tormenting a child?! This is religiously forbidden! It is a crime against childhood. Neither the mother nor the father has the right to do such things to their children. On the contrary, they are obliged to care for their children and guide them on the straight path.

And what can we say about the rare instances in which innocent Sunni Muslims who have been slaughtered by Shiite mobs after their emotions were elevated to a level of crazed irrationality? Surely, such actions would not make the Prophet proud. As Imam Hasan al-'Askari said, "Fear Allah and be an adornment for us. Do not be a cause of anger for us. With your actions attract all forms of love towards us and distance all negative (people) from us (with your actions)." Rather than draw people to Shiite Islam, the advocates of blood *matam* do nothing but alienate them.

The proponents of blood *matam* claim that their ritual blood-letting helps keep the message of Ashura alive. Evidently, these individuals are oblivious to the fact that neither the Imams nor their Companions engaged in pre-meditated ritualized blood-letting nor are they aware that blood *matam* has only existed in recent centuries. As Grand Ayatullah Fadlullah recognizes, "These practices do not trace back to the lives and teachings of the Imams." Even if it were true that some fanatics had drawn blood for Husayn 1400 years ago, such action would not set an acceptable precedent. It would have been just as wrong then as it is wrong now. Simply because you do something *haram* for a long time does not make it *halal*.

The message of Ashura was passed down for over one thousand years, from the 7th century to the 19th century, without people engaging in self-flagellation and self-mutilation. While the Imams who followed Husayn all encouraged their Shiites to mourn the martyrdom of Imam Husayn, it was initially a private practice. It was only in 962 C.E. that the first public demonstration of Ashura took place in Baghdad and Egypt. In both cases, the processions involved chants of *Ya Husayn*, chest-beating, and the recitation of elegies. The participants did not draw blood.

As any religious historian can confirm, blood *matam* is very much a modern *bid'ah* or religious innovation with no basis in the Qur'an and Sunnah of the Prophet, the Imams, and the Companions. In Lebanon, blood *matam* rituals only trace back to the early 20th century. Just as the message of Imam Husayn was preserved for ten centuries without blood *matam*, Ashura can continue to be commemorated without the senseless shedding of blood. As Imam Khamene'i has said, "*Tatbir* is not *azadari*; rather, it is a wasting of *azadari*;" namely, "The shedding of blood is not mourning; rather, it is a wasting of mourning." As Grand Ayatullah Fadlullah has rightly observed, the swords of the Shiites should be directed towards their enemies, not towards themselves. As Fadlullah has stated, blood *matam* is not a proper way to mourn the death of Imam Husayn. The true devotees of Imam Husayn are those who fight, are wounded, and die in the battlefield against the enemies of Islam. Surely, the young Shiites who practice blood *matam* should channel their energy and enthusiasm constructively, as opposed to destructively.

Cutting one's forehead open while hypnotically chanting does nothing to preserve and promote the message of Imam Husayn. Grand Ayatullah Muhsin al-Amin, it should be remembered, used to boycott such ceremonies and organize his own sessions in which the authentic story of Imam Husayn was conveyed to the people. It is information, and not self-mutilation, that spreads the message of Karbala. As surveys of Shiites conducted during Muharram have confirmed, the traditional modes of commemoration are more cultural customs than religious rituals. When asked why they were attending mourning gatherings during the month of Muharram, 90% of Shiites responded that it was a cultural custom, and that they were there to see friends and family. A mere 10% reported that they were there to mourn the death of Imam Husayn. In fact, many of the participants only attend the mosque a few times per year for Ashura and Eid. As violently defensive as they may be when it comes to blood *matam*, the majority of participants in ritual self-flagellation and mutilation are ignorant, uneducated individuals, many of whom do not pray, do not fast, and could not name the Twelve Imams if their lives depended upon it. Rather than mourning Husayn, they seem to be doing penance for their own serious set of sins or are bent on showing off that they are the most Shiite of Shiites.

The proponents of blood *matam* point to the fact that Zaynab, the sister of Imam Husayn, allegedly hit her head against the bars of the cage in which she was held, causing blood to flow from her forehead, in the presence of Imam Zayn al-'Abidin. Since the Imam did not reproach her, they take this incident as evidence of its permissibility. The proponents of blood *matam* also point out that Uways al-Qarni, the Companion of the Prophet, broke his tooth when he heard the news that the Prophet had broken a tooth in battle. Since the Prophet did not reproach him, they take this incident as evidence of permissibility. However, there is a fundamental difference between a spontaneous expression of grief, anger, and despair, and pre-meditated, planned, and performance-centered act of self-flagellation and mutilation which has historically been performed in exchange for payment.

The alleged incidents involving Zaynab and Uways were not habitual, ritualized religious acts replicated by others: they were one-time events, not actions that were taken up again and again in a fallacious show of piety or grief. A mother who wails after the death of a beloved child will not scream and cry in the same way fifteen years after the event. She will remember the adored one and weep quietly to herself. Why? Because the emotion in both cases is real: not contrived. Taking the argument further, even if Zaynab and Uways had repeated their actions; the behaviors would have been customs of ordinary individuals and not the Sunnah of the

Infallibles. After all, Shiites are followers of the Prophet and the Twelve Imams. As authenticated traditions confirm, the Prophet Muhammad never beat himself or drew blood over the future death of Husayn. On the contrary, he cried, demonstrating a dignified manner of mourning.

Although many Shiites blindly accept the tradition regarding Zaynab's spontaneous blood-letting as authentic, hadith scholars confirm that it contains an incomplete chain of narrations. Not only are these "brotherhoods of blood" following a hadith, rather than the Qur'an, they are adhering to one that does not uphold the necessary authority. In fact, according to authentic traditions, Imam Husayn specifically prohibited his sister from scratching her face and tearing her clothing in the event of his martyrdom. Verily, there is a large body of sacred sayings from Allah, the Prophet, and the Imams prohibiting wailing over the dead.

Those who promote blood *matam*, however, view Shiism as a religious banquet, where they can pick and choose what suits them. If they really wanted to follow Uways al-Qarni, then they should smash the teeth out of their mouths on the day the Prophet was injured in battle. Using that hypothesis, we must assume that, according to the mindset of certain Muslims, the Messenger of Allah would be pleased to see masses of toothless Muslims marching around.

The proponents of blood *matam* insist that their gory rituals form an integral part of their cultural traditions. In reality, blood *matam* is not Arabic, Persian, nor Indo-Pakistani in origin. As scholars have confirmed, blood *matam* is of Turkish origin. Instead of being Islamic, the practice is pagan in origin and seems to have spread to Shiism via Christianity. As scholars have established, the practice of blood *matam* originated among the Turks of Azerbaijan where self-flagellation was introduced in the mid-1800s. It was the inhabitants of Karabagh, the very heartland of the *Ghulat*, extremist Shiites who believe in the divinity of 'Ali, who first practiced excessive flagellation and who later proceeded to spread these customs in Tabriz and other Iranian towns.

The blood-letting rituals reached Iran during the late Safavid period with more extreme forms becoming official during the Qajar dynasty. Blood *matam*, as we know it today, reached Iraqi Arabs in the early 19th century, Indians in the mid-19th century, and Lebanese Arabs in the early 20th century. The Lebanese were introduced to the practice by Iranian immigrants while the Indo-Pakistanis learned the ritual from immigrants of Qizilbash and Iranian origin. In Iraq, Arabs did not participate in blood *matam* processions until the mid-twentieth century. Prior to then, blood *matam* was limited to Iraqi Turks, Sufis, and Kurds from western Iran. There is no evidence that blood *matam* was practiced in Najaf or Karbala before the mid-19th century, having been first performed by Qizilbash Turks, a notorious tribe of *Ghulat* Shiites. Like many *Ghulat* sects, the beliefs of the Qizilbash contain elements of Shamanism, Mithraism, and Yazdanism, along with Christian influences of Armenian origin. The practice of blood *matam* was also adopted by the Akhbaris, a semi-*Ghulat* group that believes in *tahrif al-Qur'an*, namely, that the Qur'an was corrupted, and who profess that the Usulis, that is, the vast majority of Twelver Shiites, are infidels. If the blood *matam* rituals in Iraq, Iran, and Lebanon are contaminated with pagan, Zoroastrian, and Christian elements, the blood *matam* rituals in India and Pakistan are contaminated with Hindu elements. In fact, some Hindus and Sikhs actively participate in blood *matam*.

The proponents of blood *matam* seem to have confused the means with the end. *Azadari* or mourning is neither a ritualistic activity nor a means of atonement. The goal of *azadari* or lamentation for Imam Husayn is to revive the basic values of Islam. Ashura is not a ritual; it is a philosophy. Although many Shiites state that "Every day is Ashura, and every place in Karbala," there is no such hadith in traditional sources. On the contrary, trustworthy sources assert that there is no day like Ashura. There are times to rise up in revolt just as there are times to be patient and practice pious dissimulation. There are times for war and there are times for diplomacy.

Ashura is not simply a yearly event; it should be actualized in daily life. It should instruct our socio-political and economic perspectives. It should guide Shiite Muslims to perpetually side with the oppressed of the earth. If Shiites embraced the true meaning of Ashura, they would not tolerate injustice; they would struggle against it using the most appropriate method for each circumstance. As Dr. 'Ali Shariati pointed out, the proponents of blood *matam* are black Safavid-style Shiites who content themselves with reenacting religious rituals which pose no threat whatsoever to the enemies of Islam. The true Shiites, in the eyes of Shariati, are the red Shiites, the revolutionary Shiites, those who put the teachings of Karbala and Ashura into practice. As Shariati eloquently expressed, Black Shiism is the religion of mourning while Red Shiism is the religion of martyrdom.

Islam, it should be remembered, is a religion of moderation. Muslims should be neither extremely lenient nor extremely severe in religious matters. As we read in the Holy Qur'an, "Allah burdens not a person beyond his scope" (2:286); "[Allah] has not laid upon you in religion any hardship" (22:78); and "Allah does not want to place you in difficulty" (5:6). As Almighty Allah warns in the Holy Qur'an, "Do not exaggerate in your religion" (4:171). The Qur'an also warms believers to "Beware of extremism in your religion" (5:77). In essence, Muslims are expected to be "a justly balanced nation" (2:143).

Although some scholars may argue that the admonition against extremism contained in the Qur'an applies to Jews and Christians, the Messenger of Allah demonstrated that it was also directed to Muslims. In fact, he warned his followers to "Beware of extremism in your religion for it is that which destroyed the nations which came before you" (Nasai and Ibn Majah). In another tradition, he stated that "The religious extremists are destroyed" (Muslim). And again, "Let it be known, the religious extremists are destroyed" (Abu Dawud). The Messenger of Allah also warned: "There are two groups of people from my Ummah who will not receive my intercession: oppressive rulers, and religious extremists" (Tabarani).

As the embodiment of the Qur'an, the Prophet Muhammad was a moderate man. When faced with two equally acceptable alternatives, he always opted for the one which was the most straightforward. As the Messenger of Allah explained, "The religion is indeed easy, and no one contends with the religion except that it will overwhelm him" (Bukhari). He also warned, "Do not cause the worship of your Lord to become hateful to you" (Bayhaqi). The Prophet also taught that moderation is the order of the day in all aspects of religious practice. After teaching a Bedouin how to perform the ritual ablution, the Prophet warned him, "This is the ablution. He who does more than this has done wrong, transgressed the limit, and oppressed himself" (Tirmidhi, Nasa'i, Ibn Majah, and Abu Dawud). Furthermore, the Prophet clearly condemned the deviant interpretations of Islam made by religious extremists. As he explained, "Religious knowledge is protected from every deviated direction: the distortion of the extremists flees from it, as does the false assumptions of the infidels, and the misinterpretation of the ignorant" (Bayhaqi).

If Almighty Allah and the Prophet denounced all forms of religious extremism, so did the Twelve Imams. As Imam 'Ali warned, "Two types of people will be destroyed because of me: the extremist and the enemy." He stated that "The best stance towards me belongs to those who choose a moderate way." Imam Muhammad al-Baqir professed that "There are two categories of my Ummah which do not benefit from Islam: the extremists and those who believe in predestination." As Imam Ja'far al-Sadiq warned, "Beware of the exaggerators lest they deviate your children." He stated that "The smallest thing that diverts a believer from his faith is sitting next to an extremist, listening to him, and confirming his words." As Imam 'Ali al-Rida said, "We, the Household of Muhammad, are the middle nation.

The extremists cannot reach us, and the laggard cannot keep up with us."

Proponents of blood *matam* will inevitably argue that these traditions denounce the extremist beliefs of the *Ghulat* who deify the Imams. However, the Imams also extended the definition *ghuluww* or "exaggeration" to include those who believed in delegation and predestination. Furthermore, if one examines these traditions attentively, one inevitably notes that many of them denounced extremist actions as well, such as the fabrication and false attribution of traditions to the Imams. Extremist beliefs go hand in hand with extremist practices. And what can be more extreme than engaging in self-flagellation and self-mutilation? While many of the individuals who engage in blood *matam* are mainstream Twelver Shiites in belief, they are unquestionably engaging in a ritual which originated among extremist Shiites, the very *Ghulat* whose infidelity was denounced by the Imams. Why, then, should any Shii seek to perpetuate a practice which originated among Shiite extremists who fall outside the framework of Islam?

When faced with such arguments, the proponents of blood *matam* resort to emotion as opposed to reason and academic evidence. Rather than focus on this single objectionable aspect, they claim that the opponents of blood *matam* are opposed to *azadari* or mourning and seek to destroy Ashura. For many Indo-Pakistani Shiites, anybody who opposes blood *matam* is a Wahhabi or a CIA agent who deserves to die. This is where one finds the main difference between those who oppose and those who defend blood *matam*. While the advocates of blood *matam* readily curse, condemn, threaten, and sometimes kill the opponents of blood *matam*, those who object to extremism do not accuse the other side of being infidels nor do they seek to harm them in any way. They may believe that advocates of blood *matam* are ignorant, misguided, extremists and fanatics. They will never, however, accuse them of being infidels and issue death threats against them.

Simply because scholars oppose blood *matam*, known alternatively as *zanjir*, *tatbir*, and *qama zani*, it does not mean that they oppose *matam*, and *azadari*. On the contrary, those who oppose blood *matam* are staunch defenders of *azadari* and Ashura. Rather than oppose mourning ceremonies, they seek to purify them from un-Islamic cultural practices of pagan origin. Ashura ceremonies expressing sorrow and grief, and which include the recital of elegies (*marsiya*), chest-beating (*matam*), mourning processions, parading the biers, models of the mausoleum, and the dramatic reenactment of the tragic events are acceptable according to Islamic law so long as they are correct in both content and form. The one and only objection which is raised revolves around self-injury, whether it involves severe blows to the head with one's hands or fists, lashes caused by whips, slashes caused by razor blades, and flesh wounds to the forehead caused by swords. Since these more extreme expressions are so limited in size, accounting for less than a fraction of 1% of Shiite mourners, their loss will do nothing to hamper the overwhelming power of Ashura.

It is high time that Twelver Shiites move from ignorant practices to educated practices, from low culture to high culture, from passivity to activity, from manifestations of machoism to modesty, from popular entertainment to devotion, from confrontation to composure, from despair to discipline, from irrationality to rationality, from impurity to purity, from the destructive to the constructive, from frenzied sectarianism to intrafaith fraternity, from outlandish actions to organization, from the past to the present, from theory to application, from extremism to moderation, from otherness to unity, from the ahistorical to the historical, and from traditional commemoration based on emotion, legends and lies, to authenticated commemorations based on intelligence, understanding, and empirical evidence.

CHAPTER SIX

YOU DA BOMB!
THE SHEER STUPIDITY OF SUICIDE BOMBING

Suicide bombings are not heroic; they are stupid. Suicide bombers are not martyrs; they are imbeciles, misguided self-professed Muslims who were manipulated by corrupt clerics who would never personally engage in so-called "martyrdom" operations or even encourage their own children to do so. Suicide, the intentional taking of one's own life, is categorically prohibited in the Qur'an. If such crimes are committed, it is only as a result of politically-motivated hermeneutics of deceit and deception that some scholars have propagated in an attempt to legitimize suicide bombings, which they have repackaged as "martyrdom operations." While driving a dynamite-laden truck into the military base of an enemy might be justified as a necessary and unavoidable act which will result in the loss of life of a Muslim combatant, there is no acceptable reason to kill oneself in order to blow up a café, a restaurant or a bus filled with unarmed civilians: men, women, and children. Such acts are nothing short of sheer evil.

I have met many self-proclaimed Muslims who were maniacs, psychopaths, repressed serial-killers and mass-murderers who extolled the virtues of suicide bombing. To be fair, I found these fanatics among both so-called Sunni and Shiite scholars. I have also met some sincere, but seriously misguided men and women, who seek the advice of their *shaykh* prior to taking a position on any issue. "Suicide bombings are *haram*," I told a man known for his piety. "Let me see what Maulana says..." he replied. "If you need someone to tell you that it is wrong to kill civilians, you are seriously astray from the path," I responded. "If your *shaykh* tells you that slaughtering non-combatants is *halal*, you are both stupid and misguided." Right is right and wrong is wrong. And it is always wrong to intentionally kill unarmed men, women, and children. Whenever any scholar argues otherwise, I would advise any Muslim to take refuge in Allah, distance themselves from Satan, the Rejected, and seek guidance from someone else.

CHAPTER SEVEN

THE OBLIGATION OF ENGLISH

In the mid-1980s, an African American *shaykh* was leading a group of pilgrims on the Hajj. While in the sacred precinct of the Ka'bah, he was explaining the ritual rules of the pilgrimage in the English language. When listening to the *shaykh* speak English, a local Arab man proclaimed: "I take refuge in Allah from the language of Satan." The *shaykh* shook his head, glared into the eyes of the xenophobic Arab, and retorted in Classical Arabic: "Praise be to Allah! The language of Satan has become the language of Allah!"

The response of the African American *shaykh* was not without wisdom. He was well-aware of the spurious traditions which claimed that Arabic was the language of Allah and the language of Adam, notions which are dismissed by authentic Islamic sources and historical linguistics. The African American *shaykh* was also highlighting an increasingly inescapable reality: English was no longer *a* language of Islam; it had become *the* language of Islam, that is, the predominant language of Islamic scholarship and the *lingua franca* of many Muslims.

If we consult World Cat, a digital online database containing the catalogs of 71,000 libraries from 112 countries, including all the major Muslim majority nations, the preeminence of English as an academic language is empirically established. According to a search conducted in 2010, this catalog contained over 150 million unique titles in 470 languages. There were 325,416 books on the subject of Islam in all languages: 117,153 of them were in the English language; 61,838 were in the Arabic language; 21,648 were in the French language; 13,464 were in the German language; 12,712 were in the Persian language; and a mere 3,292 were in the Spanish language.

As the evidence establishes, there are nearly twice as many books about Islam in the English language as there are in the Arabic language in research libraries throughout the world. The other major Western languages, like German and French, lag far behind the English language in the field of Islamic Studies, while the Spanish language is particularly low in scholarly proclivity. Although Persian is often described as the second language of Islamic scholarship, and though Iran is currently publishing as much scholarship as the entire Arab world combined, it still pales in comparison to the academic accomplishments embodied in English language texts.

While no sane scholar wishes to undermine the importance of Classical Arabic to the field of Islamic Studies--after all, the major sources in the field are found in that enthralling language--the inherent predominance of English, as a language and a world resource, is becoming all the more manifest. While one cannot claim any scholarly credibility in the field without a working knowledge of Classical Arabic, if not a perfect proficiency in this ancient idiom, not a single researcher or writer can be considered a complete, credible scholar without also achieving advanced reading proficiency, if not a full skills mastery, of the English language.

As the Prophet Muhammad preached, "Seek knowledge, even in China" (Bayhaqi, Ibn 'Abd al-Barr, and Khatib) which essentially means, "Seek knowledge, even in Chinese." It is the obligation of all Muslims, especially Islamic scholars, to seek knowledge regardless of the language in which it might be found. While knowledge of Arabic, and in some cases Persian, has been required of Shiite seminarians, an English language requirement should also be contemplated and rigorously implemented for the sake of scholarly currency. To put it plainly: scholars who do not have access to English language information cannot possibly remain in tune with academic advances in the field. As if frozen in time, they are condemned to an antiquated understanding of the sources of religion.

When faced with modern matters, this linguistic handicap becomes particularly perilous, impeding a just and objective *ijtihad*: the interpretation and application of Islamic principles to current questions. Since virtually all scientific knowledge is now delineated by the vast expanse the English language; how can a jurist, however brilliant he may be, deliver an edict on any subject if he can scarcely understand the language in which it is most cogently and broadly explained? This is not an issue of a personal lack of intellectual prowess, but one that arises due to a lack of data in his native tongue. It is for this very reason that virtually every rigorous graduate program on the planet requires reading comprehension of the English language. If scholars and scientists cannot remain current in their fields unless they understand English; how can people who speak only Arabic and/or Persian, however respected their ancient roles may be, expect to achieve an adequate comprehension of critical issues?

Whether one likes it or not, English is the most widely published language in the world. According to the latest available statistics from

UNESCO, the U.K., the U.S., Canada, and Australia combined publish an average of 400,000 English language books per year. The Chinese publish approximately 136,226 books per year while the Russians publish 123,336. The Spanish speaking nations of the world release an average of 102,250 works per year. The Germans and the Austrians publish roughly 104,000 books per annum. The Japanese churn out some 45,430 books on a yearly basis. Yet, all the Arab countries combined publish a mere 15,000 books per year, many of which are in French and English. While this is a sad commentary on the role of scholarship, creativity, and outreach within the Arab world, it is more importantly a clear signal of a sea change in intellectual pursuits. English is the ship knowledge comes in on.

If the number and type of books published per language per year is an important standard index of education, the English language has overwhelmingly become the language of culture, civilization, and science in the 21st century. As important as they may be, languages like Mandarin Chinese, Russian, Spanish, German, and Japanese, lag far behind the English language in influence. Although it is spoken by 250 million people in 28 countries, and is the liturgical language of 1.5 billion Muslims, the Arabic language has long lost the privileged role it once had in the transmission of knowledge, culture, science, and civilization. Much has changed since the eras when the libraries in Islamic Spain churned out as many as 60,000 Arabic works per year. Because so few books are translated into the Arabic language, and even fewer books are translated from Arabic into other languages, monolingual Arabic and Persian speakers are very much isolated from the waves of information that speakers of culturally dominant languages take for granted. This begs two questions: 1) Should we not expect Shiite, Sunni, and Sufi scholars to read and understand religious and secular works in English? And 2): How can those seminarians argue from an informed position if they rely only on Arabic or Farsi materials?

Chapter Eight

Sell-Out Scholars: The Uncle Tom *Ulama*

While the religion of Islam commands respect for scholars, many Muslims adopt an uncritical attitude of reverence towards the ulama without resorting to critical thinking of any kind. Religious scholars, in reality, are human beings like those in any other collective. Just like there are good lawyers, there are also bad lawyers. The same dichotomy exists among jurists; there are both good and bad. Unfortunately, many Muslims make the mistake of believing that all scholars are inherently pious and well-informed. Simply because someone wears a mantle and a turban does not make him a sage and a saint. There are brilliant scholars and there are mediocre scholars. There are pious scholars and there are impious scholars. There are scholars who are sincere and there are scholars who are hypocrites. There are good theologians and there are bad theologians. This litany of the obvious has failed to register with too many people and is the cause of both social and religious upheaval. Many Muslims fail to realize that merely because a person is a legal authority does not mean that he is a spiritual authority.

While some might condemn this critical attitude towards the ulama as an act of irreverence, that is certainly not the case. As Almighty Allah explains in the Holy Qur'an, there are Imams who lead to Heaven (21:73), and there are Imams who lead to Hell (28:41). As the Messenger of Allah said, "There are two types of people who, if they are good, then the Ummah will be good, and, if they are bad, then the Ummah will be bad: the scholars and the rulers." He then added, "Do not ask me about the bad, but ask me about the good." After repeating this three times, he said, "Verily, the worst of people are the scholars, if they are bad, and verily, the best of people are the scholars, if they are good" (Abu Nu'aym and al-Darimi). In short, both the Qur'an and the Sunnah urge Muslims to employ critical reasoning to evaluate the righteousness or lack thereof of their religious leaders. If we survey the history of Islam to the present, we can easily confirm the damage that has been done by misguided mullahs at the service of the Umayyad, 'Abbasid, Safavid, and Ottoman empires, not to mention the current congregation of court ulama at the service of despotic regimes throughout the Islamic world.

One web definition of critical thinking encompasses the active relationship people are encouraged to have with their beliefs and actions. It says,

> Critical thinking is self-guided, self-disciplined thinking which attempts to reason at the highest level of quality in a fair-minded way. People who think critically consistently attempt to live rationally, reasonably, [and] empathically.

Alas, this criterion is at odds with the tendency among humans of "wanting to believe" those with whom they feel a connection. That is where the snare exists, in our default to belief. Ironic, when one considers how often we are led astray by everyone from politicians to snake-oil salesmen. Yet, the Prophet cautions us, saying that not all scholars are saints and that righteousness can be a winning and destructive disguise.

CHAPTER NINE

SHIISM IN CHINA

When many Muslims think of China, they think of Chinese food. In fact, the vast majority of Muslims seems oblivious to the fact that China is the home to some 20 to 100 million Muslims from various ethnic groups, the majority of which are Hui and Uyghur, along with smaller minorities who are Kazakh, Dongxiang, Kyrgyz, Salar, Tajik, Uzbek, Tatar, and Tibetan. While the majority of Muslims in China are Sunnis, there are tens of thousands of Shiite Muslims in the country, including Ismailis and Twelver Shiites.

Although it is alleged that Islam was first introduced to China in the year 650 by Sa'd ibn Abi Waqqas during the Caliphate of 'Uthman, the first communication about the Prophet and the Qur'an was likely at the hands of Muslim diplomats during the first decades of the Islamic era. While political contacts played a role in the spread of Islam, it was primordial business contacts that propagated the faith through Muslim settlements of Arab and Persian merchants, some of whom were certainly Shiites. China, like other remote regions such as the Maghreb and al-Andalus, was also a place of refuge for Shiites of all sorts, Zaydis, Ismailis, and Imamis, who sought to escape Umayyad and 'Abbasid persecution. Other Shiites, like the descendants of Syed Khamush Shah Shirazi, entered China after the destruction of Alamut in 1256, settling in Sikiang, Kashgar, Rashkam, western Mongolia, and Chinese Turkistan. Although China was a refuge for Shiites, they continued to be victimized in the country, not so much by the Chinese, but by foreign invaders like the Uzbeks who destroyed many Shiite shrines and mosques in Chinese Turkistan as an act of retaliation against the Safavids.

Ismaili *da'wah* or missionary activities in China continued into more modern times. An Ismaili missionary known as Syed Muhammad Ibrahim, who belonged to the fifth generation of Syed Sohrab Wali, is reported to have gone to China. In 1930, Syed Shah Ghulam from Chitral went to China, only to be murdered by the government, while Abdul Shah officially visited the country in 1937, delivering the *waez* or religious service on the orders of Imam Sultan Muhammad Shah. The most recent visit of an Ismaili leader to China was that of the current Agha Khan, Prince Karim al-Husayni, who visited the country over a period of twenty days in October of 1981.

While the majority of Chinese Muslims are Sunnis, many of their religious practices can be traced back to Persian Shiites. Known as *An-la* or Allah, *Zhen-Zhu* or True Lord, Chinese Muslims also refer to God by the Persian word *Hu-da*, and refer to their religious leaders as *ahong* or Teacher, which derives from the Persian *akhund*. One of the most popular Muslim surnames in China is Ma, a shortened form of Fatimah. The Chinese Muslims celebrate *Fadimajire*, Fatima's Remembrance Day, on the 4th day of the 9th Islamic month. On this evening, women gather in mosques to hear the *ahong* speak about Fatimah al-Zahra, the daughter of the Prophet Muhammad, and the wife of Imam 'Ali ibn Abi Talib. Unlike Sunni Muslims, who tend to take 'A'ishah as an example, Chinese Muslim women consider Fatimah to be a model of Islamic ethics, morality, and spirituality.

Besides celebrating Fatimah Day, the Muslims in China commemorate *Ahshula* or *'Ashura'* as it is pronounced in Arabic, the tenth day of the Islamic month of *Muharram*. While some may say that many Sunnis celebrate Ashura as a sacred day in the life of prophets like Adam, Noah, Abraham, and Moses, Chinese Muslims also commemorate the assassination of Houssainiyuce or Husayn, an aspect which is lacking from most Sunni celebrations. As scholars and historians can confirm, the Umayyads attempted to subvert the true meaning of Ashura, namely, the martyrdom of Imam Husayn, by associating it with other festive events. It would have been highly unusual for Sunni Muslims to introduce the mourning for Imam Husayn in China. Regardless of the origin of the commemoration, huge *Muharram* programs are organized in major Chinese cities such as Peking, Shanghai, and Taiwan.

Another practice of Shiite origin observed among the Chinese Muslims is that of *Chiragh-i Rawshan*, a lamp lighting ritual of Ismaili origin. One of the oldest Ismaili traditions, and one which continues to be practiced in Central Asia, the *Chiragh* appears to have been introduced into Central Asia while it was in its formative stage by Taj Mughal. The spread of the *Chiragh-i Rawshan* may also have been a testament to the fruitful activities of Ismaili missionaries in the region.

Although many Chinese Muslims appear to practice Hanafi jurisprudence, it must be remembered that Zaydi jurisprudence is almost identical to that of Abu Hanifah. One wonders whether the ancient Chinese Muslims were not first taught the rules of ablution and prayer by Zaydi Muslim refugees and merchants from the Yemen.

Shiite beliefs and practices may also have reached China through various Sufi orders. Some of the Sufis who established themselves in China included Baba Hamza Isfahani who settled in the country in the 16th century and who preached Sufism in the regions of Hezu and Dongxiang. Hezu, which is now known as Linxia, was one of the most important Muslim centers in China. A veritable melting pot of Muslims, followers of every imaginable Islamic school of thought coexisted there in mutual respect and harmony. As a result of this symbiosis of schools of thought, Hezu was known as Little Mecca by Chinese Muslims. Other Sufis of Shiite faith and practice included Zayn al-'Abidin al-Shirvani (1790-1837), the head of the Nimatullahi Sufis. Although it was a Twelver Shiite Sufi *tariqah*, Ismailis, like the ancestors of the current Agha Khan, were associated with the Nimatullah Order. Although they are Hanafi Sunnis in jurisprudence, the members of the Kubraviya Sufi Order of China have been strongly influenced by Twelver Shiism. To this day, the Kubraviya continue to recite qawwalis or devotional chants which invoke the Twelve Imams, and engage in other Shiite rites.

Another practice which seems unusual in a Sunni setting is the existence of mosques reserved for the exclusive use of women under the direction of female Imams. Unlike some currents of Sunni Islam, which have a history of hostility towards women, evidenced by banning them from mosques according to the edict of Abu Hanifah, or confining them to restricted quarters as second class Muslims, Shiite mosques have always been open to women. In fact, rather than relegate women to a dirty room in the back or in the basement, Shiite mosques are often equally divided into male and female sections. Furthermore, while Sunni Islam has produced few women scholars, a wide range of leading female scholars and jurists can be found in the ranks of Shiite Islam.

Although the egalitarian attitude towards women manifested by Chinese Muslims forms a fundamental part of Chinese culture, it may also have been reinforced by Persian Shiite and Sufi influence. As further confirmation of the Iranian influence on Chinese Islam, most of the Muslim manuscripts on *fiqh*, *tasawwuf*, and *tafsir*, namely, jurisprudence, Gnosticism, and Qur'anic commentary, available in China are written in Persian as opposed to Arabic. The traditional Chinese style of reciting the Qur'an is also strongly influenced by Persian mispronunciation of Classical Arabic. Moreover, the Uyghur language contains a large number of Persian words.

While the history of Shiism in China traces back to the 7th century, the current Shiite community in the country is composed primarily of Ismaili Shiites, with a small minority of Twelver Shiites. The Chinese Ismailis are predominantly Tajiks who live in an autonomous region in the Pamirs. Despite the difficulty they have communicating with the Agha Khan, they are Nizari Ismailis as opposed to Musta'ali Ismailis. Numbering in the tens of thousands, these ethnic Tajiks are concentrated in the northwestern part of the Xinjiang-Uighur Autonomous Region, where they are isolated from the worldwide Ismaili community.

Kept under a watchful eye, as are the rest of the Muslims in communist controlled capitalist China, the authorities only allow a single Ismaili mosque to operate in the district capital of Tashkurgan, observed and dictated to by the observant eye of a state-appointed Imam. Although the Agha Khan visited the region in 1981, the secular government prevented him from providing any economic assistance to his followers. Even though Tashkurgan is only 60 miles from the Chinese-Pakistani border, the Chinese government does not allow Ismaili preachers from Pakistan to work in China. Tajikistan is in close proximity to the Ismaili community of Xinjiang, but it has no contact with Tajik Ismailis. While the Ismaili community in the nearby Gorno-Badakhsant Autonomous Region thrives thanks to the generosity of the Agha Khan, the Chinese Ismailis are left to languish.

Besides the Tajik Ismailis, China also has a Twelver Shiite minority of Azeris and Ironis which inhabit the autonomous region in the Pamirs. Twelver Shiites are also found along the Chinese/Kashmir border in the area surrounding Siachen. If other Muslims in China find themselves in difficult circumstances, the plight of the Shiites is even more severe, particularly that of the Twelver Shiites who have no religious representation of any kind. Unlike the Ismailis, who are not viewed as a political threat, the Twelver Shiites are perceived as potential allies of the Islamic Republic of Iran. Viewed as a destabilizing element in Central Asia, the Twelver Shiites seem to suffer far greater than the Sunnis and are apparently controlled much more closely. The sole exception, perhaps, is the *Shia Ansa-l-Ashri* or *Shi'ah Ithna 'Ashari* community of Hong Kong, founded in 1985 by East Indian Twelvers, and which appears to operate with greater freedom due in large part to the special status reserved for the former British colony.

Chapter Ten

Syrian-Lebanese Settlers in the Dakotas

Meet Mr. Hassan Abdallah. He was 80 years old in 2015. He is a farmer. He looks like any one of my neighbors in the rural Midwest. Note the name. It is Arabic. It is Islamic. And it is entirely American. He is not an immigrant. He is an Arab-American Muslim of Lebanese ancestry. He is the son of one of the first Muslim families to settle in the United States. And he lives in Ross, North Dakota, where Muslims gathered for the first communal prayer in a home in the year 1900, and where Muslims built the first mosque in the United States in 1929.

Wow! But who knows anything about Arab-Americans anyway? Casey Kasem, Khalil Gibran, Edward Said, Tony Shalhoub, Danny Thomas, James Zogby, Ralph Nader, John Sununu, Doug Flutie, Jeff George, Joe Robbie, Paul Anka, Tiffany, Paula Abdul, Frank Zappa, Jamie Farr, Marlo Thomas, William Blatty, Jacques Nasser, Joseph Abboud, Paul Orfalea, Candy Lightner, Christa McAuliffe, are all Arab Americans. In fact, I cannot even find someone who knows that Shakira is a Lebanese Colombian or that Salma Hayek is a Lebanese Mexican. So, let us rewind a bit and enter quietly into this well-hidden history.

Settlers who came to the United States and the Midwest were from all over the world. In the Dakotas, we hear about Germans, Norwegians, the Irish, the English, and dozens of other groups: a veritable ethnic mosaic. But we never hear about Arabs. We never hear about the Syrian-Lebanese. Yet they came to the Dakotas in droves.

The first Arabic-speakers to reach what is now the United States accompanied the Spanish explorers of the sixteenth century. Arabs also actively traded with the early colonies by the late 1700s. North African countries formed political and economic alliances with American revolutionaries. It was the Algerians who exported horses to replenish George Washington's cavalry, a force depleted by the War of Independence. In 1779, an Algerian ship wrecked off the coast of the rebelling colonies, and the mariners chose to settle in North Carolina. The Wahab family of

North Carolina therefore claims to descend from the first Arab settlers in the United States. Morocco was the first country to officially recognize the independence of the United States in the *Treaty of Friendship* between Mohammad III of Morocco and George Washington in 1787.

The Centennial Exhibition of 1876 drew almost 2,000 Turkish and Arab vendors who won, as a group, 129 awards, more than all the exhibitors except those from the U.S. and Britain. Many of these merchants remained in America. Other Arabs who settled in the U.S. included Jeremiah Mahomet in Frederick, Maryland; Antoun Bishallany in New York in 1854, and Hadji Ali, a camel driver known as Hi Jolly, in Arizona in 1856. The first significant wave of Arab immigrants, however, started to arrive in the U.S. in 1885. By 1892, *Kawkab Amrika*, the first Arabic newspaper in America was founded in New York City and ran for seventeen years. Around the same time, in 1893, the Columbian Exposition in Chicago drew merchants from the Arab world, many of whom stayed to establish peddling settlements in the Great Lakes region.

By 1900, the Syrian population of Manhattan and Brooklyn surpassed 10,000. Wills have been found in Washington, D.C., archives, written between 1900 and 1917, which begin with the Islamic formula, "In the Name of God, Amen," with names like Hannah Henderson, Fontaine Mahmood, James Moore, Mary Newman, Edward Quader, and Anne Yarrow, thus indicating the reach of Arab culture and hints of Islam as well. The 1904 St. Louis Exposition brought another group of merchants from Arab lands. In fact, the oh-so American ice cream cone made its debut thanks to a Syrian waffle maker who came to the aid of an ice cream vendor short on plates or bowls for serving the cold concoction. In 1907, the Immigration Department reported that Syrians sent home more money per capita than the immigrants from any other country and that 94 percent of Syrian immigrants who came to America were joining relatives already here. It was also in this year that the first Syrian American Club was established.

By 1914, more than 100,000 Syrians found their way to North America, 15,000 of them serving as American infantrymen in World War I. After this, immigration dropped to a trickle, due to the Quota Act of 1921 and the Johnson Reed Immigration Act of 1924 which banned all immigrants from Asia, and drastically reduced the numbers permitted from Southern and Eastern Europe, as well as the Ottoman Empire. Still, by 1924, there were approximately 200,000 Arabs in the United States, most of them from the Levant, with smaller numbers from Yemen, Iraq, Morocco, and Egypt. By the 1930s, there were more than 50 Arabic publications in the U.S. Later, 6000 Palestinians arrived as refugees during the 1950s and 1960s. Broader Arab immigration would only resume in the 1960s. In fact, between 1965 and 2001, half a million Arabs immigrated to the U.S. Currently, according to the 2000 Census, 615,000 Americans speak Arabic.

Most of the early Arab settlers, from the late 1800s to early 1900s, settled in the Midwest. Many of them were drawn by the Homestead Act of 1862 which offered free land to anyone who could farm it. Arabs, anxious for their own land, took the offer and established farming communities in the Dakotas. Some of them even went to Alaska and the Canadian Arctic. Peter Baker, born in 1887 in Lebanon, operated trading posts at various locations along the Mackenzie River, in addition to traveling by dog-team and canoe, and going among hunters, trappers, and fishermen in their camps. He was known as the "Arctic Arab" and ended up serving as a member of the Northwest Territories Legislative Assembly from 1964-67. He wrote a book: *Memoirs of an Arctic Arab: A Free Trader in the Canadian North: The Years 1907-1927*. The Arctic being a bit chilly, let us head south to the Dakotas to warm up.

The Arab presence in the Dakotas goes back to the time the state was exclusively inhabited by Native Americans plus a motley crew of French Canadian and Métis hunters and trappers. In the 1860 territorial census, among French, Norwegians, and German, names, we find a single Arabic name, Najim, a 49-year-old hunter born in the Washington Territory. This Arab was there before many of the European settlers, having worked, like many other groups, to build the railway, eventually completed in 1873 and 1874. Records thus place this intrepid Arab's date of birth at 1825.

From the late 1800s to the early 1900s, thousands of Arab immigrants settled in the Dakotas. They entered North America via Halifax, Montreal, and New York City. Some stayed in the port cities of the Great Lakes or the East Coast, but many of them continued on to the Prairies, the Great Plains, and the Midwest. There were two main routes to the Dakotas, the Zahle route, which passed through Chicago and St. Paul into Fargo and Grand Forks, and the other route, known as the Ain Arab route, which went from Chicago to Cedar Rapids, to Sioux City, to Sioux Falls, and on to Aberdeen, finally crossing into North Dakota.

Strangely, it seems that most of the Christian Arabs took the northern route. Most of the Muslims took the southern route. Why? Well, Cedar Rapids, Iowa, has the oldest Muslim community in North America and was, therefore, a Medina for most Muslim immigrants. One of the oldest mosques in the U.S. was built in Cedar Rapids in 1934. Amazingly, hundreds and hundreds of caravans of Muslim Arabs passed through South Dakota. In the late 1800s and early 1900s, Sioux Falls had a large

Arab community. Eastern Sioux Falls was known as the "Arab" part of town. Many of the existing buildings are the former businesses of Arab immigrants. Most continued on, however, founding farming communities, along with stores and shops, in the East River area and even West River. Still others continued on through Aberdeen to North Dakota where twice as many settled. The Muslim Arabs were concentrated in Mountrail, Rolette, Foster, McIntosh, Pierce, and McHenry counties. The Christian Arabs settled mostly in Williams, Sheridan, Pierce, Towner, Walsh and Counties, as well as Polk County in Minnesota.

In the early 1900s, there were approximately 2,000 Arabs in North Dakota, and 1,000 in South Dakota. By 1943, however, there were only 266 Arabs left in South Dakota, spread throughout the state, and found in virtually every county, with the largest concentration remaining in Minnehaha County. According to the 1970 Census, 309 South Dakotans spoke Arabic as their mother tongue, yet only 68 of them were foreign-born. The rest were either children of Palestinian refugees or descendants of the early Arab pioneers. In North Dakota, at the same time, there were 422 speakers of Arabic, only 125 of whom were foreign born. Presently, there are 380 Arabic speakers in South Dakota, and most of those are recent immigrants. So, what happened to those larger populations of Arabs? Two catastrophic events: The Great Depression and the Dust Bowl. By the 1930s many of the children and grandchildren of these early Arab settlers were compelled to relocate to big cities, particularly Chicago and Detroit. Most of the Dakotan Arabs had moved to big industrial cities and joined the labor force of the Midwest. While most South Dakotan Arabs left, some stayed, and some are very well-known. Case in point: James Abourezk was born in Wood, South Dakota, to parents of Lebanese descent who were homesteaders and pack peddlers. His parents opened two general stores and settled on a Sioux reservation, where Abourezk grew up. He served in the Navy during the Korean War, later studying engineering and law. He served as a Democratic United States Representative and United States Senator. In fact, he was the first Arab-American to serve in the U.S. Senate. He represented South Dakota in the U.S. Senate from 1973 to 1979. In 1980, Abourezk founded the American-Arab Anti-Discrimination Committee, a grass-roots organization, committed to empower Arab-Americans and designed to encourage a balanced U.S. foreign policy in the Middle East. Abourezk works as a lawyer and writer in Sioux Falls, South Dakota.

James Abnor is another politician from the state of South Dakota. Born in Kennebec, South Dakota, he served in the U.S. Army during World War II and from 1956-1968, he was a member of the South Dakota

Senate. He was the Lieutenant Governor in 1969 and 1970. In 1972, he was elected to the House of Representatives as a Republican. He ran against George McGovern for the U.S. Senate, in 1980, defeating him by a large margin. He won a re-election primary campaign against Bill Janklow and finally lost his Senate seat in 1986 to Tom Daschle. Abnor also served as a respected political advisor to John Thune.

In conclusion, this brief glimpse clearly establishes that the Dakotas have a long and rich Arab heritage. Despite this, when doing an anecdotal survey on campus at Northern State University in Aberdeen, I could not find a single university student from South or North Dakota who knew that Arabs had settled those two states. In fact, I found but a single professor who was familiar with this fact, and he was a Jordanian-Palestinian immigrant! Arabs are not the only group to have made extensive contributions to the nation and yet not be recognized for their efforts. Almost any non-European ethnicity could make the same, unfortunate claim. This tendency gives the impression that the United States is an ethnocentric, inward-looking nation, suffering from collective historical amnesia. Being inward-looking is not necessarily bad, so long as you do not stop at Lewis and Clark, so long as you go back to the French, the Spaniards, the Métis, and the Amerindians. Considering the rich cultural, linguistic, ethnic, and religious origins of the Dakotas, all we really have to do is look into ourselves to develop of full appreciation of diversity. We can look inward to look outward.

CHAPTER ELEVEN

STYLISTIC ANALYSIS OF PROPHETIC ARABIC

As the second source of authoritative information on Islam, the study of the Sunnah is of paramount importance. Known as *'ilm al-rijal* or the science of men, the study of the Sunnah revolves around authenticating chains of narration in order to establish their reliability. Based on an analysis of their *sanad* or chains of narrators, hadith scholars, known as *muhaddithun*, categorize traditions as *sahih* (authentic), *hasan* (good), *da'if* (weak), *mu'allaq* (suspended), *mursal* (hurried), *mu'dal* (omitted), *munqati* (broken), *munkar* (denounced), *shadhdh* (irregular), *mudtarib* (shaky), and *mawdu'* (fabricated). Traditions are further categorized as *ahad* (sole narration), *mashhur* (well-known), *'aziz* (double narration), *gharib* (single narration), and *mutawatir* (successive narrations).

While the *isnad* or chain of a tradition is important, it should not be the sole indicator employed to determine the acceptability of a hadith. It is particularly problematic when scholars focus on the narrators and ignore the content of the tradition. A comparison to this tendency might be to believe that a ten dollar Gucci watch is authentic merely because it bares the brand name. Traditions, like products, can easily be falsified. Even the most elementary student of *'ilm al-hadith* or the science of traditions can construct a perfectly sound *isnad* or chain. Just because the chain is authentic does not mean that the hadith is authentic. Just because the chain is incomplete does not mean that a hadith is fabricated. As a result of focusing on form, as opposed to content, many spurious traditions have been embraced as authentic while many authentic traditions have been dismissed due to some technical shortcoming.

Although it is a good beginning, concentrating on both chain of narration and content is insufficient according to modern scholarly standards, since information on the majority of narrators is extremely scarce. Simply because a person was a faithful follower of *Ahl al-Bayt* or the Household of the Prophet does not mean that he was honest. In fact, many misleading traditions are the product of pious lies perpetrated by individuals who had the best intentions in mind. In other cases, however, they were the work of hypocrites who sought to advance their individual agenda or to undermine Islam. Computerized cross-referencing can expose weaknesses in chains of narrations. They cannot, however, establish whether a person was telling the truth in the first place.

Increasingly, it would seem, Muslim scholars need to embrace new, scientifically-sound, approaches to the study of hadith literature. Besides focusing on logic and reason, as stipulated by *usuli* principles, modern *muhaddithun* should focus on the scientific study of prophetic Arabic. As any linguist or literary scholar can confirm, no two persons express themselves in an identical fashion. So long as you have one authentic, representative example of a person's writing or rhetoric, it is perfectly possible to determine other works that were written or uttered by the person. Since every person has his own idiolect or particular pattern of language use, including vocabulary, syntax, grammar, and so forth, it is possible to engage in author identification.

Although more research needs to be done in the field, Muslim scholars should be at the forefront of forensic linguistics. Then, and only then, will they be able to conclude that a particular text is consistent with the unique mode of expression of the Prophet Muhammad. This would lead to the introduction of two new terms in hadith terminology: "conclusive," demonstrating that the text is consistent with the Messenger of Allah, or "inconclusive," demonstrating that the Prophet is ruled out as the author.

Chapter Twelve

Advances in Arabic Pedagogy

Classical Arabic is, without a doubt, one of the most difficult languages to learn. And what makes it doubly difficult to learn is the lack of adequate language learning material at all levels. From kindergarten to college, Arabic language instruction is a barren desert with only a rare oasis of intellect-quenching educational resources.

The traditional method used to teach children how to read in the Arabic world is the "whole word" method. The focus is not on phonics, but rather on identifying the entire word. As one Arab professor argued, "One sees the forest before one sees the trees." Instead of starting with letters, syllables, small words, medium words, and long words, Arabic teachers commence with the Qur'an, the most complex work in the entire language! This is like using Chaucer to teach literacy to English children.

Children's literature is virtually non-existent in the Arab world. What passes for children's literature are ten to thirty-page tales from centuries past which are written at an adult level. Good luck finding baby books, cardboard books, vocabulary learning books, cartoons, and novels for young readers. If there is a scarcity of works of fiction and non-fiction for adults, imagine the situation for infants, children, adolescents, and young adults. This is not to say that such material does not exist. There is some material available, virtually all of which was produced by Westerners or Arabs who live or have lived in the West for extended periods. It is, nonetheless, very limited and usually more expensive than it should be. If few of the adult Arabs who can actually read, do read, it is because a love for reading must be instilled at an early age. With rare exceptions, Arab parents do not read stories to their children.

"We are an oral culture," is the excuse an Arabic teacher offered to explain the lack of dictionaries, thesauruses, grammar books, and verb conjugation charts. "We do not need books," he claims; "We learn by ear." "And how do Moroccan students do in Arabic?" I inquire. "Dismal," he responds, "They cannot even construct a grammatically correct sentence in Classical Arabic." I had made my point but he perceived it not.

If Arab children suffer from the lack of language material in their home countries, the situation is even more acute for those who live abroad and attend schools in which the language of instruction is other than Arabic. Arabs have the infamous reputation for being the most quickly assimilated of all immigrants. One byproduct of this cultural adaptation is that knowledge of Classical Arabic is never passed on to the children. The colloquial dialects of Arabic, of which there are myriad, are transferred but typically without knowledge of reading and writing. When they reach adulthood, these children retain knowledge of an imperfect form of *'amiyyah* or colloquial Arabic whilst living in environments in which they are surrounded by English, French, Spanish, and German... By the time we reach the children or grandchildren of these first immigrants, they are monolingual speakers of some other language and have lost any connection to the Arabic language of their ancestors.

Learning other languages is important and, in the case of immigrants, essential. However, it should never be at the cost of one's own language, culture, and identity. When Arabs who live in the West lose Arabic, they lose not only part of their heritage; they also lose a part of their religion, so closely is Arabic tied to Islam at all levels of expression. In order to help slow or even stop this process of language attrition and assimilation, Arabic-speakers must concentrate on creating high quality books in Arabic for learners of all levels. Allah may have told us to "Read!" (96:1), but He also commanded us to write.

Chapter Thirteen

Bye, Bye Burstad and *Ahlan* Abboud!

Students of Arabic: I pity them. Tens of thousands of them subjected to the torture of *al-Kitab fi ta'alim al-'arabiyyah*, *The Book for Learning the Arabic Language*. Marketed as the most cutting-edge approach in Arabic language instruction, the work was born in the torture chambers of academia. This soft-covered monstrosity is as ugly as it is pedagogically unsound. A book now used in the second millennium, the text's art work, drawings, and cartoons appear to have been created in the 1970s with an Atari computer. Its protagonist, Maha, is an ugly, clinically depressed Egyptian with whom students can scarcely identify; the young lady's male friend takes the term *loser* to lows never imagined.

Visuals aside, the grammatical instructions in the book are ill-expressed, relying on an annoying mixture of Egyptian colloquial and Classical Arabic. The readings are far too advanced from the onset instead of gradually increasing in complexity. Much of the vocabulary introduced has a low functional yield. Students who complete a couple of these *Kitab* textbooks are often devoid of even basic, high frequency, terminology. Unfortunately, options for Arabic language study are scarce. *Ahlan wa sahlan* by Mahdi Alosh is more pedagogically sound than Burstad's book. Still, it is a far cry from the quality found in French, Spanish, and Italian language textbooks. Sadly, *Elementary Standard Arabic* by Peter Abboud and company is still one of the best Arabic learning texts available, demonstrating that little progress has been made in Arabic language instruction over the past forty years. If his grammatical explanations are completely and utterly worthless, the exercises and activities are engaging and effective and the readings are truly excellent.

CHAPTER FOURTEEN

WHO SPEAKS ARABIC?

"So when are you finally going to learn Arabic?" a frustrated elderly Moroccan woman asks me in *darijah*, the Arabic dialect of her country. "But I speak Arabic," I respond in astonishment. "I mean, *our* Arabic. When are you going to speak *our* Arabic?" Of course, by "our Arabic," she means the colloquial Arabic dialect spoken in Morocco and which is commonly known as *darijah*. This is not the first time that I face this annoying reality. Most Arabs that I have met, and I have met thousands from all parts of the Arab world, cannot last longer than five minutes in *fushah* or Classical Arab before becoming hopelessly lost. Sure, there are exceptions: most Muslim scholars speak High Arabic; some passingly well; others, barely the basics; and yet others with varying degrees of reading comprehension. Many intellectuals are also proficient in *fushah*. The same, however, cannot be said of professionals who studied the sciences. Whether they were family physicians or specialists, all the medical doctors I met knew only their Arabic dialect and the European language of their medical instruction; typically, French or English. To say that those who speak Classical Arabic do not speak Arabic is silly. This is tantamount to saying that Shakespeare could not speak English. We speak the Arabic of the Qur'an and the Arabic of the Prophet. We speak the literary and intellectual language of Islam. Considering how far Arabic dialects have deviated from the classical norm, to the point of being mutually unintelligible languages, we must ask ourselves who actually speaks Arabic. "I speak Arabic," I proudly affirm to the little old lady, "So when are you going to learn how to speak Arabic?" I ask.

Chapter Fifteen

Monotheistic Indians of the Americas

"Indians did not believe in God," said Professor R.J. Glickman during a class at the University of Toronto in the early nineties, "they were all polytheists." Suddenly, my indigenous blood started to boil, my Métis *taqiyyah* or pious dissimulation kicked in: feign to be French Canadian, claim to be Catholic, hide your roots and your identity among these wicked *Wasichus* or white devils. If there is a time to remain silent, there is a time to speak out. And the time to speak out has come. Let me then instruct you about the ways of my people: the aboriginal inhabitants of the Turtle Island, the continent you know as the Americas.

It cannot be denied that many indigenous peoples were polytheists. There is no point gainsaying that the Aztecs and the Mayas, among many others, were idol-worshippers who engaged in unsavory religious practices, including the ritual sacrifice of human beings. For this, no excuses can be made and no defense is due. It is wrong, however, and categorically untrue, to assert that all indigenous people were polytheistic. On the contrary, many tribes or populations were monotheistic. My ancestors, the Indians of the Eastern Woodlands, believed in Manitou, the Great Spirit. The Iroquois also believed in the Great Spirit, whom they called Hawenneyu. To clarify, some also believed in spirits or invisible agents, but Muslims also believe in Angels and Jinn. Our God, the Creator, was very much one, and such was the case with the Lakota who worshipped Wakan-Taka, the Great Mystery. Nezahualcóyotl, the leader of the Acolhua, was also an outspoken and most articulate monotheist. Like all other tribes and nations, we received prophets, messengers, and holy men who taught us about the Creator and how to live our lives in balance. As the Prophet Muhammad taught, all human beings were created with a monotheistic nature. This includes my people, the First Nations, Métis, and Inuit.

CHAPTER SIXTEEN

THE PATH OF PRECAUTION: *FIQH* FOR THE 21ST CENTURY

Taqlid, namely, the act of following a source of emulation in matters of jurisprudence, has only existed in its current form for approximately one hundred and fifty years. It is a valuable and enviable system that has served Twelver Shiites well. It has ensured that Shiites are well-informed regarding their religious obligations and the proper methods of observance. Historically, Sources of Emulation, the Grand Ayatullahs, as they are now known, were uncommon. Often, there were no more than a few of these persons at a given time and, in some instances, there was a single authority recognized universally as the most learned. The situation, however, has utterly changed.

Among the many achievements of the Islamic Revolution of Iran was the revival of the religious sciences. During the 19th century and the first three quarters of the 20th century, the life of a student of the religious sciences was a difficult one. Resources were few. Funding was scarce and prospects were poor. The only people who devoted themselves to seminary studies responded to a deep spiritual calling. With the advent of the Islamic Revolution, the *hawzah* or religious seminary was re-organized and revitalized. Its curriculum was updated and enhanced. Buildings were constructed. Modern residences were erected. Funding was increased enormously and scholarships became relatively generous.

As a result of this infusion of state funds and improved management, the religious sciences became more accessible and higher ranks more easily attainable. Within a question of decades, the number of jurists had grown exponentially. While there was never a shortage of scholars among the Shiites, there might be one scholar per community. Now, in the 21st century, jurists have literally become a dime a dozen. Since the number of jurists has increased, so has the number of those who rise to the rank of Ayatullah and Grand Ayatullah. For the first time in history, Twelver Shiites have not one, two, or three Grand Ayatullahs, but literally, dozens and dozens of *maraji' al-taqlid* or Sources of Emulation. For many *muqallidun* or followers, this is a blessing as it increases the diversity of opinion. For others, however, it is a blessing with a flip side, fractioning the Shiite community into numerous sub-groups that follow different Grand Ayatullahs. As Dr. Liyakat 'Ali Takim has shown, the institution of the *marajiyyah* or Religious Authority has not been a source of unity among Shiites, but rather a source of division. In many communities, mosques have been divided among the followers of Khamene'i, Sistani, Fadlullah, and others.

Since there are so many high-ranking religious authorities, and a greater degree of specialization has taken place, the custom of following a single *marja* or source of emulation has started to decline. Rather than follow one religious authority, a growing number of Shiites are now adopting the path of precaution, examining diverse rulings, and following the safest route. Others, however, now opt to follow different Grand Ayatullahs on different issues. If the 20th century was one of *taqlid* or emulation, it seems that, increasingly, the 21st century might be one of *ihtiyat* or precaution if not comparative jurisprudence based on critical thinking, hinting at a degree of intellectual evolution among the Shiite community.

CHAPTER SEVENTEEN

WILL THE REAL SUNNIS PLEASE STAND UP?

Sunnism, true Sunnism, is a beautiful belief system. Unfortunately, in certain circles, traditional Sunnis seem to stand side by side with the tiger, the rhinoceros, and the polar bear as an endangered species. "But I'm a Sunni," some Muslims will say in unison. "Are you sure?" I will respond. "Or are you really a bunch of Salafis?" And that is the beauty or perhaps the horror of thing: thanks to billions of Saudi dollars, some Muslims, who believe that they follow *Ahl al-Sunnah*, have actually become the unwitting followers of Muhammad ibn 'Abd al-Wahhab and his foreign doctrines. They falsely believe themselves to be following the 1400-year old teachings of Muhammad ibn 'Abd Allah, the Messenger of Allah, when, in reality, they are following the deviant doctrines of a brutal heretical cult created a mere two centuries ago.

The first form of Islam to which I was exposed was what supposedly passed for Sunnism. I studied and socialized with so-called Sunnis for several years. I was taught a dry, arid, ritualistic doctrine, which was devoid of spirituality of any sort. It was literalist, fundamentalist, and essentialist. It rejected anything but the surface meaning of the text even when the literal meaning was nonsensical and only an allegorical interpretation was plausible. I was taught to reject all authorities, modern and ancient, be it Maulana Mawdudi, Ghazali, Rumi, or Ibn 'Arabi. One of the few scholars I was told to accept was Ibn Taymiyyah. My associates hated Jews more than Hitler did. They denounced Christians as polytheists who should be put to the sword. Sufis were dismissed as heretics who were worthy of death. Shiites were infidels and heretics whose blood was *halal*. Yes, my self-professed Sunni friends were a bunch of fun-loving guys. They taught me their three key creedal concepts: *haram*, *bid'ah* and *takfir* [prohibition, innovation, and excommunication]. And they encouraged me to join the jihad…

Praise and thanks be to Allah, I left these demented fundamentalists in the dust after I came across the Twelver Shiites who, strangely enough, actually followed the Sunnah. They balanced religiosity with spirituality. They encouraged, as opposed to repress, intellectual inquiry. Their scholars actually engaged in hermeneutics. They were open to debate and discussion. They encouraged critical thinking and intellectual analysis. They approached Islam from a scholarly perspective. They performed their obligatory prayers and their supererogatory prayers. They showered the Prophet with *salawat* or prayers and blessings. They sent their salaams or salutations to the Prophet. They performed *dhikr* or remembrance of God. And they recited the most beautiful of supplications. They were, by far, more Sunni than the so-called Sunnis I had encountered.

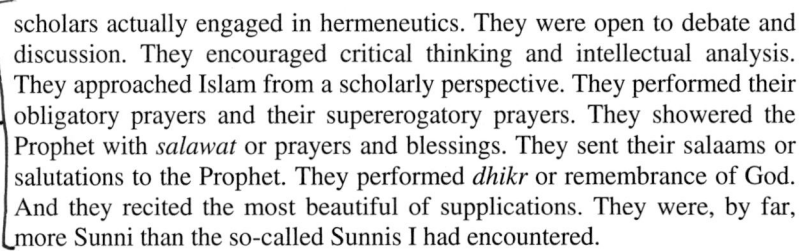

To be honest, the first people I came across who adhered to true Sunni beliefs and practices were the Sufis and by Sufis I mean *Ahl al-Sunnah wa al-Tasawwuf*, the People of Tradition and Spirituality, who combine sharia with *'irfan* or Gnosis and not deviant pseudo-Sufis who deny the obligations of Islamic law. These real Sufis, namely, those who balance the *zahir* and the *batin*, the inner and the outer, the esoteric and the exoteric, were virtually identical to the Shiites in devotional matters. The only difference was that most of them adhered to one of the Sunni schools of jurisprudence. In contrast, most of the so-called Sunnis I had met previously all insisted that they were not *madhhabi*, namely, that they did not follow schools of jurisprudence. They claimed to directly follow the Qur'an and Sunnah. However, these were all incurious, ignorant people. Most of them had no higher education in any field. Some had not even completed high school. How on earth were they qualified to interpret the Qur'an, determine the authenticity of traditions, and derive principles and rulings of jurisprudence?

Eventually, I came to the realization those who professed to be Sunnis were, in actuality, Salafis. They were naught but pseudo-Sunnis, so-called Sunnis; Wahhabis who paraded around as Sunnis in order to lead, or mislead, the followers of *Ahl al-Sunnah wa al-Jama'at*. I had studied Islam for years before taking my *shahadah*. I knew Islam from the Qur'an and the Sunnah. I knew Islam before I knew any Muslims. While I was perplexed by these people at first and highly suspicious of what they said, as it made no logical or spiritual sense, it became increasingly obvious that the ideology to which they adhered was an absurd misrepresentation of Islam. It was false marketing. It was a sham and a fraud. It made a mockery of the religion of Muhammad.

While I did not know who they were, nor what they stood for, when I first met them, their dogmas assaulted my intellect and soiled my soul. This was not Sunnism, I realized, but Salafism, and Salafism is not and will never be Sunnism. For some, it is certain, their Salafism was only skin-deep. They were people of Sunni background who had been forced fed a steady diet of Salafi ideas. The so-called Sunnism they were taught at school, through books, and via the media, was tainted and adulterated. Rather than nourish the soul, it caused spiritual food poisoning. For others, however, they had been so fully brainwashed with Wahhabi ideas that they could never conceivably be considered followers of the Sunnah. They knew full well who they were. They had complete conviction. They were hard-core Salafis, Wahhabis, and Takfiris committed to spreading spiritually-transmitted diseases. And this, my friends, is one of the single greatest crimes committed against Islam; the classic sleight of hand, the trickery and deviousness of presenting Salafism as Sunnism.

As a result of continued study and experiential knowledge gained through travel and human contact, I came to learn that most Sunnis actually hated Salafis, Wahhabis, Takfiris, and Jihadis. There was no Sunni Muslim society on earth that had been spared from the sadistic crimes of the Salafi Jihadists. If these Salafi subversives operated clandestinely in many Muslim nations, where they were always under the watchful eye of state surveillance, they had functioned freely in the Western world for decades thanks to Saudi/American sponsorship.

The Saudis, like the British, the Germans, and the Americans, were never enamored with the Wahhabis. On the contrary, they considered them to be useful idiots, rabid Rottweilers that they could sic on command. In the same way that the Takfiris served the British in their quest to dismantle the Ottoman Empire in the 19th and early 20th centuries, we saw them serve the Americans in Afghanistan since 1979, fighting on their behalf. And despite the fact that these Takfiris attacked the United States on September 11th, 2001, we saw them resurface in Syria, Iraq, Libya, Yemen, Somalia, and Nigeria, in the early 21st century, at the service of regional and global powers. As many Sunni Muslims have come to realize, mercenaries are mercenaries whether they are called Blackwater, al-Qaeda or Daesh. After all, what's in a name? Takfiri terrorists may claim to fight for Islam; however, the question must be asked: Who's your daddy? If this is the case, and Sunni Muslims are increasingly able to distinguish between real Sunnis and fake Sunnis, then we can proudly profess that the real Sunnis are slowly but surely standing up.

Chapter Eighteen

Terrible Translations: Weakening Islam from Within

While it may be an obligation to disseminate Islam, it is also an obligation to do it well. For far too long, generally well-intentioned Muslims have produced, in a myriad of languages, hundreds and even thousands of books aimed at non-Muslims. The problem, however, has not been one of intention; it has been one of quality. Many Muslim groups and publishers seem to be of the mind that quantity takes precedence over quality when the contrary should be the case. How Muslims could have forgotten this critical point is puzzling. After all, they have the Qur'an as their example. The revelation that the Prophet Muhammad received is a miraculous literary masterpiece, a work that is literally not of this world. Imagine how the Arabs would have reacted to his message if the Prophet had come down from Mount Hira reciting some played-out poetry with bad meter, weak rhymes, and dull content. Not only did the Qur'an far surpass any poetic competition, the Prophet himself, in his speeches, sermons, and sayings, exhibited a true mastery of many rhetorical modes. Only Allah was more eloquent than the Prophet. So when trying to attract non-Muslims to Islam, it is important to present them with works that are accurate, intelligent, and written or translated in a flawless linguistic form. Time and again, I have seen Muslims present non-Muslims with books with errors peppering every page: the spelling, the syntax, and the style were all appalling. Some of these texts were respected classics in original Arabic; however, due to garbled translations, their rebirth in other languages made them worthy of contempt. In short, the message was lost in the medium. Muslims! Remember: quality is of the essence.

Chapter Nineteen

Universal Islam: The Faith of the Future

Muslim converts are curious characters. Some are remarkable while others are demonstrably risible. The most ridiculous new believers are those who blindly adopt beliefs, cultural traits, and characteristics from Muslims from other nations: black men who take on the plumage and mannerisms of Pakistanis; white men who pretend to be Arabs; formerly liberated women who cloak themselves in chadors and niqab, seeking to emulate ignorant, illiterate, and oppressed women. This is a sad spectacle.

If Muslim converts merely modeled the positive features of cultural Islam that would be one thing; the problem is that they imitate that which is most noticeable and often bad. This is an overarching theme, a display of the most repugnant traits of deluded Muslims, namely their intolerance and sectarianism. How many times have I heard converts call Shiites and Sufis infidels? How many times have I heard them profess that their blood is *halal* or legal to shed? If this is Islam, they can keep it. If anything, their ideology of intolerance is the antithesis of Islam and completely unsupported by the teachings of the Qur'an and the wisdom of the Prophet Muhammad.

Fortunately, not all Muslim converts are Muslim-trons and Wahhabi wannabes. Not all Western Muslims want to imitate Eastern Muslims. Many Western Muslims are highly educated. They have, at the very least, bachelor degrees. Many have Master's degrees and an impressive number have doctoral degrees. Even those without formal education are informally trained and have attained high levels of culture. If these people value one thing, it is reason. It was reason, after all, that drew them to Islam. Many of them were dismayed, or perhaps even withdrew from the Islamic community, when the so-called Sunnis they encountered tried to instill in them racism, bigotry, and prejudice directed, not only toward non-Muslims, but towards Muslims as well, particularly Shiites and Sufis.

I place myself and these others in a group for whom, Allah is one, Islam is one, and Muslims should be one. Unfortunately, our inclusive approach is not shared by all. Many Sunnis hate Shiites. Some Shiites hate Sunnis. And a large number of Sunnis and Shiites hate Sufis. Add to this racial rivalries, tribal animosity, national sentiments, and misogyny, and the Muslim World resembles nothing so much as a childish and malicious squabble of international proportions.

Since cultural Muslims have been unable to put their house in order, they are in no position to tell us how to reform our own. Since most of them are not proper representatives of Islam in the world, they are in no position to preach and teach us Islam. If anything, it is us, Western Muslims, who can give many Eastern Muslims basic lessons in Islamic beliefs, practice, morals, ethics, and etiquette.

Most importantly, large numbers of Western Muslims oppose division and disunity, preferring to promote Islamic unity. We may have accepted Islam, but we have never accepted the partisanship of Islam, focusing on the differences between groups or lumping them into Sunnism, Shiism, Sufism, and dozens of other sub-branches and sub-sects. We may take a position regarding the succession of the Prophet, but this remains, for us, a personal matter. We may follow specific schools of Islamic jurisprudence but, this again, is a personal matter. And, finally, we may follow a particular spiritual path which, once again, is a matter of individual choice.

The Islam espoused by many Western Muslims is an inclusive Islam as opposed to an exclusive Islam. It is an Islam that embraces diversity of religious expression. It is an Islam committed to critical thinking. It is an Islam committed to peace, justice, and equality. We do not deal with Islam partially; we approach Islam as a totality. For us, Islam is like a pizza pie. We are not going to accept a single slice: we want the whole thing! Islam is not a single dish but a Divine Banquet. It is not a speck of paint on a Picasso, but the entire Mona Lisa! We are not satisfied with a sip of divine wine! We have bought the entire winery!

Chapter Twenty

The Nation of Islam is not Islamic

While few individuals in the Western world allow themselves to be duped and deceived by the Nation of Islam and Louis Farrakhan, the majority of Muslims outside of the Occident remain oblivious to the true nature and beliefs of this African American movement which claims to profess Islam. Although ignorance and illiteracy certainly play a part in this acceptance of the NOI, the main culprit in the Muslim world is the Arabic and Iranian mass media which continues to portray Farrakhan as some sort of American Muslim leader. Despite the abundance of primary and secondary sources which delineate the actual beliefs of this black supremacist sect, here I will limit myself to an overview of "The Muslim Program," which is the official creed of the Nation of Islam, and which I reproduce integrally:

1. WE BELIEVE in the One God whose proper Name is Allah.

2. WE BELIEVE in the Holy Qur'an and in the Scriptures of all the Prophets of God.

3. WE BELIEVE in the truth of the Bible, but we believe that it has been tampered with and must be reinterpreted so that mankind will not be snared by the falsehoods that have been added to it.

4. WE BELIEVE in Allah's Prophets and the Scriptures they brought to the people.

5. WE BELIEVE in the resurrection of the dead--not in physical resurrection--but in mental resurrection. We believe that the so-called Negroes are most in need of mental resurrection; therefore, they will be resurrected first. Furthermore, we believe we are the people of God's choice, as it has been written, that God would choose the rejected and the despised. We can find no other persons fitting this description in these last days more that the so-called Negroes in America. We believe in the resurrection of the righteous.

6. WE BELIEVE in the judgment; we believe this first judgment will take place as God revealed, in America...

7. WE BELIEVE this is the time in history for the separation of the so-called Negroes and the so-called white Americans. We believe the black man should be freed in name as well as in fact. By this we mean that he should be freed from the names imposed upon him by his former slave masters. Names which identified him as being the slave master's slave. We believe that if we are free indeed, we should go in our own people's names--the black people of the Earth.

8. WE BELIEVE in justice for all, whether in God or not; we believe, as others, that we are due equal justice as human beings. We believe in equality--as a nation--of equals. We do not believe that we are equal with our slave masters in the status of "freed slaves."

We recognize and respect American citizens as independent peoples and we respect their laws which govern this nation.

9. WE BELIEVE that the offer of integration is hypocritical and is made by those who are trying to deceive the black peoples into believing that their 400-year-old open enemies of freedom, justice and equality are, all of a sudden, their "friends." Furthermore, we believe that such deception is intended to prevent black people from realizing that the time in history has arrived for the separation from the whites of this nation.

If the white people are truthful about their professed friendship toward the so-called Negro, they can prove it by dividing up America with their slaves. We do not believe that America will ever be able to furnish enough jobs for her own millions of unemployed, in addition to jobs for the 20,000,000 black people as well.

10. WE BELIEVE that we who declare ourselves to be righteous Muslims, should not participate in wars which take the lives of humans. We do not believe this nation should force us to take part in such wars, for we have nothing to gain from it unless America agrees to give us the necessary territory wherein we may have something to fight for.

11. WE BELIEVE our women should be respected and protected as the women of other nationalities are respected and protected.

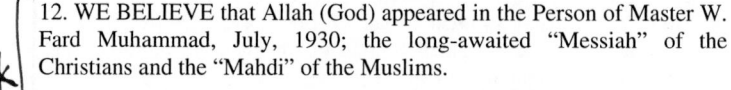

12. WE BELIEVE that Allah (God) appeared in the Person of Master W. Fard Muhammad, July, 1930; the long-awaited "Messiah" of the Christians and the "Mahdi" of the Muslims.

We believe further and lastly that Allah is God and besides HIM there is no god and He will bring about a universal government of peace wherein we all can live in peace together.

The first article of faith of the Nation of Islam, namely, that there is only one God whose proper name is Allah may mislead the unwary into believing that members of the NOI are actually Muslims. By "Allah," however, the members of the Nation of Islam are not referring to Allah, the Creator of the Universe, who has no partners, and who does not incarnate. For Black Muslims, W.D. Fard, the founder of the Nation of Islam, is literally Allah. While the members of the Nation of Islam profess that "There is no god but Allah, and Muhammad is the Messenger of Allah," they are not referring to Allah as understood by all Muslims: they are speaking of W.D. Fard; nor are they speaking of Muhammad, the son of 'Abd Allah, who lived in Arabia from 570-632 CE--they are referring to Elijah Muhammad, the Final Prophet and Messenger of the Nation of Islam who was born in 1897 and who passed away in 1975. Although they say, "There is no god but Allah, and Muhammad is His Messenger," they mean, "There is no god but W.D. Fard and Elijah Muhammad is His Messenger."

The second article of the Nation of Islam is belief in all the revealed books, the Torah, the Gospel, and the Qur'an, something which is consistent with the Muslim faith. The third article of the Nation of Islam is belief in the truth of the Bible, which has been distorted. Unlike Muslims, who rely upon the Qur'an and the Sunnah, the followers of Elijah Muhammad and Louis Farrakhan consider the Bible to be a source of law and guidance, a belief which is rejected by Muslim theologians and jurists.

The fourth article of the Nation of Islam is belief in the Prophets of Allah and their scriptures. While this may sound like a Muslim tenet of faith, it should be recalled that the Nation of Islam considers Elijah Muhammad, and not Muhammad ibn 'Abd Allah, as the Final Messenger of Allah. However, as the Holy Qur'an teaches, Muhammad, the son of 'Abd Allah, is the Seal of the Prophets (33:40), a verse interpreted by the Nation of Islam as "the Ring of the Prophets," based on the Ahmadiyyah commentary. When they say that they believe in the Scriptures brought by the Prophets, the Nation of Islam includes the teachings of Elijah Muhammad as Revealed Truth.

The fifth article of the Nation of Islam is belief in mental resurrection, as opposed to physical resurrection. The Qur'an, the Sunnah, and the scholars of Islam explicitly endorse the belief in physical resurrection, which forms a fundamental part of the belief in the Day of Judgment. The Nation of Islam also believes that black people "are the people of God's choice" while Islam does not believe in the concept of "chosen people."

As Almighty Allah and the Prophet Muhammad made clear, the "chosen people" are the people of faith, the believers, and not a specific race.

The sixth article of the Nation of Islam is belief in the judgment which will first take place in America. While this may sound superficially Islamic to some, the Nation of Islam does not believe in the Day of Judgment as Muslims do. They believe that Allah, aka W.D. Fard, will return to Earth in the Mother Ship, and destroy white America for the crimes it committed against African Americans. This is not the Day of Judgment as espoused by Islam. It is a belief in an upcoming racial apocalypse: the divinely decreed extermination of the white man.

The seventh article of the Nation of Islam is belief in racial separation while Islam has abolished racism (49:13: 4:1; 2:213; 6:98; 7:189; 21:92; 23:52). In reality, Islamic civilization was the first major cosmopolitan and multicultural society the world had ever seen. Muslims of all races and ethnicities intermixed and a multitude of languages were spoken. Rather than preach racial separation, Islam promotes unity. As Almighty Allah explains in the Holy Qur'an:

> O humankind! We created you from a single (pair) of a male and a female and made you into nations and tribes that ye may know each other (not that ye may despise each other). Verily the most honored of you in the sight of Allah is (he who is) the most righteous of you. (49:13)

Since the Nation of Islam believes in racial segregation, they also believe that "intermarriage or race mixing should be prohibited," an attitude which is un-Islamic. As the Prophet said in his Farewell Sermon, "All humankind is from Adam and Eve, an Arab has no superiority over a non-Arab nor a non-Arab has any superiority over an Arab; also a white has no superiority over a black nor a black has any superiority over a white, except by piety and good action" (Muslim, Ahmad, Darimi, Ibn Majah, Abu Dawud, Ibn Hibban et al.).

The eighth article of the Nation of Islam is the belief in justice for African Americans. While no Muslim would object to human equality, many would object to the Nation of Islam's belief that it can only be accomplished through the creation of a separate state or nation for blacks. Qur'anically speaking, Almighty Allah does not want countries created on the basis of a single race. In fact, most of the Muslim countries in the world are highly diversified, racially, ethnically, linguistically, and culturally. As far as the core beliefs of Islam are concerned, diversity is a good thing and racially segregated states are unacceptable.

The ninth article of the Nation of Islam is the opposition to racial integration, a dated doctrine which they should long have dropped as Black Muslims have benefited from integration for almost fifty years. The tenth article of the Nation of Islam opposes the drafting of blacks to fight America's wars, something that makes sense to most Muslims. Unfortunately, blacks, Latinos, and poor whites, continue to constitute the bulk of the American military. The eleventh article of the Nation of Islam is respect for women, a praiseworthy position. In practice, however, this respect rarely extends to white women who, for certain African Americans, "are only good for one thing."

The final article of the Nation of Islam's "Muslim Program" is the belief that Allah appeared in the Person of Master W. Fard Muhammad in July of 1930 and that he was the Messiah of the Christians and the Mahdi of the Muslims. As the "Muslim Program" further elaborates, it is God himself, namely W.D. Fard, who will bring about a universal government of peace on Earth. Despite the claims of some apologists, the Nation of Islam is explicit about its belief that W.D. Fard is the literal incarnation of Allah. The belief in *hulul* [incarnation] is the antithesis of *tawhid* [oneness of God] and the belief in a prophet coming after Muhammad is clearly inconsistent with the Qur'an and Sunnah.

On the basis of its "Muslim Program," it is evident that the Nation of Islam has little in common with Islam besides its name, and just like any imposter, the organization can profess to be Muslim to all within hearing, but the articles and practices brand it otherwise. Since they literally believe that W.D. Fard is Allah, and that Elijah Muhammad is the Final Messenger of Allah, the followers of Elijah Muhammad and Louis Farrakhan are outside of the fold of orthodox Islam. The Nation of Islam is not a legitimate Muslim sect or a heterodox branch of Islam. From the perspective of Islamic orthodoxy, it can either be considered a heretical cult which only possesses a veneer of Islam or an entirely different belief system altogether.

Chapter Twenty-One

Talk to the People in the Language of the People

According to the Prophet Muhammad, "Every prophet was sent solely to his people; I, however, have been sent to all of humanity" (Muslim). Thank God for that. And thank God for the fact that the Messenger of Allah, along with the Twelve Imams, could speak every human language. This, of course, may come as a shock to Sunni Muslims, who are taught by the Salafis that the Prophet was simply an ordinary man who received a message. However, educated and informed Shiites, Sufis, and Sunnis, for that matter, know better. They know that the Messenger was a man of miraculous abilities, talents bestowed upon him by Allah.

Language, of course, is a positive force. Its purpose is communication and it serves as a mode of education. It can, however, transform into evil incarnate when it is imposed upon others. In many countries in the West, language has actually been used as a weapon of exclusion as opposed to a tool of inclusion. In fact, in Europe and America, many Western Muslims have been subject to something called *reverse colonialism* by which Islam is controlled by foreign agents representing foreign powers and speaking foreign languages. In too many Western mosques these days, the language used from the podium is not English, French, Spanish, or any other dominant Western language, but Arabic, Urdu, or Persian, among other foreign tongues.

The justification for using these immigrant languages in Western mosques is foreign-focused: "Some of our elders do not speak English; if we do not preach in Urdu they will be left out." Unfortunately, what they seem to forget is that by speaking Urdu, the service caters to a tiny immigrant minority while it excludes the native majority. Mosque leaders also argue that the children of immigrants are losing the languages of their homeland. This may be the case, but the purpose of a mosque is not to preserve heritage languages in the course of religious services. Specific classes can be organized for this purpose particularly during Sunday school.

In the United States and Canada, for example, American and Canadian Muslims have been subjected for decades to mosques in which only Arabic, Urdu, Persian, or other foreign languages were spoken. These mosques might as well post signs saying, "No dogs or Westerners allowed" as they effectively exclude the participation of Western Muslims. Some imams, when complaints reached their ears, have made some specious "compromises," namely, to throw in five minutes of English in a sermon that is fifty-five minutes long. Some Western Muslims endure such arrangements; however, most of them view it for what it is: tokenism. "If more English-speaking brothers would come to the mosque," said one imam, "I could speak more in English." This ignores the fact that 99% of his Pakistani congregation spoke English, while 0% of the Canadian converts spoke Urdu. As a result of such patronizing attitudes, most Western Muslims simply ceased to attend these mosques, and sadly have lost potential connections to their international brothers in Islam.

The problem of foreign language imposition is not unique to North America; it remains preponderant in much of Western Europe. In Switzerland, a majority of the 180 Imams working in the country are not proficient in the languages of the regions where they reside. In the United Kingdom, most of the imams were born and educated abroad, in non-English speaking countries. Since many speak limited English, most deliver their sermons in Arabic, Urdu, Persian, or other languages. In France, two-thirds of the country's 1,200 imams are foreign born and less than half of them speak French. In Germany, the situation is similar: most imams come from abroad, typically Turkey, and many of them do not speak German. In addition, they have little knowledge about the country, and understand virtually nothing about its mores.

Not only do many of these Muslim preachers who work in the West ignore the national language of the country in which they live, most of them are unfamiliar with other Western languages as well. In fact, according to some sources, fewer than 5% of imams working in Europe are familiar with other Western languages. Consequently, they understand little to nothing about Western culture and civilization beyond stereotypes and prejudices. The end result is clear: if imams speak only Arabic, Urdu or Persian from the pulpit, they effectively disenfranchise the Western Muslims who are entitled to worship at the mosque. In some cases, this result is secondary, a sort of collateral damage caused by ignorance. In others, the result appears to be the intended result of a deliberate policy of exclusion: keep the converts out in order to keep the mosque under the control of immigrants.

While most Western Muslims value multilingualism, it should never be at the expense of national languages. After all, Almighty Allah says that "Among his Signs is the creation of the heavens and the earth, and the variations in your languages" (30:22). As one illustration of this lack of openness, you will hear some Muslim immigrants insist that, "Canada is multicultural; hence, we have the right to speak our own languages." Yes, but you are also expected to speak one of the two official languages: English or French. When we ask such people to preach in an official language, we are not discriminating against them. On the contrary, it is they who discriminate against us when they impose their foreign language upon us and exclude us from fully participating in the affairs of the Muslim community.

Language, for many Muslim leaders, is a sign of allegiance. Most Arabic-dominated mosques are directly or indirectly under the control of Saudi Arabia. Many Urdu-dominated mosques are directly or indirectly under the influence of Pakistani forces. And many Persian-speaking mosques are directly or indirectly under the control of the Islamic Republic of Iran. This is religious colonialism. Mosques in the Western world must be controlled by Western Muslims and deliver their sermons in the language of the people. Some will certainly cry "racism," but when we speak of "Western Muslims," we are speaking of all people born and raised in the West, regardless of race or country of origin. We also speak of those who are naturalized citizens, who no longer pledge allegiance to foreign powers, and who identify fully and completely as Westerners.

The use, and abuse, of Arabic, Persian, and East-Indian languages in Western mosques is not only in poor taste and an overt disinclination toward hospitality, it is actually, completely and totally un-Islamic and counter-Qur'anic. As Almighty Allah says in the Qur'an al-Karim, "We sent not an apostle except (to teach) in the language of his (own) people, in order to make (things) clear to them" (14:4). If the Prophet Muhammad was sent to the Arabs, then he spoke to them in Arabic. If Jesus was sent to the Jews of his time, then he spoke to them in Aramaic. If Moses was sent to the Hebrews, then he spoke to them in Hebrew. Muslim imams must always endeavor to speak to the people *in the language of the people*. This cannot be stressed enough. "The language of the people is the language of the congregation," a Muslim once insisted. But who, then, was the racist? Was it I who simply asked to be included or this foreigner who clearly implied that those who did not speak Urdu were not members of the congregation? Islam, as this man could not understand, is not the personal property of Pakistanis. As Almighty Allah says in the Qur'an al-Karim, "Had We sent this as a Qur'an (in a language) other than Arabic, they would have said: 'Why are not its verses explained in detail? What! (A

Book) not in Arabic...?" (41:44). Just like the Arabs would have been dismayed to be presented with a revelation in a language other than Arabic, we Western Muslims have every right to ask: "What! A sermon in a foreign language in our own country?"

For Muslim immigrants who still cannot fathom what on earth I am talking about, I point them to a few fundamental facts from Islamic history. According to the Imams of *Ahl al-Bayt*, the Prophet Muhammad could read and write in seventy languages. According to the *sirah* [biography] and Sunnah [example] of the Prophet, the Messenger of Allah ordered his companions to learn the languages of the people belonging to different religions and nations. Believe it or not, this even included Hebrew. When the Prophet communicated with Jewish tribes, he used to send them letters written in Hebrew. Although he initially used Jewish scribes, he eventually asked Zayd ibn Thabit to learn the writing of the Jews so that he could communicate with them on his behalf. According to Sunni traditions, the Prophet used to speak to Hasan and Husayn in Persian. Imam 'Ali himself was able to communicate in any language used in the Caliphate. Imam al-Hasan once said that "I know all languages." In one tradition, Imam 'Ali says that "The Imam is blessed in his majesty with the knowledge of all languages." Thus, there is no question that the Prophet, the Imams, and many Companions of the Prophet and Followers of the Companions were multilingual. Unlike many shaykhs who preach in the Western world today, the early Muslims actually practiced what the Qur'an and the Prophet preached: speak to the people in the language of the people.

Chapter Twenty-Two

Tahrif:
The Problem of Pious Lies

Tahrif is an Arabic term which means, in the context of Islamic Studies, the deliberate distortion of a text by changing something from its proper place to another place, rearranging the syntax of a sentence, or giving a meaning other than its true intended meaning. For Muslim scholars, the term *tahrif* is typically applied to the distortion of sacred scriptures, be it the Torah, the Gospel, or the Qur'an, but also applies to changes made to prophetic traditions or any other published work.

As a staunch defender of academic honesty, Almighty Allah condemns the hypocrites among the Jews, Christians, and Muslims, who manipulate sources for their own self-interest. As we read in the Holy Qur'an, "Some of the Jews distort [*yuharrifuna*] words from their meaning" (4:46); "There is among them a section who distort the Book with their tongues: (As they read) you would think it is a part of the Book, but it is no part of the Book; and they say, 'That is from Allah,' but it is not from Allah. It is they who tell a lie against Allah, and (well) they know it!" (3:78); "They change the words from their (right) times and places" (5:41); and "The transgressors among them changed the word from that which had been given them" (2:59; 7:162).

If Almighty Allah condemns the distortion of revealed scripture, the Prophet Muhammad also condemned liars, distorters, and fabricators of all sorts, linking lying with infidelity. In fact, when the Prophet was asked "Can a believer be a liar?" he responded "No" (Malik). The Messenger of Allah also warned, "Do not tell a lie against me for whoever tells a lie against me will surely enter Hell-fire" (Bukhari); "Verily, one of the worst lies…is to attribute to me what I have not said" (Bukhari); and "Be mindful of transmitting sayings from me… He who intentionally lies about me will find his abode in Hell-fire" (Tirmidhi).

While nothing can be as abominable as distorting the Word of God and the words of the Prophets and the Imams, the manipulation of any information is highly objectionable, and constitutes both a serious sin and a contemptible crime against liberty of expression and intellectual property. It is therefore lamentable to find Muslim translators, editors, and publishers, who are so self-righteous that they believe they have the authority to censor the works of others without their permission. While the problem is prevalent around the globe, we can point to a single work for the sake of example: the English translation of *The Voice of Human Justice* by George Jordac, the Latinized form of his Arabic name, Jurj Jurdaq or Jurji Zaydan.

Originally published in Arabic as *al-Imam 'Ali, sawt al-'adalah al-insaniyyah*, the work was translated into English by M. Fazal Haq, edited by Amirali Aini, published by the Islamic Seminary of Pakistan, and then republished by Ansariyan Publications in Iran. Although a complete and honest translation of the work would have been an important contribution to scholarship, *The Voice of Human Justice* has been the subject of extensive and inexcusable *tahrif*. As the original publisher of the book readily admits,

> The author is an enlightened man of letters and has written the book with perfect sincerity. However, at times, he has said things which do not accord with the facts of history. In such cases necessary clarification has been made in the foot-notes and at places some paragraphs have been deleted altogether. (11)

While translators or editors have the right, indeed, the obligation, to include a prologue or a preface, along with explanatory notes of all kinds, it is unethical and even illegal for them to change the original meaning and suppress content without the written permission of the author and copyright holder. Although including footnotes is an allowable means for editors and translators to express divergence of opinion, deleting entire paragraphs is outrageous. This is what has happened to *The Voice of Human Justice*, which is not simply ironic but an egregious abuse of editing. Simply because one does not agree with a person's interpretation of history does not grant one the right to delete what has been written. While the publisher's footnote may give the impression that only a few paragraphs have been removed, the work has been substantially censored from start to finish. The original Arabic version of *The Voice of Human Justice* is actually a five volume work while the English translation has become a poor abridgment masquerading as the full text. Unless authorized by the author, the role of translators is to accurately convey the entirety of the work, not leave their own personal touch. Suppressing and censoring content is both dishonest and deceptive. We can only conclude by saying, "O ye who believe! Fear Allah and be with those who are truthful" (9:119).

Chapter Twenty-Three

Where Work Needs to be Done

Da'wah, da'wah, da'wah. Tabligh, tabligh, tabligh. Calling to Islam and preaching. Speeches, brochures, and books. Blah, blah, blah. Yada, yada, yada. Enough already. While there is no question that conferences, publications, videos, websites, and other modes of communication can play a role in spreading Islam in the West, these approaches, some of which have been used for over one century, have serious shortcomings and have not produced the expected results. Certainly, there have been converts. And now, there are many third and fourth generation Muslims who trace back to a Western convert. Millions of African Americans have embraced Islam. Over the past few decades, over one hundred thousand Latinos have entered the Muslim faith in the United States. And hundreds of thousands of Europeans and Caucasian-Americans have entered into the Ummah or Muslim Community. For many, this speaks of success. For me, however, it is a monumental failure. It is estimated that over one hundred thousand Muslims performed the final pilgrimage with the Prophet Muhammad. If we assume that one-tenth of Muslims perform the *hajj* on a yearly basis, then that would mean that he brought one million people into Islam in a little more than twenty years. Since one-tenth is probably a gross exaggeration, it is conceivable that there were actually millions of Muslims when the Prophet passed away.

So, if we are Muslims, then our model is the Messenger of Allah. He is the example we seek to follow. While we cannot compare ourselves to him, nor can we ever expect to accomplish what he did during such a short period, we must, at least, strive to emulate him. Looking, then, at the spread of Islam in Western Europe and the Americas, we must ask ourselves: have we truly done our best to disseminate Islam? If one man, the Prophet of Allah, brought one million people into Islam, how many have each of us brought into Islam? With the exception of a few zealous missionaries, virtually all of whom are Muslim converts themselves, the overwhelming majority of Muslims have not brought a single soul into the fold of Islam. There is no excuse for such apathy as *da'wah*, the dissemination of Islam, is an obligation on all Muslims within the limits of their abilities. Malcolm X, for example, brought 40,000 people into the Nation of Islam, most of whom eventually followed him into mainstream Islam after his pilgrimage to Mecca in 1964.

If Malcolm X succeeded in attracting so many converts, it was because he was able to relate Islam to the experiences of African Americans. He was able to make it relevant not only on a theoretical level but also on a practical plain. He was able to concretely show people how Islam could benefit them personally, professionally, socially, and economically. He made Islam attractive and appealing. And, most importantly, he demonstrated that Islam was a doctrine that was totally American and totally Western. He never projected Islam as being anything foreign. And he always, always, linked Islam to the socio-political concerns of the people.

If the spread of Islam is to succeed in the West, it will succeed solely on the basis of being presented as something authentically Western. For far too long, Islam has been presented as an "immigrant religion." It has been and still is perceived as being spread by brown or beige people who speak with funny accents. Westerners attempting to learn about Islam are still confronted with foreign languages they cannot comprehend when they go to mosques. In some cases, they are subjected to reverse racism; not to mention overt sexism. Many Western women have been forcibly ejected from mosques, offering a truly wonderful image of a religion that prides itself on giving women equal rights. When attempting to learn about Islam, many Westerners are fed a bunch of cultural crap that is completely unrelated to Islam. It is not enough, it seems, to convert Westerners to Islam; no, these beckoners to Islam also want to turn them into Arabs, Iranians, or Pakistanis in the process. The next thing you know, you have these ridiculous African, Caucasian or Latino Americans walking around proudly in Pakistani garb, eating curry with their hands, and using Urdu terminology. Next thing you know, they are off to Kashmir to fight the infidel Hindus, instead of fighting the oppressor at home, while those who converted them continue to covet the American dream…

For far too long, mosques have been teaching an Islam burdened with human agendas and biases. The problem is that what they preach, for the most part, in these mosques, is not even Islam. While they present it as "Sunnism," what most mosques have actually been teaching is Salafism, the nice word for the bad word, Wahhabism. Drawn into Islam because it was a "religion of tolerance," many of these converts become the most intolerant people you could ever come across. Suddenly, you find previously tolerant people possessed with hatred for Jews, Hindus, Shiites, and Sufis. Suddenly, you find people who believed in gender equality overtly espousing the most sickening of sexism. Some sincere seekers may be duped into joining this parody of Islam. Good luck getting the average Westerner to buy into such odious nonsense.

While many Muslim converts are educated, intelligent, socially-conscious and committed individuals, some of whom may also be critical of Western foreign policy, this does not mean that they harbor any ill-will towards their countries. To be clear, we may vehemently oppose certain policies espoused by Western powers, but that does not mean that we do not love our countries. If we embrace Islam, it is because we hope to guide our countries on the right path. So, when Muslim immigrants come to our countries, and tell us how much they hate Canada, the USA, the UK, France, and Germany, we get sick to our stomachs. The aspect that irritates us most is the sheer hypocrisy of a segment of this population. Some are greedy, materialistic people, who came to the West, not to spread Islam, but to get rich quick and try to return to their "homeland." They actually make it quite clear that, regardless of the Canadian, American, UK or EU citizenship that has been generously bestowed on them by welcoming nations; they are, first and foremost, Lebanese, Pakistanis or whatever. They are, for all intents and purposes, just trying to use our countries. God forbid they would ever criticize their own kings, dictators, and despots. How defensive they become when we criticize King Mohammed VI, King Hussein, or King Fahd! Yet they have the audacity to insult and abuse our leaders and institutions while guests in our homes and residents or naturalized citizens of our countries?

For Islam to spread in the West, it is Islam, true Islam, original Islam, and traditional, civilizational, Islam that must spread, not the culturally-contaminated versions of Islam espoused by the Saudis, the Pakistanis, and others. Keep your culture in your closet. Keep your politics in your home. Keep your prejudices under lock and key. We may embrace Islam but we do not embrace your racism, prejudice, and sexism. This is not to say that we wish to spread "American Islam," namely, an Islam at the service of the Empire. What we want is Universal Islam; not Saudi Islam, Pakistani Islam, or Somali Islam. And in order for Islam to be embraced in the West, it must be associated with Westerners, and not with newly-arrived immigrants or foreigners who demonize our nations and culture. All mosques and Islamic organizations and associations should be directed by Western Muslims, loyal to the West, and not at the service of foreign interests. Consequently, the message of Islam must be disseminated in our national languages, and not in Arabic, Urdu, Persian, or other foreign tongues. And Islam must be connected to the social, political, and economic concerns of Westerners. In other words, Islam should not simply be spread by preaching and teaching: it must be spread by concrete action, by showing that Muslims care for Westerners, regardless of their religion.

Chapter Twenty-Four

Freedom of Expression in Islam

The Muslim world is a place where freedoms are few, where Ministries of Religious Misguidance manipulate the message of the Prophet Muhammad to suit their own political agendas, to keep Muslims passive, and submissive, not to Allah, but to a worldly political power, where blind following, as opposed to understanding, prevails, and where creative thought, original expression, and critical thinking have been stifled before the very moment they could bud. Such is the condition of much of our Ummah. Such is the state of the Muslim world.

Islam, despite what some million-dollar-earning, mind-manipulating mullahs may think, is a religion of critical and spiritual thought. The Holy Qur'an commands Muslims to think, to analyze, to ponder, and to question, over eight hundred times, in fact, throughout its pages. Submission is not blind in Islam. Submission is the end product of critical thought. It is the realization that Allah is All-Encompassing and Inescapable. It is the spiritual dissolution of the individual "I" into the divine "We." Without freedom of thought, and freedom of expression, no social, political, economic, or spiritual development can take place. The human being is always in a state of flux. To contain a human is to kill a human. To limit movement and growth is to cause atrophy. Yet, this is precisely what has happened in the Muslim world.

Once upon a time, a long, long time ago, Muslims were actually tolerant and incredibly open. The Prophet taught by practice not by prohibition and imposition. He never told a person, "Do not do this," but rather, "It would pain me if you did such and such a thing." He actually embodied the ethics he espoused. He inspired by example. His mercy always prevailed over his wrath. He was open to discussion. He would engage in debate. He would convince people of the rightness of his cause. The spirit of the Prophet, which is the spirit of Islam, would continue, in a slightly diminished form, for centuries to come. Muslims were open and eager to learn from others. They studied ancient and modern languages. They translated and interpreted texts from pagans, Jews, Christians, Zoroastrians, Buddhists, and Hindus. They specialized in various sciences, expanded upon them, and expounded upon them. They were not threatened by the other. They absorbed anything and everything that was beneficial to Muslims and created a magnificent Islamic civilization.

Muslims may have been united in their common beliefs; however, they differed on a multitude of secondary and tertiary issues. Despite this, they did not demand uniformity and conformity. They appreciated the value of diversity in all domains. They understood that it enriched them and that debate, discussion, and dialogue were essential to development. Eventually, this open system started to constrict, namely to close in on itself. Scholars and scientists, who had once been flexible, became increasingly rigid and uncompromising in their views. The door to the independent interpretation of Islamic jurisprudence was closed. Free-thought and philosophy were forbidden. Experimentation ended and old scientific theories were treated as dogmas. Anything new or novel was deemed a prohibited "innovation." Science succumbed to superstition. Minds that were open became closed. People were compelled to conform.

Flash forward a few centuries and here we are. From the leading civilization on the planet, the Muslim world has become the bastion of backwardness. From the most intellectually and scientifically fertile part of the world, the Ummah, the World Community of Islam, has become arid, save a small oasis here and there. Even the prosperity produced by petroleum had done nothing to stimulate critical thought in the Arab World. The Gulf Arabs, as arrogant as always, build multi-billion dollar universities and scientific research centers which do not even employ their own people. Their faculty members come preferably from the United States, Western Europe, and then, perhaps from Egypt, Lebanon, and elsewhere. Rather than create knowledge, the Gulf Arabs think they can buy it. Knowledge is acquired and produced; not owned.

If the Muslim world has failed to rise out of the ruins of colonialism and imperialism, its own narrow-mindedness, and the desert of ignorance in which it remains, one of the main reasons resides in the lack of freedom of expression. With rare exception, most of the Muslim world is ruled by oppressive regimes, some more benevolent than others, but all of which limit freedom of expression and which discourage freedom of thought. In most Muslim countries, speaking your mind, and criticizing the State, can land you in prison, get you tortured, or cost you your life. I am not, of course, speaking about spreading evil ideologies or inciting people to violence. I speak of the simplest efforts to question the status quo and the most honest efforts to improve socio-economic and political conditions. With their obsession with security, the forces of repression that keep Muslims in check react swiftly and brutally to any effort to exert positive change. And so, everything stays the same... Tyrants may change, but everything stays the same...

CHAPTER TWENTY-FIVE

TO REFORM OR TO DEFORM?

Supported by the enemies of Islam for decades, faux Muslim reformists continue to gain influence in East and West, North and South. Claiming to be "renewers" of Islamic tradition, they operate from outside the Islamic tradition: their ideas are not rooted in Islam but outside of it. Intellectually, philosophically, and methodologically, they operate according to Western norms. They hide not the fact that they seek to create the equivalent of a Protestant Reformation at the heart of Islam. They pretend to be progressive when they are really regressive. They claim they want us to advance, when, in truth, they wish to bring us into modern backwardness. They say they want Muslims to evolve while they do nothing but cause the religion to devolve.

If Islam has enemies, they are of two kinds: internal and external. The external enemies are the easiest to identify. They are those who invade, occupy, and colonize the Muslim world. The internal enemies are the friends and allies of the external enemies. They are the despots, dictators, and democrats who operate from within but whose allegiance is to those who manipulate from without. We do, of course, have enemies of our own making: the ultra-conservatives whose only reaction towards external and internal threat is to freeze, to become mortified, calcified, and fossilized. When faced with a natural fight or flight reaction to the unexpected, new, or strange, they decided to play dead and became dead. While trying to protect and defend Islam, they condemned it to perpetual stagnation: they prevented it from breathing, from growing, and from living.

Islam, in many parts of the world, is faced with two equally ugly faces: the face of the Westernized liberal secularized democrat and the face of the retrograde neo-fundamentalist and extremist. Both claim to be fighting for the soul of Islam. Unfortunately, neither knows a solitary thing about Islam. The former, while claiming to stand for Islam, is really rooted in Western values. The latter, while claiming to stand for Islam, cannot distinguish between culture and religion, between what is true and what is false, between what is right and what is wrong, and between what is good and what is evil. This person claims to defend Islam but what he defends is a monstrosity that does not resemble the Islam of the Prophet Muhammad in the least. What is more, these Takfiri terrorists advance the aims of the enemies of Islam. Liberals and conservatives, moderates and liberals, reformists and deformists are all extremes employed to undermine Islam.

Truth, in my estimation, is not found in extremes. These two ugly extremes which are confronting one another across the Muslim world are two forces of evil. Neither will succeed as neither has the truth. In fact, real Islam may actually be reborn from the ashes of these enemies. Those who seek to reform do nothing but deform. Those who claim to defend and protect Islam do nothing but destroy it in the process. Both in belief and practice, they are the polar opposite of the teachings of Islam. The real Islam is neither the ultra-conservative culturally-contaminated Islam espoused by the neo-fundamentalists nor the secular liberal Islam advocated by the reformists. True Islam is the balance between extremes, it is the original Islam espoused by the Prophet, contained in the Qur'an, and protected by the Axis of the Age. It is an Islam that is long overdue but whose return draws closer with every millisecond.

CHAPTER TWENTY-SIX

THE MISGUIDED AND THE MADRASA

On one particular occasion, while I was reluctantly mingling with mercenaries responsible for mass murder, Protestant missionaries who seek to Christianize Muslims, and linguists from the Defense Language Institute, I was soon legitimately incensed at the ignorant comment made by a parochial, self-righteous slob, who sat across from me: "If we are to defeat terrorism we must shut down the madrasas." "And why is that?" I ventured to ask. "Because that is where they train terrorists," she asserted. "Have you ever been to a madrasa?" I inquired. "No," she responded, shaking her head as she scrunched up her face. "Well, if you ever visited a madrasa you would know that the only thing they teach there is how to read the Qur'an. It's like Sunday school; not an al-Qaedah training camp."

Alas, this is the reality in which we live, a time in which the most basic Islamic terminology has been soiled. Thanks to Takfiri terrorists, the *tabkir*, the cry of *Allahu Akbar* or God is the Greatest is no longer associated with divine praise but has become the background cry that accompanies beheadings and suicide bombings. Saying that someone is Muslim is like saying that someone has the plague. Thanks to reactionary fear-mongers and the actions of Wahhabi and Deobandi lunatics, the term sharia or Islamic law, which once stood for an enviable socio-economic and political system, is now associated with the most brutal form of backwardness. For Muslims, the sharia is what the *halakha* is for Jews or the *Catechism* or Canon Law is for Catholics: a religious code of conduct. When Muslims enquire whether one follows the sharia, they want to know whether one is an observant Muslim or not. A person who follows Islamic law performs five daily prayers, fasts during the month of Ramadan, pays charity, performs the pilgrimage if possible, fulfils religious obligations and avoids religious prohibitions. When Muslims speak of sharia, they speak not of lashing fornicators, cutting off the hands of thieves, or stoning adulterers. Like the term sharia, the word hijab or headscarf has equally become stigmatized as a form of imposed oppression. For most Muslim women, hijab simply stands for piety, modesty, and submission of God. Add to those, the very concept of the madrasa, which simply signifies "school," is under attack by the enemies of Islam.

From the time the Prophet Muhammad received revelation over 1400 years ago, the madrasa has been a central feature in every Muslim community. The madrasa was often connected to the mosque. In many cases, the mosque was the madrasa, where children learned to read the Qur'an at the hands of a *faqih* or jurist. The madrasa was the place where children learned their alif-bas or ABCs. It was the place they learned to read and write. The madrasa system was so successful that during the Golden Age of Islam it would have been difficult to find a small girl who could not read or write. The madrasa ensured that the Muslim masses all had a basic level of literacy. The madrasa eventually served the function of both elementary and secondary school and in some cases even constituted a university at the heart of the mosque.

When Western imperialists invaded Muslim lands, they set out to deliberately destroy the madrasa system. By closing the madrasas, they condemned generations of Muslims to illiteracy. To keep Muslims permanently disadvantaged, the European colonialists never replaced the madrasa network with Western-style schools. They did open some schools to which only the elite were invited to attend, those most likely to become tools in the colonial machine. What was missing after the demise of the madrasas were learning opportunities for the poor. For centuries, they had been able to sit in the circle, take up the slate, chant the suras, and learn along with their more affluent brethren. Afterward, barriers were erected and the balance of community was lost. Most Muslims were thus destined to be illiterate in both their native languages and the language of the oppressor. Even after independence, many Muslim nations have continued to struggle with the blight of illiteracy. In fact, some have still to recover.

The madrasa, as understood by most Muslims, is simply a school: a place where one learns to read and write using the Qur'an as the textbook of instruction. In some cases, madrasas also impart basic Islamic education, namely, the five pillars of Islam, along with basic legal rules: how to perform the ritual ablution, how to perform the daily prayers, the rules governing fasting, and so forth. Small children who attend madrasas sing songs, learn poetry, and do drawings. Unless one is dealing with madrasas under the control and command of the Taliban, al-Qaedah or ISIS, bomb-making and terrorism are not part of the curriculum. We need to recognize the relative rarity of such establishments. To condemn all madrasas for the misuse of a very few would be like closing American public schools due to increasing problems with guns and killings. In fact, to take these terrible exceptions and treat them as a general rule and apply it to the Muslim world as a whole is a huge injustice. Regrettably, this is the reality. Thanks to the propaganda disseminated by the mass media, many Westerners honestly believe that kids who attend madrasas, be they in Canada, the United States, the UK, the UAE, Malaysia, or elsewhere, are tiny terrorists. While it is one thing for ignorant, prejudiced, Westerners to look at Muslim men or women as "terrorists," it is another thing altogether for them to consider Muslim children as enemies. By demonizing the madrasa, the mass media demonizes Muslim children and desensitizes Westerners to the humanity inherent in over one and a half billion Muslims on the planet. If the children who follow Islam are portrayed as miniature enemies, and tiny terrorists, who, then, would object to the killing of Muslim kids or empathize with them if they are murdered? In fact, in recent years, the murder of Muslim children has been openly advocated by the radical right in the United States. "Muslims are training their children to be terrorists," affirmed a caller on a right-wing radio station, "if we do not kill them, they are going to kill us when they grow up." If such sentiments are not disturbing enough, they were in response to the incendiary rhetoric of Donald Trump, a 2016 American presidential candidate, who proudly promised that he would kill the family members of terrorists. Although killing combatants is permitted according to international norms, the targeting of civilians, in pre-emptive or retaliatory attacks, is a war crime. As we read in Ezekiel, "The son shall not suffer for the iniquity of the father, nor the father suffer for the iniquity of the son" (18:20). Rather than oppose madrasas or schools, we should help spread them far and wide, ensuring that they are in the hands of qualified, moderate, Muslim educators. If anything, increasing education can help stem the tide of extremism, a destructive disease that feeds on ignorance.

Chapter Twenty-Seven

The Muhammadan Covenants: A Revolutionary Revelation

The Covenants of the Prophet Muhammad will come as a revelation to most Jews, Christians, and Muslims. This is no coincidence. In fact, the Messenger of Allah makes it explicitly clear that the covenants in question were not the product of his own human initiative, not the outcome of divine inspiration, but rather the actual consequence of divine revelation.

The Covenants of the Prophet Muhammad, which I have brought to light in this period of darkness, constitute an entirely new genre in the Islamic canon. While they do not form part of the Qur'an, the divinely-dictated book granted to Muhammad ibn 'Abd Allah by means of the Angel Gabriel, they go beyond the narrow sense of Sunnah or hadith as they are not simply orally-transmitted sayings or accounts of actions. The Covenants of the Prophet are actually unique in that they are primary sources, including both originals and copies of original documents, which were dictated, signed and sealed by Muhammad, the Messenger of Allah, himself, and written down, and witnessed, by his Companions and the scribes of revelation.

According to Islamic scholarship, the Prophet received various forms of revelation: 1) the Qur'an, which was memorized and compiled during his lifetime; and 2) sacred sayings or *ahadith qudisiyyah*, which represent revelations not included in the Qur'an. These typically commence with "the Messenger of Allah said that Allah said." To these two categories, it appears, we would have to include a third form of revelation: The Covenants of the Prophet Muhammad which, according to the documents themselves, were revealed to him in the form of divine visions and revelations.

If this is truly the case, then the Covenants of the Prophet Muhammad cannot be dismissed as inauthentic aberrations due to the fact that they do not fit into existing categories. If anything, they break the existing molds. If they are indeed authentic, in word and spirit, then they would come second only to the Qur'an in importance. The implications, of course, are astounding as the Covenants of the Prophet Muhammad require a radical re-envisioning of the Ummah or Muslim Community and a realigning of existing thought patterns.

Traditional Sunni, Shiite, and Sufi scholars have generally agreed that the Prophet did not provide a specific model for an Islamic State. Many models have been proposed. Many models have been tried. All of them have fundamentally failed. If we are to believe the Covenants of the Prophet, and there is no reason that we should not considering the plethora of proof provided during the past fourteen centuries, Muhammad never attempted to establish an exclusively Muslim State. On the contrary, he strove to create an Ummah or Community, a type of federation of tribes and nations from a multitude of different backgrounds and belief-systems, all operating under the protective banner of Islam.

The brilliance of this design can only have been the product of a mastermind, Muhammad, the Messenger of Allah, and not half a dozen different forgers from distinct Christian denominations, operating in different languages, and working in disparate geographic reasons during different centuries. It is simply implausible that six different falsifiers could have conceived such a sophisticated societal model.

In fact, when confronted with the Covenants of the Prophet and the *Constitution of Medina*, some scholars have suggested that Muhammad ibn 'Abd Allah was the founding father of secularism. They come to this conclusion because the Ummah he created was multi-ethnic, lingual, racial, and creedal, with equal protections provided to all. The difference, of course, was that the Ummah was not the product of the division between Church and State. On the contrary, the Ummah was a divinely-inspired socio-economic and political system which was ordained by the Creator of the Universe.

If this was indeed the plan of the Prophet Muhammad ibn 'Abd Allah, Muslims have seriously veered away from this magnanimous model over the course of the past 1400 years. If the Messenger of Allah were to return to the world today, he would find the systems operating in the Muslim world to be completely and totally unrecognizable, including and especially, the so-called Islamist models where intolerance prevails over tolerance and where exclusivity prevails over universality. Allah was, indeed, the Best of Planners (8:30), and, as history can confirm, Muslims were, indeed, the worst of heirs and executors.

Chapter Twenty-Eight

How Has a Religion of Beauty Been Presented as Ugly by ISIL?

The Muslim world is currently experiencing unprecedented persecution at the hands of fringe, extremist, ideologically-driven, groups. Whether it is Boko Haram in Nigeria, al-Shabab in Somalia, al-Qaedah both in North Africa and the Arabian Peninsula, the Taliban in Afghanistan and Pakistan, or ISIL in Syria and Iraq, mainstream Muslims, from all the major and minor schools of law and spiritual paths in Islam, are being targeted by violent militants who view them as infidels and apostates whose blood can legally be shed. Although these terrorists also target non-Muslims, unjustly and unjustifiably, the overwhelming majority of their victims are innocent Muslims.

With the exception of some misguided souls, no Muslim can identify with any of these mercenary movements that pretend to be fighting for Islam and the Caliphate. As their ideas and actions show, these death cults are the antithesis of Islam and its diametric opposite. In fact, they relish the fact that they violate Islamic legal, moral, and ethical norms, and take pride in attributing their actions to the Muslim faith, thereby soiling the image of Islam, and inciting a backlash against believers on a global scale. How, then, has a religion of beauty been rendered so ugly?

For those who may have forgotten, the Prophet Muhammad, the Messenger of Allah, was a gentle, caring, and tender man with a message of love. His soul was pure and spotless, shinning with spirituality. His primary approach to spreading Islam was preaching and setting an inspiring example. When attacked, he defended himself, but was also just and equitable. If he ever waged war, it was to liberate, not subjugate, and to bring justice instead of injustice. The Prophet's mercy prevailed over his wrath.

If God has given us the Qur'an, He has also given us the Sunnah, the example set by the Prophet in his words and actions. Although ignored by the majority of Muslims, one of the most important aspects of the Sunnah consists of the letters, treaties and covenants between the Prophet and communities in and around Arabia. It is in these sources that the vision of the Prophet Muhammad is most clearly and meticulously articulated. How does one spread Islam? How does one treat non-Muslims? Every aspect of the Prophet's domestic and foreign policy is to be found in the covenants he concluded with the Christians of the Sinai, Egypt, Najran, the Levant, Assyria, Armenia, Persia, and the world. These documents stipulate the rights and obligations of both Muslims and non-Muslims, protecting life, liberty, and property.

The Covenants of the Prophet Muhammad were respected by the rightly-guided Caliphs as well as many of the empires and dynasties that ruled the Islamic world thereafter. Renewed on a regular basis for nearly 1400 years, the Covenants of the Prophet formed the basis of interfaith relations in Islam. As a result of the conditions of social justice, stability, and fraternity that they created, the Covenants of the Prophet played a major role in the rise, spread, and success of Islamic civilization.

The Covenants consist of official documents recording the words of the Prophet as issued during his lifetime. They possess authority equal to canonical traditions and since they confirm, as oppose to contradict, the Qur'an and the Sunnah, they can serve as a source of legal guidance and inspiration while showing the true spirit of Islam.

The Covenants of the Prophet shed an enormous amount of light on the biography of the Prophet and early Islamic history. They demonstrate convincingly that the Muslim model is one of tolerance, pluralism, and peaceful coexistence.

The written words of the Prophet Muhammad are a central part of his message. They should sit side by side with the Qur'an in both mosque and home. If Muslims are to renew their understandings of Islam and undergo a collective awakening, these covenants of hope will play a major part in that restoration.

The disease of extremism is a sickness that plagues the modern world. More than ever, Muslims need to become reacquainted with the Covenants of the Prophet as they consist of the best antidote to repel this disease which is becoming pandemic in our world.

CHAPTER TWENTY-NINE

THE STATE OF OUR UMMAH

As a Native North American and proud member of the Métis Nation, freedom is something fundamental for me. It flows in my blood and veins. It is very much my life force. In Michif-Cree, the Métis are known as Otipemisiwak which means "the people who own themselves" or "the people who govern themselves." This is because the Métis have a long history of independence, self-governance, and democratically-elected leadership. We have always fought for our rights and freedom. We have never been conquered. We have never been colonized. And we have never been broken. We may have lost some battles. We may have been oppressed. But our spirit remains strong. We are, and will always be, the People who are Free.

While I am an Aboriginal person, and identify with the First Nations, Inuit and Métis, I also acknowledge my European ancestors: primarily French and Irish. The French, in Europe, and in Canada, have a deep commitment to the cause of freedom, justice, fraternity, and equality. My family name, Morrow, belongs to the kings of Leinster in Ireland. My Irish ancestors fought English imperialists for centuries. I also honor my Andalusian ancestors, themselves of North African and Middle Eastern origin, for maintaining their faith for as long as they possibly could under the most difficult of situations possible.

As a Métis person, I am taught to honor my elders, to honor my ancestors. And this is precisely what I do. We do not deny our mixed blood: we are proud of it. We are proud of our European ancestors who married indigenous women, learned indigenous languages, embraced indigenous culture, and adopted the indigenous worldview. Their offspring, the Métis, were accepted as indigenous people by indigenous people and created a new indigenous nation: the Métis Nation which spread from the Atlantic to the Pacific. Not only are we recognized by our people, we are recognized by the Canadian Constitution and the Federal Court of Canada as Métis Indians, *li gens libres*, the Free People, as we call ourselves. Our complexions may vary, from light-skinned, blue-eyed blonds, to bronze-skin and jet-black hair; however, this lack of precise phenotype has never posed a problem for our people. We are a people and a culture; not a specific set of facial features. Identity is not determined by skin color. It is based on ancestry, history, community, and culture. It is rooted in a common worldview, set of values, and shared beliefs.

So, while I am a Muslim, and a scholar of Islam, I am also an indigenous person, racially, ethnically, culturally, linguistically, and spiritually. I can confirm that the traditional worldview of the Eastern Woodland Indians, the Indians of the Plains, and many other First Nations from the Americas is consistent with the true teachings of Islam: belief in the Creator and righteous action. If you look at *tasawwuf* or *'irfan*, the spiritual and mystical tradition of Islam, you will find that is correlates clearly with the traditional teachings of many First Nations.

So when I speak about Islam, I speak, in part, as a Native person. I speak as an indigenous person from the West, as an Aboriginal, and as a Free Person, not one who has been conquered or colonized mentally and culturally. Many Muslims, however, as the result of colonialism and imperialism, understand but two things: to oppress or to be oppressed. This is all that they know. It shows in how they interact with others. It shows in how they treat subordinates. It shows in how they treat their subjects. It shows in how they rule and how they respond to being ruled. If you look around the world today, you will find but two things: Muslims who oppress and Muslims who are oppressed. The Prophet Muhammad, however, warned: "Do not oppress and do not be oppressed."

It takes a person such as I hope to be, a person with a pure heart, a person who strives to be objective, a person with perspective, a person with a mind that is fresh, unsoiled, and unspoiled, a person free of mind and thought, to present Islam as it truly is. Some will say that I am being pompous when I am simply being frank. Some will say that I lie when I simply state the truth. Some will say that I am an outsider when I am truly an insider. "There is no greater jihad," said the Prophet Muhammad, "than to tell the truth" (Ahmad). And this is what I intend to do, however much it may scandalize certain sectors. I say it clearly, without shame, and without fear: the ulama have failed the Ummah. The religious scholars have failed the Muslim Community.

As a group with vested interests, the ulama can, at times, operate like the mafia. They are, in some senses, like the police force. They tend to protect the interest of their group. So, what I say is going to infuriate certain people. Well, as the saying goes, "if the hat fits, let them wear it." When I say that the ulama have failed the Ummah, I do not speak about the true ulama, the righteous ulama, and the rightly-guided ulama. They love me and I love them. We are in this struggle together. I am talking about court clerics. I am talking about professional mullahs out for money.

I am talking about the agents of the Empire. I am talking about sell-out scholars and Uncle Tom ulama. That is who I am talking about.

So, what am I saying when I state that the ulama have failed the Ummah? Well, let me put it in the words of the Prophet: "Every one of you is a shepherd and is responsible for his flock" (Bukhari and Muslim). "The ulama are the heirs of Prophet," said the Messenger of Allah (Tirmidhi). So, how do you judge a shepherd? Well, you judge a shepherd on the basis of his flock. If the flock is in good health, if the sheep are safe, if the lambs are thriving, then you have a good shepherd. But if half the flock has been devoured by wolves, coyotes, and bears, your ewes are being taken by poachers, your rams are being stolen, your sheep are mangy and matted, infested with parasites, starving, and dying from diseases, then I say your shepherd is inept. And while I use analogy, it is rooted in reality and personal experience for I am both figuratively and literally a shepherd with over a decade of experience in the domain.

There are, and have always been, some true ulama who have struggled against colonialism, imperialism, and neo-imperialism. There are some scholars who have never ceased to promote the good and forbid the wrong. There are some clerics who have done everything possible to protect and disseminate the true teachings of Islam and to look out for the interests of the Muslim Community. Still, many would maintain that they remain in the minority. Collectively, however, the ulama have failed. They have failed fundamentally on virtually every level. Just look at the state of the Muslim world! Look at the state of our Ummah! If we had good guides, if we had competent shepherds, we would not be in the mess that we are in today and have been for centuries. The Muslim world has suffered nothing but decline, decay, and decomposition. If our shepherds were any good, we would still be the dominant world culture. But we are not. Hence, we need to hold ourselves accountable and assume responsibility for our plight. Our leaders may have failed us but we have also failed our leaders. In fact, we have failed ourselves. "The first step toward change is awareness," wrote Nathaniel Branden, while "[t]he second step is acceptance." The third step, I would add, is to take action.

One of the most moving experiences in my recent past took place at the Reviving the Islamic Spirit Convention that was held in Toronto, Canada, in December of 2013. I was invited to attend a lecture by al-Shaykh al-Habib 'Ali al-Jifri, a spiritual guide of Yemenite origin. It may seem courageous for me to blame. That is an easy game. It takes even more courage to apologize. And that is exactly what Shaykh al-Jifri did: he apologized on behalf of the ulama. "Forgive us," he said, "if we have failed you." "Forgive us," he said, "if we taught you the verses of jihad without properly contextualizing them." "Forgive us," he said, "if we have created of a generation of young Muslims who have no respect for human life whatsoever; forgive us." The man made me cry. I was moved by his courage to speak the truth. And I was touched by his complete and total humility. In short, I was stunned by his sincerity.

What do we, as Muslims, have to offer the world? Yes, we can offer spiritual development and personal salvation. And that is plenty. But, in terms of socio-economic, cultural, scientific, and political power, we have little to nothing to offer. We used to lead the world. We were the bastion of culture and civilization for over a thousand years. The entire world wanted to be like us and imitate us. Muslims are no longer leaders, they are followers, and, unfortunately, a large number of them only seem to follow bad things and bad examples. If they adopted the positive aspects of Western civilization and culture, that would be great. However, if anything, many of them only accept negative elements from the West.

Many Muslims are always quick to blame. Blame the West! Blame the US! Blame the Zionists! How about blame yourselves? Germs may infect the human body, but if you have ruined your immune system with filthy habits, can you blame the germs? People are ultimately responsible for their own fate and destiny. Have you ever heard the saying, "people deserve their leaders?" They do nothing but blame the West, but they are the first to imitate the West and move to the West. If Muslims who live in the West hate the West so much, they should immigrate to a Muslim-majority country. Go back to Africa. Go back to the Middle East. And go back to Asia. It is one thing for me, as a Westerner, to criticize my country and its shortcomings. However, I find it particularly offensive when we open our doors to immigrants who have little love or loyalty for our nations. I am very critical of foreign policy issues. But never, ever, assume that I harbor any ill-will towards the land of my ancestors. As a person who loves and appreciates diversity, I am not expressing racist or anti-immigrant sentiment. I support immigration and I love all immigrants who genuinely love their countries of adoption. I love immigrants who are loyal to the countries that granted them citizenship. In my experience, that would be most of them. It is the subversive Islamist/Jihadist minority that I charge with treachery and treason.

Yes, the West is to blame. There is no doubt. History speaks for itself. But, yes, Muslims are equally to blame. Who has soiled the image of Islam in the world? The Jews? The Americans? Who has soiled everything that we hold sacred? The *shahadah*, the testimony of faith that "There is no god but Allah and Muhammad is the Messenger of Allah," the traditional black banner of Islam, the very symbol of the Prophet, is now associated with al-Qaedah, al-Nusrah, and ISIS. If I decided to fly the flag of the Prophet Muhammad on my property, the FBI would come knocking on my door while my conservative Christian neighbors might burn a cross on my lawn and try to lynch me.

Ramadan. What can be more beautiful than Ramadan? A month of fasting, spiritual purification, charity, brotherhood and sisterhood. Now, it is the symbol of slaughter. I live in the Midwest, close to a relatively large urban center. Typically, when it is Christmas season, grocery stores put out holiday displays. They do the same for Easter, Thanksgiving, and Hanukkah. Well, some grocery stores put special items on display for Ramadan: for example, dates and other items. They had to take them down due to all the complaints they received. What did people object to? "How on earth can you celebrate Ramadan, the month of beheadings?" The month of *beheadings*? Yes, Ramadan, the month of beheadings. Thanks to those Salafi serial killers from Iraq.

Now we have these terrorists from Boko Haram. I call them *awlad haram*, "sons of sin," as we say in Arabic or "bastards" as we say in English. Burning churches, slaughtering Christians who are celebrating mass, kidnaping, raping, and selling Christian girls: all in the name of Islam. "That's part of their religion," I have heard people say. "That's Islam." And do not even get me started about Syria and Iraq, where these Takfiri terrorists have been destroying mosques, churches, and sacred sites. And do not even get me started about Pakistan, where they burn down churches, kill Shiites, kill Ahmadis, and kill Sufis. And do not even get me started about the attacks against Shiites and Christians in Egypt, not to mention women, who were being sexually-assaulted in the streets of Cairo to chants of *Allahu Akbar*. The same wretched thing that happened to women in Algeria and Afghanistan. And the same sickening thing that is being committed by some so-called Muslim refugees in Europe.

In the event anyone is oblivious to the fact, in 2012, a retired Egyptian army general, by the name of Ahmed Ragai Attiya, obtained 71 administrative orders demanding the destruction of the Monastery of St. Catherine. He claims that the monastery was only built in 2006 when, in reality, it was built in the 6th century. He alleges that the monastery is a threat to national security. As all informed parties are aware, St. Catherine's Monastery houses the *ashtinameh*, a charter of privileges and protection that was granted personally by the Prophet Muhammad. To destroy the Monastery of St. Catherine, a UNESCO World Heritage site, would be a crime against humanity, a crime against the Divinity, an affront against decency, and a clear and blatant violation of the *Covenant of the Prophet Muhammad with the Monks of Mount Sinai*.

So, what does this covenant contain? What does it state? Here are a few choice citations:

> This covenant was written by Muhammad, the son of 'Abd Allah, the proclaimer and warner, trusted to protect Allah's creations, in order that people may raise no claim against Allah after [the advent of] His Messengers for Allah is Almighty, Wise.

Allah entrusted the Prophet to protect all of creation. He was sent to defend not only Muslim but all of humanity. He came to grant universal rights and freedoms:

> He has written it for the members of his religion and to all those who profess the Christian religion in East and West, near or far, Arabs or non-Arabs, known or unknown, as a covenant of protection.

The *Covenant of the Prophet* was made with Christians as a whole. In fact, the Prophet made treaties with all of the major Christian denominations of the time. It was a covenant of protection, not a covenant of oppression and persecution. The Messenger of Allah continues:

> If anyone breaks the covenant herein proclaimed, or contravenes or transgresses its commands, he has broken the Covenant of Allah, breaks his bond, makes a mockery of his religion, deserves the curse [of Allah], whether he is a sultan or another among the believing Muslims.

Anyone who violates the treaty offends Allah, insults the Prophet, and incurs the wrath of Almighty Allah. Those who persecute Christians in the name of Islam are actually outside the fold of Islam. As the Prophet states:

> If a monk or pilgrim seeks protection, in mountain or valley, in a cave or in tilled fields, in the plain, in the desert, or in a church, I am behind them, defending them from every enemy; I, my helpers, all the members of my religion, and all my followers, for they [the monks and the pilgrims] are my protégés and my subjects.

To fight peaceful Christians is to fight the Prophet Muhammad. To oppose one religion is to oppose every religion. The People of the Book form a fundamental part of the Ummah or Muslim Community. As the Messenger of Allah states:

> A bishop shall not be removed from his bishopric, nor a monk from his monastery, nor a hermit from his tower nor shall a pilgrim be hindered from his pilgrimage.

And yet Christian priests, monks, and nuns are expelled from their monasteries in Syria, Iraq, and Nigeria. The Prophet proceeds:

> Moreover, no building from among their churches shall be destroyed, nor shall the money from their churches be used for the building of mosques or houses for the Muslims. Whoever does such a thing violates Allah's covenant and dissents from the Messenger of Allah.

And yet Takfiri terrorists destroy religious establishments in clear violation of the *Covenant of the Prophet*. In Syria, they have ransacked churches and monasteries and plundered their property. And again, in the words of the Messenger of Allah:

> Neither poll-tax nor fees shall be laid on monks, bishops, or worshippers for I protect them, wherever they may be, on land or sea, in East and West, in North and South. They are under my protection, within my covenant, and under my security, against all harm.

And yet in Syria and Iraq, in areas controlled by Takfiri terrorists, the *jizyah* has been imposed on Christian monks, bishops, and worshippers in defiance of right. In the following segment, the Prophet extends his mercy to his Christian friends and allies:

> And with the People of the Book there is to be no strife, unless it be over what is good. We wish to take them under the wing of our mercy, and the penalty of vexation shall be kept at a distance from them, wherever they are and wherever they may settle.

The Prophet Muhammad promised peace, mercy, and justice to his Christian subjects. Takfiri terrorists have brought nothing but terror, injustice, intolerance, oppression, and bloodshed. As the Messenger of Allah commanded:

> If a Christian woman enters a Muslim household, she shall be received with kindness, and she shall be given opportunity to pray in her church; there shall be no dispute between her and a man who loves her religion. Whoever contravenes the covenant of Allah and acts to the contrary is a rebel against his covenant and his Messenger.

And yet Takfiri terrorists in Nigeria forcibly convert Christian girls to Islam and force them into marriage. As the Prophet said, "There is no marriage without consent" (Bukhari). A woman cannot be married against her will. Furthermore, Islam set up a system to eradicate slavery. No

Muslim has the right to enslave others. According to Islamic law, the punishment for sexual assault is death.

In Syria, the so-called Free Syrian Army took control of a Christian community and decreed: "Convert to Islam or die!" In Syria, jihadists have crucified Christians who refused to take the *shahadah* and embrace the Muslim faith. This is not Islam. Have they not read the Qur'an? "There is no compulsion in religion" (2:256). Of course not, they are Wahhabis! What do they know about Islam? Apparently nothing. They must be waiting for an illustrated Qur'an. As the Prophet of Allah continues:

> These people shall be assisted in the maintenance of their religious buildings and their dwellings; thus they will be aided in their faith and kept true to their allegiance.

Muslims are not allowed to destroy churches and monasteries. On the contrary, the Prophet has protected them. Muslims are actually supposed to maintain them. Why? Because it will keep Christians loyal. Why? Because the only way to win them is through love. And yet there have been hundreds of terrorist attacks against Christians in the Muslim world since September 11th, 2001. How can Muslims denounce that mosques are being attacked in the United States without also denouncing that churches are being attacked in the Muslim world? In the struggle against hatred and intolerance there can be no room for double standards. Either Jews, Christians, and Muslims stand together in defense of religious freedom or we will all perish alone.

Ironically, I was once accused of inciting hatred against Muslims. Seriously now? I am a Muslim. I am a deeply committed Muslim and a scholar of Islam. Am I inciting hatred against myself? Only hatred of those who hate the truth, but that is to be expected. As a Muslim, not only do I condemn the crimes and atrocities that Christians have committed against Muslims, but I also have a moral and ethical obligation to denounce the crimes and atrocities that Muslims have committed against Christians specifically when they are committed in the name of Islam. People look at the actions of a microscopic minority of self-professed Muslim militants and claim that "This is Islam." They may be small in numbers; however, terrorists make a lot of noise. Unfortunately, the disproportionate amount of media attention they receive, following the adage that "if it bleeds it leads," actually helps terrorists. They get free marketing, 24/7, from their so-called enemies.

While the media complex gives the impression that terrorists pose an existential threat to Western civilization, there are, in reality, only about 100,000 of these Takfiri terrorists in the world who, in turn, are passively supported by about 7% of so-called Muslims. These self-professed Muslims may not necessarily agree with the methods employed by these extremists; however, they support them since they falsely believe that they are fighting the enemies of Islam. Alternatively, it is quite possible that this 7% consists, in part or in whole, of Salafis, Wahhabis, and Takfiris, in which case they should not even be classified as Muslims. Even if we assume that this number consists of terrorist sympathizers, it still represents a small segment of the people surveyed.

As statistical studies demonstrate, over 93% of Muslims oppose extremism and terrorism. And, furthermore, according to FBI statistics, only 6% of terrorist attacks in the United States are perpetrated by Muslims. In fact, 42% of terrorist attacks in the country are committed by Latinos, 24% by extreme left wing groups, 7% by Jewish extremists, 5% by communists, and 16% by a variety other groups. Media coverage of so-called Muslim terrorism provides a distorted image of reality.

I am not attacking, have not attacked, and would never attack Islam or Muslims. The overwhelming majority of Muslims are good, decent, human beings. I love them and they love me. I want to make it explicitly clear that I am only targeting 0.001% of so-called Muslim terrorists along with their sympathizers which may, or may not, reach 7%. Frankly, I do not even consider them to be Muslims in the first place. While there are some who will accuse me of engaging in *takfir*, namely, doing the same thing that I accuse my enemies of doing, expelling people from the fold of Islam, there is a fundamental difference. My Islam embraces Sunnism, Shiism, and Sufism. I am a tolerant person. I embrace the totality of Islam. I am only intolerant towards those who are intolerant. Sunnis are my brothers. Shiis are my brothers. Sufis are my brothers. I only do *takfir* of the Takfiris. I only excommunicate the excommunicators. Since they do not consider us to be Muslims, why should we consider them to be Muslims? If anything, they are devil-worshipping Satanists.

So let me continue with what the Prophet truly has to teach concerning the manner in which Muslims should treat Christian friends, neighbors, allies, subjects, and minorities: "None of them shall be compelled to bear arms, but the Muslims shall defend them." And yet in Bangladesh, jihadists have kidnapped Christian children in order to train them to be suicide bombers. "Whatever... The *Covenant of the Prophet* is a fake..." some will say. I say, fear God! Speak not without knowledge. Tolerance of Christians and other minorities was normative in Islam for most of Muslim history. Tolerance is the rule while intolerance is the exception. Fear Allah, I warn Muslims, for the *Covenant of the Prophet* clearly states: "and they shall never contravene this promise of protection until the hour comes and the world ends." If the *ashtinameh* is authentic, as it certainly appears to be from an academic and scholarly standpoint, then the *Covenant of the Prophet* is binding until the Day of Judgment. If that is the case, why would Muslims be willing to run the risk of violating it? After all, it is only the eternity of their souls that is at stake.

Chapter Thirty

The Roots of Takfirism: How to Confront the *Fitnah* of Takfirism

"Islam is a religion of peace," I was once foolish enough to say at an interfaith gathering in Aberdeen, South Dakota. "Yeah, right!" shouted some infuriated Christian from the back-row. And you know what? He was right. He was right to call me out. Had he thrown a shoe at my head, I would have deserved it. Islam may signify "peace and submission;" however, some self-professed Muslims are far from being the peaceful submitters that the noun denotes. Our name has been soiled. Our brand has been tarnished. If the Takfiris, Wahhabis, Salafis, Jihadis, Irhabis, Muharabis and Kharijis are Muslims, then we are not Muslims. If what they represent is Islam, then we do not want to have anything to do with it.

Ah, but the world is upside down. Everything is out of balance. We, the masses and the majority, are the real Muslims. We are the *muslimin*, the submitters. We are the *mu'minin*, the true believers. And those who make *takfir* of *Ahl al-Sunnah wa al-Jama'at*, those who make *takfir* of the Shia of *Ahl al-Bayt*, and those who make *takfir* of the *Ahl al-Tawassuf* are the real infidels, outcasts, renegades, and apostates in question. As the Prophet Muhammad said: "If a Muslim calls another Muslim a *kafir* or an infidel…then he is himself a *kafir* or an infidel" (Abu Dawud). And yet again, "No man accuses another man of being…a *kafir* or an infidel but it reflects back on him" (Bukhari).

So, with all due respect, nobody can turn around and accuse me of fighting fire with fire. I never did *takfir* of anyone. I never excommunicated anyone. They did *takfir* of me. They did *takfir* of us, the Muslim majority. Hence, the Takfiris, Wahhabis, Salafis, Jihadis, Irhabis, Muharabis, Kharijis, Iblisis, and Shaytanis did *takfir* of themselves. Through their beliefs, words, and actions, they have placed themselves outside the fold of Islam. They have expelled themselves from humanity.

We need to be explicitly clear that the members, supporters, and sympathizers of al-Qaedah, al-Nusrah, Daesh, and any similar groups, are not Sunnis. They are not *Ahl al-Sunnah.* To call them Sunnis is an insult to the Sunnah. To call them Sunnis is an insult to the Prophet Muhammad because they are far removed from the Sunnah and everything for which it stands. As we say in Spanish, *al pan pan y al vino vino*: call bread, bread; call wine, wine. In other words, let us call the Takfiris what they really are: Kharijites, the enemies of the Sunnis, the Shias, and the Sufis. And when I speak of Kharijites, I speak of the early Kharijites, the defectors who rose up in revolt against 'Uthman, 'Ali, Mu'awiyyah and other early leaders, and not the moderate 'Ibadis from Oman and Algeria, who oppose violence, and who belong to the Ummah of Islam.

We talk about Islamic unity. We talk about uniting the Ummah. Well, finally, we have grounds on which to stand and principles for which to fight. All Muslims, Sunnis, Shiis, and Sufis, as well as 'Ibadis, need to unite in the face of the Takfiri Kharijites who have resurfaced in these latter days to hasten the rise of their "Messiah," the fake Messiah, not Jesus-Christ but the Anti-Christ. By God, I pity the fool who cannot distinguish truth from falsehood. I pity the fool who cannot distinguish darkness from light, right from wrong, and good from evil. It is simply astonishing how so many pseudo-Muslim zombies have sided with Satan in this dawn of Armageddon.

The Takfiri-Khawarij rape, pillage, and plunder. The Takfiri-Khawarij destroy mosques, churches, and sacred sites. The Takfiri-Khawarij crucify Christians. The Takfiri-Khawarij behead Shiite women and children. The Takfiri-Khawarij machine-gun Shiite civilians. They systematically violate all the injunctions of the Qur'an, the Sunnah, and the sharia, as well as the rights and protections granted by the Prophet Muhammad to the members of his Ummah: all of them, Jews, Christians, Muslims, Zoroastrians, and even peaceful polytheists. And yet they find supporters? And yet some so-called Muslims approach me, saying: "I am confused about ISIS. Are they good or bad?" *Wa Allah*, there is no hope in hell for someone who cannot distinguish between God and the Devil.

Perhaps some of these so-called Muslims think that at least the Takfiris have the courage to "defend Islam from Western control." These ignorant people should inform themselves about just how much support the West has given the Takfiris. And if the Frankenstein monster created by various Western and non-Western nations has now turned on them in the case of ISIS, maybe these nations will think twice about arming terrorists in the future, and maybe those mercenaries who are tempted to join such terrorists will also think twice, seeing that those who arm and pay them today may be bombing them tomorrow.

Islam. What is Islam? Shall I share the very essence of Islam? It is time to brace oneself. It is time to hold on to one's chair. This can blow people away and blast them into oblivion: Islam is a religion of moderation. Can I possibly be clearer? This is Islam: the middle path, the pivot, the *qutb*, the axis, the center, the *wasat*, the core, the heart, and the balanced pendulum. We are not liberal. We are not conservative. We are not right-wing nor are we left-wing. We are not nominal Muslims nor are we fanatical Muslims. We are not pacifists nor are we terrorists. We are a middle-nation, justly balanced, and the pride of the Prophet.

CHAPTER THIRTY-ONE

MUHAMMAD'S LEGACY: THE COVENANTS OF THE MESSENGER OF ALLAH

The *Covenants of the Prophet Muhammad with the Christians of the World* is the story of a journey. It is very much the story of a quest: a search for the Scrolls of Hope, a voyage of discovery and rediscovery which provides unparalleled insight into primordial Islam and the living legacy of the Messenger of Allah.

Thanks and praise be to God, I was exposed to the *ashtinameh*, the *Covenant of the Prophet Muhammad with the Monks of Mount Sinai* immediately upon embracing Islam, in the mid-1980s, and professing the sweetest and most spiritually sublime words I have ever uttered, the *shahadah* of *la ilaha illa Allah / Muhammadan Rasul Allah*, the testimony of faith that "There is no god but God and that Muhammad is the Messenger of God." Consequently, along with the Qur'an and the *Constitution of Medina*, the *ashtinameh* represents the fundamental foundation of Islam.

Is Islam a religion of violence? Is Islam a religion of brutality? Is Islam a religion of misogyny, pedophilia, sexual slavery, and ritualized rape? Is Islam a religion of terror? Is Islam a religion of destruction and chaos? Is Islam a cult of death, dismemberment, torture, mutilation, and mass murder? Is Islam the manifestation of injustice, oppression, despotism, and tyranny? Some will say: "Yes, by God Almighty, yes it is!"

But I say no. We say no. The Prophet says no. The Qur'an says no. The Sunnah says no. The sharia says no and Almighty Allah, glorified and exalted be He, says no, absolutely not, never! Islam is a religion of justice. Islam is a religion of peace. Islam is a religion of tolerance. Islam is a religion of compassion. And those who argue otherwise are ignorant, misguided, or ill-intentioned: "Deaf, dumb, and blind, they will not return to the path" (2:18).

This is not to say that we are pacifists. This is not to say that we always turn the other cheek. This is not to say that we follow in the footsteps of Mahatma Gandhi. This is not to say that we are non-violent in the mode of Martin Luther King, Junior. This is not to say that there is no jihad in Islam. Let me be absolutely and categorically clear: the Prophet Muhammad said: "I smile and I fight" (Ibn Taymiyyah) and "I am the Prophet of Mercy and I am the Prophet of Battle" (Ahmad, Dhahabi, Tabari, Mawardi, and Ibn Taymiyyah).

The Prophet Muhammad came with the sword but it was the sword of justice. It was the sword of self-defense. It was the sword of the oppressed drawn against the oppressor. It was never the first option. It was always the last option and the last recourse.

The Messenger of Allah always preferred conciliation over conflict. He always opted for a diplomatic solution over a military solution. And when there was war, there were rules of war, rules of just war which governed military conflict, the treatment of non-combatants, the treatment of women, the treatment of crops, orchards, and gardens, as well as the treatment of churches, monasteries, and synagogues, all of which are being blatantly and shamelessly violated by those who have deviated from the teachings of Allah and the Messenger of Allah.

The *Covenants of the Prophet Muhammad with the Christians of the World* take us, not only to the early days of Islam, but to the days before the rise of Islam, when Muhammad, a caravan leader, used to travel the Middle East, extensively, making journeys throughout Arabia, to the Yemen, to the Sinai, to Egypt, to Palestine, to Syria, to Iraq, to Persia, and, perhaps, as far away as Abyssinia and Armenia. This is not revisionism. This is well documented in the works of early Muslim and non-Muslim historians. The revisionists are those who have deliberately ignored or suppressed these sources to suit their myopic and dogmatic vision of Islam.

We all know, from our books of hadith and *sirah*, from our books of prophetic traditions and history, that Muhammad, before he received revelation, was known as *al-Amin*, the Trustworthy, throughout the Hijaz. However, few of us are aware that his reputation extended far beyond the reaches of Arabia where he was known, respected, and loved by Christian patriarchs, abbots, bishops, priests, and monks.

According to traditional accounts, one such Christian, who was a friend of Muhammad, served as the abbot of St. Catherine's Monastery in the Sinai. One day, it is reported, when Muhammad, who was still a young man, was resting in front of the monastery, an eagle appeared. This eagle, which circled mysteriously above the young man, intrigued the abbot. He knew that the Angel Gabriel could take the form of an eagle. This is confirmed in our books of hadith or prophetic traditions.

The abbot concluded that this event was a sign from God Almighty. Consequently, he invited Muhammad into the monastery, treated him with the utmost hospitality, and asked him for a letter of protection. Muhammad, who had no power or wealth at the time, asked: "How can I protect the monastery when I am but a poor orphan?" The abbot foretold that Muhammad would become a mighty leader. "How can I grant you a letter of protection if I cannot write?" asked Muhammad. "Just give us your word," said the Abbot. He then gave him a parchment and a bowl of ink. Muhammad soaked his hand in the ink, and stamped the paper with his palm print, effectively saying: "My word is my bond."

After Muhammad received the revelation, as the abbot had predicted, and established the Islamic Ummah, the monks reportedly organized a delegation and headed off to Medina. There, they met the Messenger of Allah, and reminded him of the promise of protection that he had made. He essentially said: "I remember my promise, and I fully intend to fulfil it." He then proceeded to dictate a charter of rights and freedoms to his cousin, companion, and scribe, 'Ali ibn Abi Talib, had it witnessed by his companions, and bid the monks farewell and safe travels. The charter was placed in the monastery. It remained there until 1517 when it was taken to the Treasury in Istanbul by Sultan Selim who granted the monks a notarized copy. The *Covenant of the Prophet* was recorded in the registry of the Ottomans where it remains to this day.

The *ashtinameh* is not the only covenant of the Prophet. The first covenant of the Prophet was the *Constitution of Medina* which granted protection to all the inhabitants of the Ummah, including Muslims, Jews, Christians, and even polytheists. Yes, while it may come as news to many, the Prophet protected the polytheists who were allied with the Muslims. According to demographic studies, when the Messenger of Allah arrived in Medina, the Muslims only numbered in the hundreds: half the town was pagan and half the town was Jewish. However, he was embraced by all parties as a peace maker and conciliator. The Ummah of Islam was pluralistic and inclusive from the moment it was established. The *Constitution of Medina* granted non-Muslim citizens the same political and cultural rights as Muslims. It granted them autonomy and freedom of religion. It also granted protection to all parties. In short, "The security of God is equal for all groups."

Inspired by the *Constitution of Medina*, the first written Charter, many communities, Jewish, Christian, and Zoroastrian, approached the Prophet requesting to join the Confederation of Believers. Consequently, Muhammad al-Mustafa granted covenants of protection to the Christians of Najran, to the Jews of Aylah and Maqnah, to the Assyrian Christians, to the Armenian Christians, to the Christians of Persia, and to the Christians of the world. These Muhammadan Covenants, which were found in ancient churches, monasteries, and mosques around the Middle East, Europe, and Asia, are so similar in content, style, language, and witnesses, that they can only conceivably have been authored by the same man: Muhammad, the Messenger of Allah.

The Covenants of the Prophet grant the People of the Book, Jews and Christians, freedom of belief and freedom of religious practice. They protect places of worship: churches, monasteries, and synagogues. Not only must Muslims protect these religious sites, they must help maintain them. The Muhammadan Covenants prohibit conversion by force or any compulsion in matters of religion. While these promises of protection and privileges permit Muslim men to marry Christian women--marry them, not rape them--they forbid Muslim men from coercing their Christian wives to embrace Islam. They speak not merely of tolerance, but of love.

Islam, for those who have forgotten, is spread by the word. It is spread by the intellect. It is spread by reasoning, and, most importantly, it is spread by example. The Muhammadan Covenants also command Muslims to protect the Christians of the East until the end of times. We are not talking about Crusaders. We are not talking about colonialists. We are not talking about imperialists. We are talking about the indigenous Christian communities of the East, who were friends and allies of the Prophet Muhammad, and who have lived among us, as neighbors, since the dawn of Islam. This was always understood by true Muslims. During the Crusades, the Europeans were described as *salibis* or "Crusaders" while the Christians of the Middle East were described as *masihis* and "our Christian brothers." True, traditional, Muslims always distinguished between true, traditional, Christians who were our neighbors, friends, and allies, and fake Christians, who were our open enemies. The Christians of the East were treated as *Ahl al-Kitab*, namely, as People of the Book, who were worthy of protection, while European invaders were treated, rightfully so, as *kuffar al-harbi*, infidels at war against Islam.

While many Muslims are unfamiliar with the Covenants of the Prophet, they are well documented, and have been transmitted consecutively by both Muslims and Christians from the early days of Islam until the present. It is our duty, as Muslims, to familiarize ourselves with the Sunnah of our beloved Prophet. This includes, not only hadith or traditions, but also *tarikh* or history, as well as the *Watha'iq*, namely, the letters, treaties, and covenants of Muhammad ibn 'Abd Allah, the Prophet and Messenger of Allah. Let us revive the Covenants of the Prophet

Muhammad and show the world the true teachings of Islam, a religion of justice, a religion of compassion, and a religion of love for God and all of humanity.

Chapter Thirty-Two

ISIS versus Islam: What would the Prophet Muhammad do?

ISIS versus Islam. Islam versus ISIS. The topic is timely. It is very much a matter of life or death. If, God forbid, we listen to right-wing radio headed by hate-mongers who follow in the footsteps of Paul Joseph Goebbels, or read the writings of political pundits who pretend to be experts on Islam, we will have inevitably come to the conclusion that Islam is the mother of all evil and that ISIS is the embodiment of Islam. To be fair, you will come to same conclusion, namely, that Islam is inherently evil, even if you listen to the liberal media.

For educated individuals, however, with a capacity for critical thinking this conclusion is unwarranted, ignorant, and ill-informed. There is a great deal of anti-Jewish propaganda yet I have never accepted it blindly. There is a great deal of racist propaganda yet I have never accepted it blindly. As intelligent adults we have an obligation to investigate matters, to question claims, to seek verification, and to examine counter-arguments. We need to see all sides of a story. We need to draw our information from credible sources. We need to come to a balanced and informed conclusion concerning any topic.

When I see Western powers invade, occupy, and colonize the Americas, leading to the death of 80 million indigenous people, my people, I do not blame the Cross despite the fact that the perpetrators of this physical, religious, cultural, and linguistic genocide claimed to act in its name. When I see up to 100 million Africans enslaved by self-professed Christians, I do not blame the Gospels. When I see the suffering caused by Western imperialism and colonialism all around the world, I do not condemn the Christian faith. When I see self-professed Christian fundamentalists and Dominionists promoting hatred and racism, I do not blame Jesus. When I see images of the Ku Klux Klan terrorizing African Americans along with Irish and French Canadian Catholics, I do not blame Christianity.

When I see so-called German Christians exterminate Jews, Muslims, gypsies, homosexuals, and the disabled, I do not blame Christ. When I see nuclear bombs dropped on civilian populations in Hiroshima and Nagasaki--Nagasaki, which was then the most Christian city in Japan, whose cathedral towers were used by the B-29 crew to mark ground zero-- in two of the greatest acts of terrorism the world has ever seen, I do not blame the Bible. When I see millions of Vietnamese civilians massacred by the US army, I do not blame the Church.

When I see the Israeli Defense Forces bomb schools and hospitals and kill civilians by the thousands, I do not blame the Torah. I do not disrespect Judaism. When I see over one million Iraqi civilians murdered in the course of two illegal and criminal invasions of a sovereign state, I do not blame Christianity. When I see the brutal government in Burma strip its indigenous Muslim population of its citizenship, confine Burmese Muslims to concentration camps, engage in pogroms, and expel them from their country in a campaign of ethnic, linguistic, and religious cleansing, I do not blame the Buddha. Likewise, when we see the likes of the Taliban, al-Qaedah, al-Nusrah, and ISIS committing war crimes and acts of genocide, we should not be so quick to condemn the Prophet Muhammad, the Qur'an, and Islam.

My intention is not to offend. My intention is to clear the table. Set things straight. Get God out of the picture. Get religion out of the picture. Get the Prophets of God out of the picture. And put the blame where the blame belongs: on human beings regardless of their race, ethnicity, nationality, culture or religion. I will admit that things are not always clear, particularly when the criminals in question commit atrocities in the name of Allah, in the name of Muhammad, in the name of Islam, in the name of the Qur'an, and in the name of the sharia. Yes, even generally well informed people, good, kind, generous and tolerant people, can get confused, and can entertain doubts about the true nature of Islam. We need to remind ourselves of what Islam really is and what Islam really teaches.

Murder

Islam prohibits murder. ISIS murders indiscriminately. As we read in the Qur'an: "Whosoever kills a human being for other than murder or corruption in the earth, it shall be as if he had killed all humankind, and whoever saves a human life, it is as if he had saved all of humankind" (5:32).

Killing Civilians

Islam prohibits the killing of civilians. ISIS encourages the killing of civilians. They even kill non-combatants while they are engaged in prayer.

Killing the Elderly, the Sick, and the Blind

Islam prohibits killing the elderly, the sick, and the blind in times of military conflict. ISIS encourages such cowardly crimes. The Prophet Muhammad said: "Do not kill old men" (Muslim and Bayhaqi). Abdullah Azzam, the godfather of global jihad and terrorism, and the teacher of Osama bin Laden, wrote that: "Those who can be useful to the unbelievers and to others must be killed, whether they are old people, priests or invalids." This is the exact opposite of what the Prophet teaches.

Killing Women

Islam prohibits the killing of women during times of war. ISIS not only kills women, they make sure to rape them, to degrade them, and to humiliate them before doing so.

Killing Children

Islam prohibits the killing of children. ISIS encourages the killing of children. In fact, Islam prohibits the use of child combatants. However, ISIS is eager to use child combatants and even go to schools, with a handy "apostate" or "infidel" in hand, to show children, hands on, how to behead a so-called unbeliever. The Prophet, however, said: "Do not kill children" (Ahmad, Tirmidhi, Muslim, and Bayhaqi). "He is not one of us," warned the Prophet, "who shows no mercy to children" (Tirmidhi and Abu Dawud). As Takfiri terrorists have shown repeatedly, they could not care less about the psychological, emotional, and physical well-being of children. In fact, they take pride in corrupting them.

Killing Prisoners

Islam prohibits the killing of prisoners. The only exception is made for combatants who have been condemned to death by a court for having committed war crimes. ISIS, however, routinely executes prisoners using methods that are as cruel as they are creative.

Rape

Islam prohibits rape. ISIS encourages rape. ISIS terrorists go door to door in search of girls to sexually assault. If they resist, they are gang-raped, crucified or decapitated. Tens of thousands of girls have been sold into prostitution by ISIS, some for as little as a pack of cigarettes. ISIS encourages its fighters to enslave Yazidi women, Christian women, and apostate women. By apostate, they mean Muslim women who are not Wahhabis. They have allowed a single girl or woman to be owned collectively by a group of men, all of whom have the right to rape her even if she has not reached the age of puberty. According to ISIS ideologues, the right to rape female prisoners is a reward from "God." As can be appreciated, the only "God" they invoke is the Devil.

Disrespecting Christians

Islam commands Muslims to respect Christians. ISIS has nothing but contempt for them. As Almighty God says in the Qur'an: "Verily, you will find the nearest in love to those who believe to be those who say: 'We are Christians.' That is because there are among them priests and monks, and they are not proud" (5:82). For ISIS, however, Christians are infidels whose blood is legal to shed.

This is not to say that there are no bad Christians. That would be like saying that there are no bad Muslims. The world, however, is not black and white. Islam's view of the other is more nuanced. As Almighty God says in the Holy Qur'an:

> They are not all alike. Among the People of Book is an upright community, who recite the verses of God in the watches of the night, and who prostrate [to Him]; they believe in God and the Last Day, enjoin the good and forbid the evil, and hasten unto good works; they are among the righteous. (3:13)

Unlike modern-day terrorists, early Muslims distinguished between Christians, who were friends and allies, and pseudo-Christians, who were enemies. In the Middle East, Muslims, Christians, and Jews, fought together against their common foes. After all, Western Christian Crusaders massacred not only Muslims and Jews but Eastern Christians, as well, whom they viewed as schismatics and heretics.

Killing Christians

Islam prohibits the killing of Christians. ISIS encourages it. As the Prophet Muhammad said: "Whoever kills a *mu'ahid* [a person who is granted a covenant of protection], shall not smell the fragrance of Paradise though its fragrance can be smelled at a distance of forty years [of traveling]" (Bukhari). As Abu Bakr, the first Caliph, said: "Beware not to kill those who benefit from the protection of Allah for Allah will ask you about His protection and will cast you into the Fire face-first" (Hajjar).

Killing Monks

Islam prohibits the killing of monks. ISIS encourages it. The Prophet said: "Do not kill monks" (Abu Dawud, Ahmad, and Tirmidhi). Abdullah Azzam, the forefather of al-Qaedah, al-Nusrah, and ISIS, said: "Monks living in society must be killed." He wrote this in his ironically titled *Morals and Jurisprudence of Jihad*, a work written by a man who was manifestly devoid of morals and values.

Oppressing Christians

The Messenger of Allah said: "If anyone wrongs a man or a woman with whom a covenant has been made, curtails any of his rights, imposes on him more than he can bear, or takes anything from him without ready agreement, I shall be his adversary on the Day of Resurrection" (Abu Dawud and Abu Yusuf). The Messenger of Allah said: "Whoever oppresses a *dhimmi* [a Christian or a Jew], I will testify against him on the Day of Judgment" (Bukhari and Abu Dawud). The Messenger of Allah said: "He who causes damage to a Muslim or a non-Muslim is to be cursed" (Abu Yusuf). The Messenger of Allah said: "Observe scrupulously the protection accorded by me to non-Muslim subjects. Whoever oppresses non-Muslim subjects shall find me to be their advocate on the day of Resurrection (against the oppressor)" (Muslim and Mawardi). 'Umar ibn al-Khattab, the second Caliph, was even more explicit: "I warn you concerning those who have been placed under the protection of Allah for the protection of your Prophet covers them" (Hajjar). Christians living under Muslim rule have rights: the right to life, liberty, and the pursuit of happiness. Salafi Jihadists offer nothing but death, slavery, suffering, and misery.

Destroying Churches and Monasteries

Islam prohibits the destruction of churches and monasteries. Not only does ISIS destroy churches and monasteries, they take particular pride in blowing up mosques, without bothering to remove the Qur'ans that were inside, of course, showing how much they really respect the Word of God. They take pleasure in blowing up the graves of Prophets, Messengers, Companions of the Prophet, and other saintly figures. How much respect do they have for these figures if they desecrate their graves and scatter their remains? They are at war with the religion they claim to profess.

Converting People by Force

Islam prohibits converting people to Islam by force. ISIS encourages it. As Almighty Allah says in the Holy Qur'an: "To you your religion and to me mine" (109:6). ISIS routinely offers people the choice of conversion or death. In 2015, they crucified a Christian boy because his father refused to convert to Islam.

Torture

Islam prohibits torture. ISIS tortures people for pleasure. They torture prisoners routinely and they torture the populations under their control. As the Messenger of Allah said: "The punishment by fire does not behoove anyone except the Master of the Fire [God Himself]" (Abu Dawud). What right does ISIS have to burn prisoners alive? Who do they think they are? God? The Prophet Muhammad is also reported to have said that "He who tortures people will be tortured by God" and "Those who torture people in this world will be tortured in the other world" (Abu Yusuf). And yet we find ISIS gouging out people's eyes, throwing people off buildings, crucifying them, drowning them, dousing them with gasoline, and burning them alive. We see them make a mockery of sharia punishments, which are supposed to be swift, hacking away at a man's hand or neck with a dull knife in a deliberate and sadistic effort to increase pain and suffering.

Cannibalism

Islam prohibits cannibalism. The terrorists from al-Nusrah, however, include criminals who cannibalize corpses and ISIS terrorists have forced prisoners to eat their dead relatives.

Islam versus Anti-Islam

How much more ridiculous can this get? Asking Muslims to prove that they are opposed to the immorality of ISIS is like asking Christians to oppose fornication, adultery, murder, pornography, and pedophilia. Following this line of reasoning, Christianity should be blamed for any action committed by a Christian. We, as Muslims, should not be forced to apologize for crimes committed by Muslims any more than Jews, Christians, Buddhists or Hindus should be forced to apologize every time a person who claims to profess their faith commits a sin or a crime. If I get mugged by a Christian criminal in New York City, I do not expect the Catholic Bishop to issue an apology on behalf of the Christian community.

Although we speak of Islam versus ISIS or ISIS versus Islam, it is clear that we are speaking of Islam vs. Anti-Islam. When we are talking about ISIS, al-Nusrah, al-Qaedah, and the Taliban, these modern-day Kharijites and Nawasib, we are not talking about misinterpretations of Islam. When we are talking about Takfiris, Wahhabis, Islamists, and jihadists, we are not talking about aberrations of Islam.

The Islamic State is not Islamic: it is Satanic. ISIS is not Sunni. ISIS is an existential threat to Sunni Islam. To put things into a Christian framework, it is like comparing Christianity to the Klan, Christianity to apartheid or Christianity to white supremacy. You insult Christianity by considering such people to be Christians. Let us take some of the Ten Commandments, for example, something Jews, Christians, and Muslims all agree upon, many of which are principles at the basis of secular society.

God says: "You shall have no other gods but Me and You shall not make idols." And then you have someone who usurps divine authority, acts like God, arrogantly believing that he can judge a person's faith, acting as judge, jury, and executioner.

God says: "You shall not take the name of the Lord God in vain." And then you have these people who invoke the name of God, blasphemously, while they rape, torture, mutilate, and murder, soiling the name of God and spitting on the name of God.

God says: "Remember the Sabbath day, to keep it holy." While there is no Sabbath in Islam, there are plenty of holy days, days that have been desecrated along with sacred celebrations like Eid al-Adha that have been outlawed.

God says: "Honor your father and your mother." And then you have someone who disrespects his mother, his father, his family, and his community, by accusing them of being apostates who deserve to die. You do not honor your mother by calling her an infidel. You do not honor your father by calling him an unbeliever.

God says: "You shall not murder." And then you have someone who murders and promotes murder.

God says: "You shall not commit adultery." And then you have someone who rapes, gang-rapes, traffics women, and forces them into sexual slavery and prostitution.

God says: "You shall not bear false witness against your neighbor." And then you have someone who bears false witness against his neighbors, accusing them of infidelity, heresy, and apostasy, in order to get them executed, and to steal their homes.

God says: "You shall not covet." And then you have someone who robs, steals, and pillages, and who profits from the sale of archeological and historical treasures.

If Judaism has a certain set of beliefs and practices, and a person, who professes to be Jewish, violates them all, not simply as a sinner, but with conviction, can he be considered Jewish? If Christianity has a set of beliefs and laws, and a person, who professes to be Christian, does the complete and total opposite and holds beliefs that are diametrically opposed and contradictory, can that person truly be considered a Christian?

Certainly there are different interpretations of Judaism, Christianity and Islam: there is a spectrum. Some people are at the center. Some people are center right. Some people are center left. Some people are on the periphery of both sides. And then, there are people who are outside of the religious tradition completely and totally.

There are different interpretations of Islam. There are different schools of thought, law, and theology in Islam: but they all form part of the Islamic Tradition. Takfiri terrorists, however, people like the Pseudo-Islamic State systematically violate the teachings of the Qur'an and the teachings of the Prophet. Consequently, they cannot be remotely connected to Islam.

As al-Shaykh al-Habib 'Ali al-Jifri said to me, "We must make a clear break between Muslims and Takfiris." They are not Sunnis. They do not belong to *Ahl al-Sunnah wa al-Jama'at*. It is not even an issue of them having left the Community of Believers. They were never part of it to begin with. In fact, they have declared war against *Ahl al-Sunnah wa al-Jama'at*. They have destroyed hundreds of Sunni mosques and they have executed hundreds of Sunni Imams.

Islam is a religion, a world religion, founded by a man of sublime character, Muhammad ibn 'Abd Allah. ISIS, on the other hand, is a diabolical death cult that serves imperial interests. So, what can we do? What can be done? We do not have private armies. But we have our voices. And our voices need to be heard.

Although many people feel helpless and hopeless, there are some simple actions that they can take in order to make a difference. These include: 1) spreading the Covenants of the Prophet; 2) Engaging in interfaith work; 3) endorsing the Covenants Initiative; and 4) signing the Genocide Initiative.

Interfaith Work

In the spirit of the Covenants of the Prophet, I encourage Jews, Christians, and Muslims, to engage in interfaith work. Get to know your neighbor. While it may surprise some Christians, most Muslims are perfectly normal human beings. While it may surprise some Muslims, most Jewish people are perfectly normal human beings. I know that some people think that interfaith work is pointless. Some think that it is counterproductive. Some think that it weakens and dilutes different religious traditions. No, on the contrary, unity does not mean uniformity. What is more, interfaith work has shown its power.

Dozens upon dozens of armed, anti-Muslim, protests were organized throughout the United States in 2015. It could easily have gotten ugly. Do these thugs and bikers think that we are not willing and able to respond to threats of force with some serious force of our own? God have mercy on anyone who dares aim a gun at our women and children. It is called an eye for an eye and a tooth for a tooth and a life for a life.

But we did not respond to threats of violence with more threats and more violence. Why? Because the Qur'an does not teach us to fight fire with fire. Because the Qur'an teaches us to fight evil with good and to fight wrong with what is better. So, we greeted people, who were misled by violent, ignorant bigots, racists, and hate-mongers, with hugs, with tea and crumpets, and with hospitality. And we won many of them over. We brought them into our mosques. We gave them tours. And they saw that we are university professors, lawyers, engineers, medical doctors, business owners, entrepreneurs, and hard-working loyal Americans who love this country and who would not hesitate to fight anyone who tries to harm it.

How ironic it is that some of the people who came to protest Islam actually ended up embracing Islam or, at the very least, realizing that what was being falsely presented as Islam, by certain sectors in the mass media and political establishment, was not, and is not, Islam. Muslims are not all terrorists. They are, however, all scapegoats. They are a "convenient enemy" used to justify imperial action abroad and to curtail civil liberties and privacy rights at home. They are a wedge used to push previously liberal, democratic, societies, towards the right. They are a pretext used to create a surveillance state and to provoke popular support for fascism and totalitarianism.

People of faith, Jews, Christians, and Muslims must come together and pose a united front against anti-religious globalists and secular fundamentalists. Interfaith work begins with the recognition of our mutual humanity; the next step is the recognition of our common enemy: ISIS, for example, along with its outside supporters whose names and agendas we should learn. The third step is to begin to talk about concrete plans for our mutual defense.

The Covenants of the Prophet Muhammad

Besides interfaith work, concerned people are encouraged to read, study, and spread *The Covenants of the Prophet Muhammad with the Christians of the World*. The work provides an overview of Christian-Muslim relations from the time of the Prophet to the present, focusing on the treaties and covenants that he concluded with the Christian, Jewish, and Zoroastrian communities of his period.

The full study, which is available in English, Spanish, Italian, and Arabic, is nearly 500 pages long. There is also a shorter booklet, titled *Six Covenants of the Prophet Muhammad with the Christians of His Time*, which is available in English, French, and Spanish, as well as Italian, Arabic, Portuguese, and Russian, among other languages.

As the Covenants of the Prophet make abundantly clear, ISIS does not speak for Islam. ISIS does not represent Islam. It is the Prophet Muhammad who speaks for Islam. Hence, we must invite people to read the rights, privileges, and protections that the Messenger of Allah granted to non-Muslim minorities, Jews, Christians, and others.

The Prophet Muhammad did not persecute the People of the Book. On the contrary, he granted covenants of protection to Jews, to Zoroastrians, to Greek Orthodox Christians, to Assyrian Christians, to Syriac Orthodox Christians, to Coptic Christians, to Armenian Orthodox Christians, to the Christians of Persia, and to the Christians of the whole wide world.

The Messenger of Allah granted non-Muslims freedom of religion, freedom of belief, and freedom of religious practice. He protected churches, monasteries, and synagogues. He protected monks, priests, and rabbis. He granted them religious autonomy. He protected pilgrims. He prohibited forced conversions. He prohibited economic oppression. He prohibited Muslim men from taking non-Muslim women by force or coercing them into marriage. In the event that a Muslim man married a

Jewish or Christian woman, he was obliged to respect her religion and take her to church or to the synagogue. He commanded Muslims to help Jews and Christians maintain and rebuild their places of worship in order to help keep them loyal to their alliance. He exempted clerics from military service. He commanded Muslims to treat non-Muslims with love and care. He prohibited Muslims from oppressing them. In the case of conflict, he commanded dialogue and urged reconciliation. He commanded Muslims to protect Jews and Christians from their enemies. Finally, he made these covenants binding upon all parties until the end of times and prohibited Muslims from changing them.

The Covenants of the Prophet are found in Jewish sources. They are found in Christian sources. And they are found in Muslim sources. They all confirm each other. For those who want Arabic and Muslim names, I will give them names: Waqidi, Ibn Ishaq, Ibn Hisham, Tabari, Mas'udi, Abu Yusuf, Yahya ibn Adam, Abu 'Ubaydah, Abu Dawud, Baladhuri, Ya'qubi, Ibn al-'Athir, Shaykh al-Mufid, Fakhr al-Din al-Razi, Qalqashandi, Ibn Kathir, and Ibn Hawqal. These are only some of the early Arab and Muslim sources that support the Muhammadan Covenants.

For those who want Christian names, I will give them names: Latin names, Greek names, Assyrian names, and Armenian names: Sebeos, Sahak, Yohanes, Samuel, Kirakos, Grigor, Ahmad ibn Yusuf, Abu al-Fida', Ibn al-'Amid, Habib, Bar Hebraeus, Mari ibn Sulayman, Nektarios of Sinai, Amrus, Assemani, Scaliger, and Sionita. These are only some of the early Christian sources that support the Muhammadan Covenants.

The Covenants of the Prophet were respected by the Four Rightly Guided Caliphs and by all the righteous rulers who followed them. This is not to say that all the Caliphs abided by them. Just like we have had good presidents and bad presidents, benevolent kings and oppressive kings, we have had good Muslim rulers and bad Muslim rulers. However, if one looks at Islamic history as a whole, we find that most Muslim rulers respected the Covenants of the Prophet to varying degrees. Some rulers were more severe. Others were more lenient. However, by and large, all Muslim rulers recognized that the People of the Book were protected communities that were granted privileges by the Prophet and only an occasional reprobate attempted to revoke and rescind their rights.

The Muhammadan Covenants were well known throughout most of Islamic history and were renewed until the end of the Ottoman Empire. However, after the collapse of Islam as a political power, a mere century ago, the Covenants of the Prophet were forgotten and fell into oblivion. It is therefore our duty, as Muslims, and as non-Muslims, to resurrect these covenants of protection as they represent a solution to many of the problems we face today in the Islamic world.

The Covenants Initiative

In order to promote the Covenants of the Prophet, all Muslims should be encouraged to sign the Covenants Initiative. Simply put, the signatories agree to abide by the letter and spirit of the Covenants of the Prophet in their dealings with the People of the Book. The Covenants Initiative, available at www.covenantsoftheprophet.com, has been endorsed by hundreds of leading Muslim scholars, academics, and activists, as well as major Muslim organizations such as ISNA.

The Genocide Initiative

In order to put the Covenants of the Prophet into meaningful practice, all parties, regardless of their religion or lack thereof, are urged to sign and support the Genocide Initiative which is available on change.org (www.change.org/p/all-political-players-the-genocide-initiative).

What is the point? What difference will it make? It has already made a difference. The Genocide Initiative has been picked up by media outlets all around the world. Thanks to our efforts, and those of our partners, a resolution was introduced in Congress in September of 2015. The resolution, inspired in part by our change.org petition, is "House Congressional Resolution 75." It reads:

> H.Con.Res.75--Expressing the sense of Congress that those who commit or support atrocities against Christians and other ethnic and religious minorities, including Yezidis, Turkmen, Sabean-Mandeans, Kaka'e, and Kurds, and who target them specifically for ethnic or religious reasons, are committing, and are hereby declared to be committing, "war crimes," "crimes against humanity," and "genocide."

> Introduced in House (09/09/2015)

> Declares that:

> The atrocities committed against Christians and other ethnic and religious minorities targeted specifically for religious reasons are crimes against humanity and genocide;

> Each of the Contracting Parties to the United Nations Convention on the Prevention and Punishment of the Crime of Genocide and other international agreements forbidding war crimes and crimes against

humanity, particularly the governments of countries and their nationals who are in any way supporting these crimes, are reminded of their legal obligations under the Convention and these international agreements;

The United Nations (U.N.) and the Secretary-General are called upon to assert leadership by calling the atrocities war crimes, crimes against humanity, and genocide;

The member states of the U.N., with an appeal to the Arab States that wish to uphold religious freedom and justice, should collaborate on measures to prevent further war crimes, crimes against humanity, and genocide, and collaborate on the establishment of tribunals to punish those responsible for the ongoing crimes;

The governments of the Kurdistan Region of Iraq, the Hashemite Kingdom of Jordan, the Lebanese Republic, and other countries are commended for having undertaken to shelter and protect those fleeing extremist violence;

Those who force the migration of religious communities from their ancestral homelands, including specifically the Nineveh Plain and Mount Sinjar, should be prosecuted in accordance with the laws of the place where their crimes were committed and under applicable international criminal statutes and conventions.

This is only one of several resolutions that have been presented to the House and Senate in the United States of America. Thanks to our efforts, and those of our partners, the US government officially accused ISIS of genocide in March of 2016. Across the Atlantic, the European Parliament declared in 2016 that the slaughter of Christians and other religious minorities by ISIS was tantamount to genocide. Activism and diplomacy are critically important and effective tools. Action is essential. Apathy is objectionable and sitting still is a sin.

Conclusions

There is no more time or space in the interfaith movement for smiles, cordial handshakes, and expressions of undying friendship on the part of those who still choose to ignore the crimes and attacks of our common enemies. If we do not band together to defend ourselves against these enemies, then all our expressions of interfaith amity are worse than irrelevant: they are hypocritical. Actions speak louder than words or, as the Prophet Muhammad taught us: When you pray, pray with your hands.

Islam versus ISIS. ISIS versus Islam. What would the Prophet

Muhammad do? He would act. Hence, I call upon all to act. This is our country. This is our home. We are not leaving. We all share the same planet. We must do unto others as we would have them do unto us. We need to unite, as believers, as Jews, Christians, and Muslims--as fellow human beings--against the plague of extremism and hatred that threatens us all. To injustice and hatred with respond with justice and love.

CHAPTER THIRTY-THREE

EARLY CHRISTIAN-MUSLIM ENCOUNTERS

A child is born in Mecca in the late sixth century. Known as Muhammad, his childhood is filled with miraculous signs. Priests, monks, and mystics predict that he will be a great prophet. Twice orphaned, his life is endangered by unbelievers. Monks approach his mother, and later his uncle, offering to take him into their protective custody, and to guard and protect him in the safety of their isolated monasteries. Guarded by angels, he is kept safe. He works as a shepherd, contemplating the beauty of God's creation. He joins the caravans of his uncle and travels throughout the Middle East and beyond.

According to ancient accounts, Muhammad supplied the Monastery of St. Catherine at Mount Sinai where he discussed matters of theology and philosophy with the monks, where he visited sacred sites associated with the Prophets of the Old Testament, and where he used to meditate in the cave of Moses, on the top of Mount Sinai, emulating his prophetic predecessor.

One day, it is reported that an eagle appeared and circled around Muhammad while he was resting in front of the monastery. The majestic bird seemed to be guarding or protecting him much like the cloud that had followed him on his journeys to Syria, where he was recognized as a prophet by both Bahira and Nestor. The Abbot from St. Catherine's Monastery perceived the sign. He foretold that Muhammad would become a mighty ruler. He invited him into the monastery, where he was warmly received, and asked him to grant the monastery a patent of protection. Muhammad dipped his hand in the ink and stamped the paper symbolizing his promise of protection.

The years passed and Muhammad received revelation. He was persecuted for a decade. Finally, he established an Ummah or State in Medina. Shortly after his arrival in Medina, he created the *Constitution of Medina*. It was a social contract between the State and its citizens. It established, first and foremost, equality between all parties: Jews, Muslims, and pagans, regardless of race, gender or religion. It provided for the protection of all parties, including women and the poor. It eradicated racism, social superiority, and gender privilege. It created a multilingual, multicultural, multiethnic, multireligious, and multiracial society; a tolerant, cosmopolitan, community; an island of social, economic, and political justice in an ocean of racism, sexism, elitism, hedonism, violence, oppression, and exploitation.

Word of Muhammad's success and the creation of a new social system spread throughout Arabia and beyond. Christians, Jews, and Zoroastrians, all of whom were oppressed by the Byzantine and Persian Empires, were exposed to an entirely new idea: religious liberty, pluralism, participative democracy, and justice for all. In the second year of the *hijrah*, the monks from St. Catherine's monastery sent a delegation to Medina and reminded the Prophet of his promise. It was then and there, in his mosque in Medina, in the presence of his companions, that he dictated to 'Ali a set of rights and privileges that he was granting, not only to the monks from Mount Sinai, but to all Christians who were willing to be his friends and allies.

Attacked by the pagans from southern Arabia, the Prophet made peace with the Christians of Najran. Betrayed by a few Jewish tribes surrounding Medina, he made peace with the Jews of southern and northwestern Arabia. Persecuted by the Byzantine Empire, many Christian denominations were branded as heterodox and heretical. The Prophet Muhammad reached out to them, promising them protection from persecution and oppression. Soon, Muhammad had created a buffer zone of allies, consisting of Jewish, Christian, and Zoroastrian communities, effectively protecting him from his pagan Arab enemies as well as the two superpowers of the time, the Byzantine and Persian Empires.

Fortunately, the Prophet Muhammad had friends, companions he had made during decades of leading caravans throughout the Middle East. His reputation for righteousness extended far beyond Arabia. His supporters and sympathizers, Jewish, Christian, and Zoroastrian, served as his eyes and ears throughout Arabia and on the hinterlands of the Byzantine and Persian empires. They paid allegiance to the Prophet. They notified him of any troop movements. They prepared for liberation.

During the final four years of his life, the Messenger of Allah increased his correspondence with Jewish, Christian, and Zoroastrian leaders and intensified his diplomatic efforts. He received a regular stream of delegations from around the Middle East and from lands far beyond. He granted covenants of protection to old friends and allies and made new supporters in the process. The Prophet also reached out to the Byzantine and Persian Empires, offering them treaties of peace and alliance. Not only did they arrogantly refuse his advances, they deployed their troops to attack the Muslims.

How different the world would be today had the European Christians made peace with the Prophet. There would have been no Crusades. There would have been no colonialism. There would have been no imperialism. Christians, Muslims, and Jews, could have co-existed, as fellow monotheists, as the Family of Abraham. Peace would have prevailed.

By the time the Prophet Muhammad passed away, he had granted covenants of protection to over a dozen communities. The Covenants of the Prophet were once widely known in the Christian, Jewish, and Muslim world. During the time of the Prophet, and the early Caliphs, the Ummah or Motherland included all monotheists. It was only later, when relations between the various communities started to break down, that the People of the Book were excluded from the Community of Believers. They were still protected communities. However, they no longer fit into the new, increasingly narrow, definition of Islam.

Why did relations break down? I blame Muslims. But I also blame Christians and Jews. I blame them all. Some Muslims violated the Covenants of the Prophet. There can be no doubt. At the same time, some Jews and Christians also violated the Covenants of the Prophet. There can be no doubt. This was not, however, the will of the Prophet Muhammad who was intent on creating a monotheistic movement that embraced all people of faith under the cover of Islam.

Although the protections granted by the Covenants of the Prophet were respected, to varying degrees, by most Muslim dynasties, the spirit of solidarity and unity envisioned by the Prophet was virtually lost. After the Ottoman Empire collapsed, approximately one hundred years ago, the Covenants of the Prophet were essentially consigned to oblivion. They no longer formed part of the collective consciousness of Muslims. The Christian clerics of the Middle East, however, never forgot them, nor did a small segment of Muslim scholars.

Covenants of the Prophet can be found at the Monastery of St. Catherine in the Sinai, at the Monastery of St. George in Syria, at the Monastery of Simonopetra in Greece, in the archives of the King of France, and in the national archives in Germany. Covenants of the Prophet were found in Istanbul, Seert, Mardin, and Aghtamar in Turkey, as well as in New Julfa, in Isfahan, in Persia. Covenants of the Prophet have also been found as far away as Surat in India. There was a time when churches, monasteries, and synagogues openly displayed copies of the Covenants of the Prophet along with charters of rights and freedoms that were granted to them by Muslim Caliphs and Sultans.

There are, obviously and expectedly, those who argue that the

Covenants of the Prophet are forgeries produced by Christians, Jews, and Zoroastrians, for self-protection, or by Muslims, in order to improve the image of Islam. Some of these scholars are sincere. Others, however, have ulterior motives; namely, to eat away at Islam. Regardless of their motivations, the arguments presented by those who dispute the Muhammadan Covenants have been thoroughly and systematically refuted by a strong segment of scholars throughout the centuries.

The Covenants of the Prophet Muhammad have been passed down through solid chains of historical transmission from the early days of Islam to the present. They are mentioned, in part or in whole, in Muslim and Christian sources, from the dawn of Islam to modern times. The language and terminology that they employ is ancient and comparable to that found in one of the earliest sources of Islam, the *Constitution of Medina*. While some critics have alleged that the Covenants of the Prophet are spurious, the majority of scholars and academics, both Christian and Muslim, have asserted that they are genuine. In short, there is scholarly consensus concerning their reliability. Those who oppose the Covenants of the Prophet represent a minority.

The Covenants of the Prophet Muhammad are radical and revolutionary in the best sense of these terms. They grant freedom of religion. They grant freedom of religious practice. They provide for protection of churches, monasteries, synagogues, and temples. They prohibit compulsion in religion. They forbid forced conversions. In the event Jewish or Christian women marry Muslim men, out of their own free will, the Prophet's Covenants command husbands to love and respect the religion of their wives. Religious rights and women's rights: this is truly unprecedented. The Muhammadan Covenants outlaw excessive taxation. They free monks and priests from military service. They oblige Muslim leaders to provide for the material well-being of monks and clerics. They instruct Muslims to help maintain and repair churches and monasteries. They also command Muslims to defend the *Ahl al-Kitab*, the People of the Book, from their enemies. Reading the Covenants of the Prophet is comparable to reading the *Universal Declaration of Human Rights*, the *Charter of Rights of Freedoms* or the *Bill of Rights*, only that the Muhammadan Covenants were written over 1400 years ago. This is something truly remarkable. No wonder the Prophet Muhammad was recognized as one of the greatest lawgivers of the world by the Supreme Court of the United States in 1935.

Many have wondered why the Islamic world declined, degenerated and eventually collapsed. The causes were many. However, one of the major causes was the fact that both Muslims and the People of the Book violated, neglected, and ignored the Muhammadan Covenants, a social, spiritual, political, and economic contract that ensured congenial relations, respect, equality, justice, security, diversity, and prosperity.

Muslims have many shortcomings. Christians have many shortcomings. Jews have many shortcomings. After all, we are all human beings who are filled with faults. While we are all guilty of wronging each other, can we agree to keep God out of the picture? Can we agree to put Moses, Jesus, and Muhammad out of the picture? Can we agree not to blame Judaism, Christianity or Islam for all of our sins? Although we cannot, will not, and should not, agree on everything, can we agree that God is one? Can we agree that God is good and that God is Just? Can we, as Jews, Christians, and Muslims, agree to follow in the footsteps of Abraham, namely, to believe in one God and to do good deeds? Can we agree on the Golden Rule? Do not do unto others what you would not have them do unto you.

If Moses were to see the slaughter of civilians in Palestine, he would not be pleased. If Jesus saw millions of human beings murdered in his name, he would not be pleased. So, rest assured, if Muhammad saw the horrors being committed by Boko Haram, al-Qaedah, and the Taliban, as well as al-Nusrah and ISIS, he would not be pleased. The Prophet Muhammad prophesized that "The time will come when the only thing that remains of Islam is its name and the only thing that remains of the Qur'an is its writing" (Mishkat). I regret to inform you that the day in question has come. In fact, it came a long, long time ago...

Were Muhammad, the Messenger of God, to return to Earth today, and were he to witness the crimes and atrocities being perpetrated in his name, he would, in my mind, and without a shadow of a doubt, disown, reject, repudiate, and excommunicate all parties that falsely profess to follow in his footsteps. It is like day and night and night and day. We are talking about polar opposites: right versus wrong and good versus evil.

As Nu'aym b. Hammad records in his *Kitab al-Fitan* or *The Book of Tribulations*, Imam 'Ali warned that, "When you see the black flags, remain where you are, and do not move your hands or your feet." He foretold that "there shall appear a feeble folk" whose "hearts will be like fragments of iron." "They are the representatives of the State (*Ashab al-Dawlah*)," he revealed, noting that "[t]hey will fulfill neither covenant nor agreement." What is more, "They will invite to the truth, though they are not from its people." "Their names will be agnomens [namely, Abu So-and-so], and their ascriptions will be to villages," he added, pointing out that "[t]heir hair will be long like that of women." He also reassured believers that "[They shall remain so] till they differ among themselves, and then Allah will bring forth the truth from whomever He wills."

As one can imagine, ISIS supporters or sympathizers say that this hadith is weak and that there is a defect in its chain. How convenient a claim! The fact of the matter is that Imam 'Ali foretold the rise of ISIS over fourteen centuries ago. If the content is correct, if the prophecy comes true, then the tradition is clearly genuine. ISIS terrorists fly black flags. They are a morally weak people who do nothing but follow their whims and vices. ISIS terrorists have hearts of iron, namely, their hearts are hard. They have no compassion or mercy. The name of ISIS in Arabic is *al-Dawlah*, the State: *Dawlat al-Islam, Dawlat al-Islam*, they keep crying. Imam 'Ali identified these devils by name. ISIS claims to call to truth but they are not from the People of Truth. In other words, they are not Muslims. They are Khawarij. They have broken away from Islam. They are the infidels that they accuse others of being. Their names will be agnomens. In other words, Abu So-and-So, the Father of So-and-So. And so we find that most of their terrorist mercenaries use such names: Abu Bakr al-Baghdadi and Abu 'Umar al-Shishani. Their hair will be long like that of women. That speaks for itself.

How will this ISIS crisis end? "[They shall remain so] till they differ among themselves, and then Allah will bring forth the truth from whomever He wills." In other words, they will turn against each other, like the rabid dogs that they are. In fact, they have been at it for some time. These Takfiri/Wahhabi terrorists spend more time killing each other than fighting the Syrian army. We need not despair. ISIS will be annihilated and the Truth of God will prevail. The problem is that many of these terrorist mercenaries, who number in the tens of thousands, will return home, here, to the Western world, and tens of thousands of others will return to their home, in the Eastern world, where they will continue to foster unrest and incite violence. If ISIS is defeated militarily in Syria and Iraq, it merely means victory in battle. The war, however, will continue.

While we must confront Wahhabi terrorists militarily, we must also wage war against them intellectually. We are not dealing with a war between Islam and the West. We are dealing with a war between real Islam and fake Islam, between the followers of Muhammad ibn 'Abd Allah, the Messenger of God, who lived 1400 years ago, and Muhammad ibn 'Abd al-Wahhab, the creator of a diabolical death cult, called Salafism and Wahhabism, that was spawned a mere two hundred years ago.

It is our obligation, as Muslims, to spearhead a war against Wahhabism. We need to identify the origin of this ideology. We need to identify the parties that fund the propagation of this ideology. We need to identify the parties that use these vicious pit-bulls for geo-political purposes. And we need to hold all of them accountable at the International Court of Justice in The Hague. Let there be no rest for the wicked. Let us hunt-down every murderous mercenary, every rapist of Yazidi girls, every crucifier of Christians, and every destroyer of churches, monasteries, and mosques. The criminals in question will never escape the justice of God. Let us ensure that they do not escape the justice of Man and Woman.

If you combat so-called Radical Islam with Islamophobia, you simply reinforce the narrative of the radicals. You add fuel to the fire. You justify their ideology. You push people into their camp. We are faced with two forms of Islam, true, traditional Islam, as espoused by *Ahl al-Sunnah*, *Ahl al-Tasawwuf* and *Ahl al-Bayt*, namely, by traditional Sunnis, traditional Sufis, and traditional Shiites, and a fraudulent form of Islam known as Salafism, Wahhabism, Jihadism, and Takfirism. If you are given an option between an Islam that is just, peaceful, compassionate, caring, and liberating, and an Islam that is unjust, heartless, merciless, brutal, despotic and psychotic, should you not side with the former?

Islam is not going away. We are 1.5 billion strong and growing. We represent one fourth of humanity. We are a force to be reckoned with. Non-Muslims need to work with us and not against us. Let us make common cause. Let us call Muslims back to the Qur'an and the Sunnah. Let us call Muslims back to true, traditional, civilizational Islam. Let us call Muslims back to the Covenants of the Prophet. Let us unite as Muslims, Christians, and Jews. Let us come together as the Family of Abraham. Let us see one another as brothers and sisters, children of Adam, and fellow human beings.

I commend efforts on the part of the Roman Catholic Church to promote "Interreligious Dialogue." However, for this movement to have any real impact, Christian religious leaders need to acknowledge the importance of the Covenants of the Prophet Muhammad so that we can put into place similar policies and practices. Otherwise, efforts on the part of the Catholic Church, and other Christian denominations, will amount to nothing more than "good intentions."

The Covenants of the Prophet Muhammad represent a bridge between Christianity and Islam, between Judaism and Islam, and between Islam and other world religions. They can ensure the protection of non-Muslims in the Muslim world. They can also help ensure the protection of Muslim minorities in both East and West. The government of Myanmar needs lessons on how to treat its indigenous Muslim minority. In light of all the rabid anti-Muslim and anti-Islamic sentiments being openly expressed in the United States, not only on the part of ignorant hatemongers but on the part of people who wish to govern this great nation, it is evident that many Americans can learn something from the pluralistic, inclusive, and tolerant spirit of the Covenants of the Prophet.

Adolf Hitler came to power on a racist, anti-Jewish, platform. That did not turn out so well for Jewish people or for the world as a whole. We have politicians in the US who, instead of appealing to what is best in people, appeal to what is worst in people: rallying people around hatred, racism, and sexism. Our politicians should be the best of us, not the worst of us. Are these 2016 presidential candidates the best that this country has to offer? One is a buffoon and a bigot. The other candidate is a Canadian-born Cuban who reinvented himself as a racist white Christian from the Southern Baptist Convention. Since he was not born in the United States, he should have been disqualified to even run for the presidency. And finally, we have a chameleon who assumes the colors of her corporate sponsors. If these people are the cream of the crop, the candidates we have to choose from, then there is little hope for this country. We are all headed to hell in a hurry.

Reclaim this country. Reclaim the foundations on which it was based: freedom, justice, and liberty. Our Founding Fathers were tolerant, open-minded, intellectuals. Many of them were not only bilingual, they were trilingual, and multilingual. What is more, they respected Islam. They respected the Qur'an. And they had good relations with the Muslim world. In fact, Morocco was the first nation to recognize the independence of the United States of America. The United States even signed a treaty of peace and friendship with the Ottoman Empire, a document that was modeled on the Covenants of the Prophet with the Christians.

We, Americans, were once a constructive force in the world but, for far too long, we have become a destructive force. According to President Jimmy Carter, the United States is no longer a democracy. It is a corporatocracy, an oligarchy at the service of the one-percenters. It is a country controlled by capitalist supremacists. Money does not make you masters. Might does not make right. Morals and ethics do. I appeal to what is the best in people: love, kindness, justice, tolerance, and compassion. I call people to the center, to the middle ground, and to moderation. Extremism produces more extremism. Only moderation can serve as a moderating factor.

Do not fan the flames of hatred and bigotry. Those who promote hostility and animosity against specific groups are inciting violence. You cannot demonize a community and then claim that your hands are clean when people put your words into action. If you promote criminal acts, you are a criminal. You are fully and completely justified to hate terrorists. You are not fully and completely justified to hate all Muslims. You will find nobody who hates terrorists more than Muslims. Why? Muslims are the most killed people on the planet. Muslims are the single greatest victims of terrorism. You should side with the Muslim majority against the terrorist minority.

Current conditions are untenable. Christians, Shiites, Sufis, and traditional Sunnis are being systematically exterminated in Syria and Iraq. If we fail to act, then the oldest Christian communities in the world, the Christians of the East, will be wiped off the face of the Earth, as will the Shiites, Sufis, and traditional Sunnis. We need to fight fake Islam with true Islam. We need to combat terrorists with the Qur'an, the Sunnah, and the Covenants of the Prophet. The Prophet Muhammad was at the forefront of a monotheistic movement of believers composed of Muslims, Jews, and Christians. Let us reconstitute that alliance and join forces against our common enemies for verily the enemy of one religion is the enemy of all religions. Believers of the world unite!

CHAPTER THIRTY-FOUR

CAN WE TRULY KNOW MUHAMMAD?

Can we truly know Muhammad? That is the question. According to an annoying sector of academics, who are strategically positioned in higher education for the very purpose of subverting Islam, we cannot. For some of these scholarly skeptics, whose sole professional purpose is to cast doubt on early sources, the Qur'an cannot be trusted, the Sunnah cannot be trusted, and even *tarikh* or history cannot be trusted. They are, very much, *Ahl al-Shakk*, the People of Doubt, who have devoted their lives to spreading doubt, and discord, in order to undermine God, and religion, and to reinforce atheism, secularism, and capitalism.

If, God forbid, we follow certain Western and Eastern academics along the path to perdition, we will be led to believe that the Qur'an was composed, not by God, but by Muhammad; not by God, but by Bahira; not by God, but by Sergius; not by God, but by Waraqah; not by God, but by the successors of the Prophet, decades or centuries after his passing.

If, God forbid, our *'iman* and *'aql* are feeble, and our faith and intellect fail us, we will be duped and deceived into doubting, not only the divine origin of the Qur'an, the sequence and fundamental events of the *sirah* or prophetic biography, as well as the reliability of hadith records and the sincerity of past scholars, but also the very historicity of Muhammad ibn 'Abd Allah.

Islam is a tree, the existence of which is undeniable. Its seed was sown by the Creator. Its roots are the Qur'an, the *sirah*, and the Sunnah. Its trunk is mainstream, traditional, Islam. Its beautiful branches represent its multifarious interpretations: schools of jurisprudence, philosophy, theology, and spirituality. A scientist or scholar will study the roots, study the trunk, study the bark, study the buds, and study the leaves in order to better understand this magnificent living organism.

Imagine a man, or woman, who hates the tree, who despises the tree, who loathes the tree, whose heart seethes with rage, smolders with fury, and boils with anger against the tree, a person who hates this glorious and awe-inspiring creation from root to treetop, a person who is incensed at the tree's very existence, a person who dreams of saws, chainsaws, and paper-mills.

On the one hand, you have the scholar, who is a tree hugger. He wants to understand the tree. He cares for the tree. He nurtures the tree. He waters the tree. He fertilizes and prunes the tree. He wants the tree to be healthy, to grow strong, and to live long. On the other hand, you have the scholar-for-dollars, the intellectual intelligence agent, the betrayer, the backstabber, the double-crosser, the renegade, and the fifth columnist, who is a tree hater. He or she feigns to specialize in the tree. However, she or he is determined to destroy the tree. And how does one destroy the tree? By destroying its roots. "The only way we will understand the tree is by uprooting the tree." "The only way we will understand the tree is by cutting down the tree, chopping it into logs, sawing it into wood, and turning it into toilet paper." Shame on those who would shred a sequoia.

Rest assured. Have no doubt. These people are nor arborists. They are arsonists, out to set the whole forest on fire, raze it to the ground: scorched earth. They do not work for the tree farm or the nursery. They work for the paper mill. In fact, they probably work for Monsanto: "Let us kill off the created tree and replace it with a genetically altered tree that we can own and control;" "We can insert terminator technology into the tree to ensure that its offspring is sterile: to kill it off for good."

I do not mean to offend the tree huggers. But I do indeed mean to offend the tree haters. Since my goal is to reach a broad audience, I speak directly, bluntly, and frankly, teaching by means of analogy and imagery, educating, as Aboriginal people do, by means of story-telling. The true teacher is one who can distill complicated matters and make the essence understandable to anyone and everyone. So remember the story of the tree, the tree lover and the tree hater, the one who is hell-bent on destroying its roots.

As scholars of Islam, whether we are academics, clerics, or both, we have an obligation, a divine duty to protect and defend Islam at all times and in all places using the best means possible. There are plenty of Muslim professors, who specialize in Islamic Studies, but who approach Islam according to Western methodology. Far too many operate on the basis of Western interpretations or should I say misinterpretations of Islam. This poses a problem.

On the other hand, we have plenty of Muslim clerics who are only familiar with the traditional Eastern approach to Islamic Studies and who are not current with the developments, both positive and negative, that have taken place in Western scholarship. This also poses a problem. What we need is a convergence between both approaches. We cannot and must not allow non-Muslim Orientalists and their Muslim agents to dominate the discourse.

We must engage Western academia from within and from without. We must be at the forefront of an objective jihad against subjective intellectuals. This is not to say that all Western scholars of Islam are enemies of Islam. There are some who are friends and sympathizers. There are some who are seriously enamored with the subject. However, there are others who are virulently hostile to Islam and who have agendas, agendas we need to expose, and agendas we need to oppose.

Can we truly know Muhammad? Yes, absolutely, beyond a shadow of a doubt. We can know him. We do know him. And we can get to know him more and in even greater depth with every passing day. How can we know Muhammad? Through the Qur'an. Although the Qur'an is not a biography of the Messenger of Allah, Muhammad is in the Qur'an and the Qur'an is in Muhammad.

If the Messenger of Allah was the Qur'an walking and the Qur'an talking, then we can know him, understand him, and appreciate him by means of the Qur'an. It may not be much of an outer biography, but it is the most beautiful and sublime inner biography. The Qur'an descended upon Muhammad, permeated Muhammad, and saturated Muhammad. The Qur'an therefore emanated from Muhammad in all of its radiant and resplendent glory.

You do not know a person simply on the basis of their date of birth and death, physical description, and minor and major life events. How many times have we seen a wife remark that, after decades of marriage, she did not know what type of person her husband truly was? There are people who, to all outward appearances, are beautiful, charming, intelligent, kind, and loving, but who, in reality, are ugly, rude, idiotic, selfish and cruel. There are people with beautiful outsides but ugly insides.

This reminds me of a hadith from Imam Ja'far al-Sadiq. Once, when he was performing the pilgrimage, his companion exclaimed: "What a great number of pilgrims!" The Imam responded that the noise was greater than the number of true pilgrims. He then touched the eyes of his companion, and said, "See for yourself." His companion then saw that there were few human beings among the multitude. The rest were beasts, donkeys, pigs, and dogs, revealing their true inner selves. In the case of Muhammad, however, we have a beautiful inside and a beautiful outside. The Messenger of Allah was the recipient of Revelation. Consequently, the Qur'an is a reflection of the Prophet's heart and soul and a reflection of his actions.

If all we had was the Qur'an, and all our books of hadith, *sirah*, and *tarikh* were to vaporize, all of our books of prophetic traditions, biography, and history went up in smoke, we would still know Muhammad, understand Muhammad, love Muhammad, and emulate Muhammad. And yes, the accusations made against me by right-wing fascist anti-Islamites and anti-Muslimites are completely correct: I am, and always will be, completely and totally enamored with Muhammad. I am madly in love with Muhammad. I stand accused. Guilty as charged. I love the Messenger of Allah in the same manner that I love Jesus, Moses, and Abraham.

Argue as they may, dispute as they may, cast doubt as they may, and lie as they may, the enemies of Islam have never been able, and will never be able, to present definitive proof that the Qur'an was the product of a human mind and a human hand nor can they provide conclusive evidence that the Prophet Muhammad is a figment of the Muslim imagination. If you showed these skeptics the sun, they would argue that it is the moon. If you showed these skeptics the moon, they would argue that it is the sun.

If we can know the Prophet Muhammad by means of the Qur'an, let me be precise, by means of the true, traditional, interpretation of the Qur'an, we can also know him by means of the authentic Sunnah. I repeat myself, by means of the authentic Sunnah. Although the genuine nature of the Qur'an is not generally subject to dispute, and many prominent Orientalists acknowledge its prophetic provenance, the same cannot be said of the hadith literature as a whole.

If the Qur'an should be understood according to its traditional interpretation, the study of hadith must also be guided by scholarship and reason. If it agrees with the Qur'an and makes logical sense, you can accept it. However, if it contradicts the Qur'an or authentic narrations, makes no logical sense, or attributes anything improper to the Prophet, it must be rejected categorically. <u>We are not people of blind faith. We are people of faith and critical thought.</u>

This is not to say that there are no problems with our sources. There are plenty of problems. The problems being presented by professional polemicists are not new. They have not presented anything novel. They are bringing up issues that Muslim scholars have been dealing with for over 1400 years. By and large, they are questions that have already been answered.

I have studied the works of John Wansbrough, Patricia Crone, Michael Cook, Gerd Puin, Karl Heinz-Ohlig, Harald Motzki, Yehuda Nevo, Sven Kalisch, Andrew Rippin, Gabriel Said Reynolds, and others, and it is like: "Tell us something we do not know." I do not dispute the sources that they cite. I dispute their interpretation of those sources. I dispute the conclusions that they draw from those sources. Either they are ignorant of Muslim scholarship or feign ignorance to dupe and deceive their readers. They turn what are non-issues into issues.

In other words, the arguments advanced by some scholars are fundamentally flawed. It makes one wonder if they ever took Logic 101. In the *hawzah 'ilmiyyah*, namely, in the Shiite seminary, *mantiq* is one of the first courses you take in *al-muqaddimah* or undergraduate studies. I studied logic as an undergraduate student at the University of Toronto. We have senior scholars, with doctoral degree, who have not mastered basic reasoning. That is like having someone in *buhuth al-kharij* or graduate studies in the *hawzah* who has never studied logic. For us, it is an impossibility.

These professional naysayers publish so-called peer-reviewed scholarly articles and books that come across as soap operas. They leave the reader hanging. They create doubts, but do not resolve them. They ask questions, but not answer them. Their goal is not to advance scholarship. Their goal is to put up smoke screens, destabilize foundations, and to huff and to puff and to blow the house down. So, take it from an insider, who is both a Muslim, an academic and a cleric: beware of the big bad wolf who wants to blow down the House of Islam. Beware of the big bad wolf who wants to eat the three little… the three little… innocent *halal* animals. Yes, the three little lambs. We are people of *Usul*: we are *usulis*. We are scholars of sources and we are confronted by people who seek to destroy those sources, the foundations upon which we stand.

Read the Qur'an, but read it in accordance with its traditional interpretation. Read the Qur'an in context. Read various interpretations of the Qur'an and avoid all extremes. Stick to the center. Maintain moderation. Rely on logic. Read the hadith literature, but do not wander into the woods without a guide for surely you will get lost, die of exposure, or get devoured by a grizzly bear. Unless you are an experienced outdoorsman, you should stick to the city park. Limit yourselves to authenticated traditions transmitted by trustworthy sources.

And read the treaties that the Prophet Muhammad concluded with the monks of the Sinai, the Christians of Najran, Egypt, Syria, Armenia, Persia, and the world; the covenants he concluded with the Jews of Medina, the Yemen, and northeastern Arabia; as well as the covenants he signed with the Zoroastrian community. These documents provide a blueprint for the Muhammadan Ummah. They provide the lenses through which we can see the global vision of Islam. They are primary documents that allow us to truly know Muhammad's mission.

In order to provide Muslim scholars and students with the tools that they need to protect, defend, and disseminate Islam, it is imperative to compose a work that concisely and systematically refutes the allegations made by certain secular scholars whose ultimate aim is to destroy Islam in the same way that they destroyed Judaism and Christianity.

Unless you have a complete mastery of the traditional Islamic sciences from an Eastern perspective and have a complete mastery of modern, Western, contributions to the Islamic sciences, you will not be in a position to authoritatively debunk the allegations and postulations presented by scholars who are destructive as opposed to constructive.

Not only are we obliged to counter the arguments of secularists and atheists, we are also duty bound to defend Islam from the distortions of the Nasibis, the Kharijis, the Salafis, the Wahhabis, and the Takfiris. Like it or not, many people put all Muslims in the same boat. How do like that? Sharing a boat with Bin Laden? How do you like that? Sharing a ship with Abu Bakr al-Baghdadi?

As Muslims, whether we are followers of *Ahl al-Bayt*, followers of *Ahl al-Sunnah* or followers of *Ahl Allah*; as Muslims, whether we are Shiites, Sunnis or Sufis, we must disassociate ourselves from the Takfiris who seek to scuttle the *safinah* or ark of Islam.

Since the demise of the Prophet Muhammad, we have been faced with two forms of Islam: true Islam and false Islam, 'Alawi Islam and Sufyani Islam, an Islam that loves and respects the Prophet and the *Ahl al-Bayt*, and a fake Islam that, deep down, loathes and despises the Prophet and His Holy Household. They are pagans that have been parading as partisans of Prophet in order to distort and destroy Islam.

And so we see, in books of history, in books of jurisprudence, in books of hadith, in books of theology, in books of commentary, two types of Islam: one, that is beautiful, just, and edifying, and the other, that is repulsive, unjust, and dehumanizing. We have an Islam that gives rights and an "Islam" that deprives people of rights. We have an Islam that honors women and an "Islam" that degrades and debases women. We have an Islam that is tolerant and an "Islam" that is intolerant. We have an Islam that is merciful and an "Islam" that is devoid of mercy. We have an Islam of life and an "Islam" of death.

So long as we have freedom of expression, we must voice our concerns. We must reject and repudiate the Islam of Yazid and reaffirm and reassert the Islam of Husayn. And when I say so, I speak not in terms of Sunnism and Shiism. I speak not in sectarian terms. I seek not to divide. I seek to unite: to gather all Muslims around the personality of the Prophet, to bring them back to Muhammadan Islam, to the Islam that was practiced prior to the *fitnah*, the split that ruptured the Muslim Community, to original Islam, the one and only Islam. Together, Sunnis, Shiites, and Sufis, must join forces to reclaim the narrative so that we, and the world, can all truly know, and remember, the Prophet Muhammad.

CHAPTER THIRTY-FIVE

THE COVENANTS OF THE HOLY PROPHET

Happy holidays and merry Christmas! I say so sincerely, but also defiantly, as an open act of revolt and rebellion against my early teachers who, in the mid-1980s, brainwashed me into believing that it was prohibited to celebrate the birth of Jesus and even the birth of the Prophet Muhammad.

While the actual day may not be exact, and this is acknowledged by the Church and Christian scholars, it is the thought that counts. Not only is it permissible to commemorate the days of birth and death of prophets, messengers, saints, and martyrs, it is actually commendable and recommendable. In fact, the Muslims of the Middle East, North Africa, and Spain celebrated all sorts of feasts associated with pre-Muhammadan prophets and saints for over a thousand years. And those who stopped doing so only ceased because they were forced to do so by the ancient equivalents of the Takfiris of today.

Almighty Allah commands us, regularly and consistently, over 126 times in the Qur'an, to do exactly that: to remember: *adhkuru, adhkuru, adhkuru*. He commands us to be *Ahl al-Dhikr*, the People of Remembrance; so let us remember. We need to remember Allah. We need to remember the Prophet. We need to remember his faithful Companions. We need to remember the Imams of *Ahl al-Bayt*. We need to remember the great scholars of the past. We need to remember Islamic history. We need to remain connected to our religious and spiritual tradition.

If you search, far and wide, across the Muslim Ummah, you will not find a community that is as well-versed in Islamic history as the Shiite community. This is because the Shiite community commemorates every major event in sacred history. The days of birth and martyrdom of the Prophet and the Imams. The major events in the *sirah*: the biography of Muhammad. The major battles of Islam. The *Hijrah*. The Night Journey: the *Isra'* and *Miraj*. Not only does the Shiite community remember these events, they reenact some of them, like the martyrdom of Imam al-Husayn and they piously visit sacred sites associated with the history of Islam. Unfortunately, in recent history, Shiites, along with traditional Sunnis and

Sufis, have neglected certain holy places that they had once visited regularly: the sacred sites in Palestine, for example, as well as the sacred sites surrounding Mount Sinai, the land of Moses, the land of Elijah, the land of Salih, and the land of Muhammad al-Mustafa, the Seal of the Prophets.

Both geographically and historically, the Sinai was considered, since ancient times, as part of Arabia. It was also treated as part of *al-Sham* or Greater Syria. Not only was it visited by Arab traders, it was inhabited by Arab tribes. Although some scholars argue that the Prophet only left the Hijaz twice, this view is not supported by early Muslim and non-Muslim sources. If he was a camel driver, if he led caravans, for Abu Talib, for himself, and for Khadijah, then he must have been well traveled. According to a substantial body of evidence, in half a dozen different languages, recorded by both Muslims and Christians, spanning nearly a millennium and a half, Muhammad traveled to the Sinai prior to receiving revelation.

What drew him there? Trade. What drew him there? *Ziyarah* or pilgrimage. To see what? The Monastery of St. Catherine. The burning bush. The well of Moses. The site of the Golden Calf. The twelve springs that sprouted from stone for the Twelve Tribes of Israel. The Chapel of Elijah. The Gate of Repentance of Elijah. The Chapel of Aaron. The footprint of Aaron. The footprint of Salih's camel. The spot where Moses received the Ten Commandments. The Cave of Moses. The cave where he spent forty days and forty nights prior to receiving the revelation. And to do what? To pray, meditate, fast, and contemplate, in that very same cave which, since that very day, has been also known as the Cave of Muhammad. In fact, the early followers of the Prophet constructed a place of prayer, the Mosque of Fatimah, a structure that leads to the Cave of Muhammad, to commemorate this remarkable site which connects Muhammad to Moses. Not only is there a mosque on the peak of Mount Sinai, marking the Cave of Moses and Muhammad, there is a mosque, in the heart of the monastery, the Jami Mosque, which was built to mark the spot where Muhammad had once stood when he visited the monastery.

According to an impressive body of facts, the Holy Fathers from Mount Sinai knew Muhammad, and they knew him well. They foretold that he was the long-awaited prophet who would rise from Arabia. They asked Muhammad for protection and he granted them protection. As such, it is our duty, as Muslims, to become reacquainted with the *Achtiname of Muhammad* along with all the other treaties, covenants, and charters of rights and protections that the Messenger of Allah granted to the People of the Book.

In our defense of true Islam, why do we not point non-Muslims to the Qur'an? We can. We should. We must. However, the Qur'an can be used and abused. It is the primary tool used by Takfiri terrorists and by Islamophobes, both of whom share the same exact interpretation of the Qur'an: cherry-picking verses, citing them out of context, and misinterpreting them. What is more, when you give a Qur'an to non-Muslims, they believe that you are trying to convert them. They put up walls from the very beginning. Furthermore, if most Muslims have not read the Qur'an from cover to cover, how can we expect non-Muslims to read the whole thing?

The Qur'an, in the hands of the Friends of Allah, is a book of guidance. The Qur'an, in the hands of the Friends of Satan, is a book of misguidance. Everything depends on interpretation. It is not sufficient to follow the Qur'an. It is not sufficient to follow the Sunnah. It is imperative that one follows the true, traditional, teachings of the Qur'an and the Sunnah. Otherwise, it is an interpretative free-for-all. This is not to say that there is one, and only one, interpretation of the Qur'an and the Hadith. Such essentialism is the root of all extremism. *Au contraire*, the adherents of mainstream Islam rely on a long tradition of hermeneutics tracing back to the Prophet. Traditional Islam embraces diversity of interpretation.

Although we can present some selections from the hadith literature in an attempt to show that Islam is a religion of justice, non-Muslims can easily find plenty of traditions that present Islam and the Prophet in a poor light. All sources need to be subject to critical analysis. Although there is light in that ocean, do not jump into it unless you know how to swim. Falsehood will drag you down and you will drown. Although there is light at the surface of the ocean, its depths are filled with darkness and even its shores have no shortage of slime.

As much as we insist that ISIS is not Islamic, we need to acknowledge that the ideology of this death cult is rooted in Muslim sources. They draw from the Qur'an. They draw from Qur'anic commentaries. And they draw from the hadith literature. This is how they dupe and deceive naïve Muslims to convert to their criminal cause. For the sake of non-scholars, we must identify the origin of Takfiri thought. The ideology of ISIS is drawn from the Kharijites. The ideology of ISIS is drawn from the Nawasib. Takfiri thought is not derived from the *Salaf* or pious predecessors. It was not passed down by the Companions. It does not trace back to the Prophet. In fact, the ideology of ISIS is the illegitimate offspring of Yazid. They are not Muslims. They are not Sunnis. They are not Hanbalis. They are Yazidis pure and simple. They are the sons of Abu Sufyan. They are the progeny of pagans who hypocritically embraced

Islam with the objective of destroying it from within.

The Covenants of the Prophet Muhammad represent a critically important tool in interfaith and intrafaith discussions. Why? Because they predate the split between *tasunnu* and *tashayyu*, between Sunnism and Shiism. Why? Because they predate the split between *mu'minin* and *muslimin*, between believers and submitters, between the People of the Book and the Muslim Community. In the early days of Islam, the People of the Book were an intrinsic part of the Ummah. Jews, Christians, Zoroastrians, and Muslims were one entity and one community, a Confederation of Believers, united under the banner of Islam and bound by the *Constitution of Medina* as well as the Covenants of the Prophet. And this interpretation is not an innovation. It is rooted in both the Muhammadan Covenants and authenticated traditions found in Sunni and Shiite sources. Islam embraces all divinely-revealed religions.

When you give a non-Muslim a copy of the Covenants of the Prophet, you are not trying to convert them. You are reaching out to them. You are offering them friendship. You are offering them solidarity. You are defending the religion of Islam. You are defending the dignity and integrity of the Prophet of Islam. At a time when the Messenger of Allah is being maligned as never before; at a time when the Qur'an, the Sunnah, and the sharia are under attack; at a time when un-American fascists are proposing to create a Muslim registry; at a time when neo-Nazis in designer suits are openly musing about placing us in internment camps as they did with the Japanese, we need to point non-Muslims, as well as Muslims, to the Covenants of the Prophet Muhammad, and let Muhammad speak for himself. See and hear what he had to say.

The Covenants of the Prophet Muhammad, provide an unprecedented insight into early Islam. They help us reclaim the true narrative of traditional, civilization Islam, in the face of Salafi/Wahhabi subversion. Almighty Allah has brought these documents to light at the time we needed them the most. They are like a light in the darkest night. The Muhammadan Covenants are a mercy to both Muslims and non-Muslims. We must take full advantage of the bounties that God has bestowed upon us. The Covenants of the Prophet Muhammad are a blessing, a sign, and warning. Will we not pay heed?

Chapter Thirty-Six

Nightmares in Takfiristan: A Cautionary Tale

The following article addresses sensitive subjects in a frank and honest fashion. To avoid misunderstandings, it should be read as a whole and not solely in parts. During the course of my life, I have had the opportunity to meet a multitude of Muslims from around the world. I have socialized with Bedouin shepherds in the Sahara and conversed with princes in their lavish palaces. I have shared tea with simple people in souks and discussed complex jurisprudential and theological matters with the leading legal and spiritual authorities of Islam. While I have seen the good, and my experiences with Muslims have been overwhelmingly positive, I have also seen the bad and the ugly. This short memoir deals with the dark side of "Islam." However, as harsh as my criticism may be, and as shocking and scandalous as my accounts may seem, it must always be remembered that I am focusing on an infinitesimally small number of ignorant, deviant, and demonic individuals. At most, there are currently 100,000 Takfiri terrorists in the world today. However, there are 1.5 billion Muslims, the vast majority of whom are genuinely good human beings with strong faith, morals, and family values.

What good will this exposé do? Why is it important to air such dirty laundry? The importance resides in the fact that the people in question play an active role in the Muslim community. Imagine, for example, a country in which a certain ethnic group represents a mere 0.001% of the population and yet controls 80% of official positions in the country. Would that pose a problem? Yes, indeed, it would. The very same thing happens with Islam. A minuscule group of supposed Muslims, who represent a mere 0.001% of the Islamic world, hold virtually all positions of power. They are those who lead, those who speak, those who make decisions, those who criticize, and those who judge. And to add insult to injury, people mistakenly believe that this 0.001% of radicals are the representatives of Islam!

I am, I admit, acutely aware that some disingenuous individuals might read this writing and stand up and shout: "Look! Look! Even an erudite Muslim recognizes that Muslims are savages who follow a barbaric religion!" It is precisely for this reason that I have included this word of warning, clarification, and contextualization. I stress it now and I will stress it again: far from reflecting the reality of Islam as practiced by one fourth of humanity, the experiences that I relate all involved Islamist extremists--Salafis, Wahhabis, Jihadis, and Takfiris--who represent a minority in the Muslim world. And the majority of the culprits in question play these roles because they are supported and financed by those who seek to spread Takfirism. For what purpose, one may ask? To use "Islam" to destroy Islam and to use "Islam" to advance their geo-political agenda. With no further ado: Avanti! And caveat lector.

I discovered Islam on my own, *alhamdulillah*, praise be to God. Then I met "Muslims," *a'udhu billah*, I take refuge in God. For these *muwahhidun* or monotheists, as they called themselves, the pillars of Islam were three: *haram*, *bid'ah*, and *takfir*: prohibition, innovation, and excommunication. Virtually everything was *haram* or forbidden to these obscurantists: television was *haram*, music was *haram*, prayer rugs were *haram*, and prayer beads were *haram*... Killing the *kuffar* or infidels, however, was not only *halal* but *wajib*. It was not only permissible; it was obligatory. Not only was the world composed primarily of prohibitions, anything that went beyond the scope of their myopic and mentally deranged worldview was a prohibited innovation or *bid'ah*.

In fact, one of the first things that I learned after taking my *shahadah*, the profession of faith, was that only "Sunnis" were Muslims. Scholars of Islam were always keen to criticize Christianity for having so many denominations. I soon learned, however, that Islam was nearly as divided as Christianity. It was pretty much, raise your hand, said *La ilaha illa Allah, Muhammadan Rasul Allah*, "There is no god but Allah and Muhammad is the Messenger of Allah," and, "by the way, Shiites are *kafirs* or infidels." This point was even made on brochures used to invite people to Islam. In fact, one of the first books I was given after embracing Islam was *Talbees Iblees / The Devil's Deception of the Shee'ah*, translated by Bilal Philips, a Jamaican, Afro-Canadian, Saudi-serving, polygamist who reportedly recruited African American Muslims with military experience on behalf of the CIA who then dispatched them to fight with jihadists around the world.

Tellingly, one of the first lectures that we Muslim converts were invited to attend was titled "The Groups that Went Astray," or something of that nature, in which the *shaykh* went through every imaginable school of jurisprudence, school of thought, or sects, and placed them outside the fold of Islam. The event in question only served to cause confusion in the minds of both new Muslims and non-Muslims alike. I learned that, for Saudi-trained mullahs, all the various branches of Shiism were outside of Islam. Incredibly, all of the Sunni schools were outside of Islam as well. Everyone, except the members of this one and only "saved sect," was an infidel. And if that is how tolerant they were of Muslims, you can only imagine the level of hatred they had for non-Muslims.

Since only the members of this "Sunni" sect went to heaven, and all other Muslims, Jews, Christians, and followers of other faiths were destined to eternal damnation, I was told that it was my duty to try to convert my family and friends to Islam. Misinterpreting and misrepresenting the Qur'an, so-called scholars of Islam insisted that it was prohibited for Muslims to have non-Muslim friends. As one can imagine, none of this went down very well with my parents and pals. In fact, my whole life went to hell and I was soon left without family or friends. What is more, there was no Muslim community to support me in return. The people who were teaching me Islam acted like cult-leaders; namely, trying to cut me off from family and friends. However, unlike cults, which fill the void thereby created, I was left in the lurch.

"How do I handle Christmas," I inquired of my Imam and sagacious *shaykh*. "It is not permitted to give gifts to Christians for Christmas; however, you are free to accept them." How stupid and selfish does that sound? Celebrating birthdays was also prohibited causing a whole host of problems with people who cared about me. I soon found out, however, that the Imam who insisted that such celebrations were illegal in Islam had organized a secret, surprise, birthday party for his wife. We were taught that music and dancing were *haram* while the Imam's daughter was belly-dancing in Egypt. So much for being consistent. A few years later, another infamous Imam was preaching from the pulpit while his super-model daughter was posing for nude photographs. Just as there are predatory priests and rabbis, who use their power and authority for sexual purposes, I found that some fake-sheiks sought to seduce young Muslim women. One, in particular, invited a Muslim woman for a "private" *dhikr* session which moved from spiritually ecstatic to erotically orgasmic. This simply serves to demonstrate how far some sick people will go in their distortion of Islam.

I found hypocrites, not only among congregants, but among clerics as well: Imams who insisted that others eat only *zabihah/halal*, even when it violated every health regulation in existence, while they themselves would never consume meat of such dubious quality; Imams who incited young Muslims to wage jihad while they themselves would never have sacrificed their own children; Imams who encouraged others to prepare the dead for burial while refusing to even consider touching a corpse themselves; Imams who encouraged intermarriage when they themselves were entirely endogamous; Imams who encouraged converts to marry wayward women when neither they nor anyone in their communities would have touched them with latex gloves; Imams who expected women to observe strict hijab while their wives and daughters did not; and Imams who told their followers that abortion was a mortal sin, but who would coerce their own daughters to terminate illegitimate pregnancies to avoid bringing shame to their families and ruining their reputation.

When I relate such accounts, I am not suggesting that Muslims, as a whole, fail to follow the teachings of Islam. I am merely pointing out that many of those who hold positions of power and influence in the Islamic community behave exactly like non-Muslims. Evidently, this problem does not apply exclusively to Islam. The same phenomenon is found in all other religions as such failings form a fundamental part of the human condition. Why is it, we must ask ourselves, that most ordinary Muslims sincerely strive to abide by the precepts of Islam when so few of their leaders do? Leaders are supposed to be the best of the people.

I remember one young woman, a poor, pathetic, pretty, blue-eyed blonde, convert, who was perpetually pregnant, dragging her dirty, impoverished kids all over the place. She reminded me of young women who get brainwashed by cults. With her poor health, pale, anemic, skin, and history of miscarriages, she had been warned by her obstetrician that she could no longer safely have children. Despite the dangers to her life, and to the life of her potential children, she was told by her Imam, in no uncertain terms, that all forms of birth control were prohibited in Islam. Oddly enough, while their female followers had so many kids they could fill orphanages, these middle-aged Imams, all of whom were married, had no children, or merely had one or two. Unless these men were impotent or sterile, their wives appear to have been using some sort of contraceptive. Then again, they may simply have been using the rhythm method. Still, they should have explained that the Knaus-Ogino or calendar-based contraceptive method was permissible, and that there was no sin in preventing pregnancy, particularly when it was perilous.

Extremism and religious fanaticism were the order of the day. From the very moment I professed the testimony of faith, I was expected, and pressured, to fully practice every aspect of what my commanders-in-faith presented as "Islam," when, in reality, much of what they taught consisted of fabrications that had nothing to do with the true Muslim religion. While I immediately started praying five times a day, out of my own free will and devotion, I did not appreciate the threats of imminent damnation that loomed over my head if, for some reason, I inadvertently missed a prayer. Anyone who misses a prayer, I was told by my fundamentalist friends, who feigned to be Muslims, is an infidel. Even if a person were to make up his or her prayer, it would be of no avail. To miss a prayer is to reject the Prophet; to reject the Prophet is to reject God; consequently, anyone who fails to perform a ritual prayer, at its due time, is an apostate destined for eternal damnation. This was tantamount to praying with a gun held at one's head. Prayer was mandatory, I was taught, even if it meant prostrating on the sidewalk on Yonge Street in downtown Toronto during rush hour. I was surrounded by people who would pull to the side of a busy highway in a major metropolis, perform ablutions with snow, and prostrate in the slush in the freezing cold. I was surrounded by people who thought it was prohibited to prostrate on prayer rugs, but who would readily place their hands, foreheads, and noses on filthy floors, even performing their prayers in public washrooms and on private property. What kind of "God" were these persons worshipping? He was certainly not a God of love and compassion.

As fanatical as they were with their prayers, which they completed in obsessive compulsive fashion, so were they with their fasting which, in their view, was binding, not only on children, but even on pregnant and lactating women. They believed in following the sun so much that they could have been sun-worshippers. It was one thing to fast from dawn to dusk on the equator and parts of the northern and southern hemispheres; however, I came to know of Muslims who were fasting 18, 20, and even 23 hours per day, for an entire month, in the southern tip of South America and in the northern regions of Alaska and the Northwest Territories. Reasoning with such people was of no avail despite the danger they posed to both their bodies and souls. These people were prisoners of religion. Rather than follow the laws of Islam, as spiritual servants, they obeyed arbitrary and illogical reasoning as slaves. For them, the Prophet was not a spiritual guide; he was merely a drill sergeant, a despot, and a dictator. The people I frequented were truly made in the image of their "God:" they were devoid or mercy. Their ideology was more suited for psychological torture than spiritual, moral, and ethical growth. They suffocated all of the spirituality out of Islam. They inverted Islam entirely.

While I was a young, idealistic, revolutionary, I also had strong ethics. As much as I spoke of jihad and holy war, and as much as I believed in a strong legal system, I advocated a struggle for justice. I was simply scandalized by the sentiments shared by some of the so-called Muslims I met. I knew one Jordanian-Palestinian psychopath who openly fantasized about opening a slaughterhouse for the *kuffar* or infidels. I was introduced to many more who idolized Hitler. I was given anti-Semitic videos produced by extreme right-wing Protestants along with Nazi hate propaganda. What did any of this odious and despicable material have to do with Islam? Was I joining Islam or joining the Klan? Was this the Party of Allah or the National Socialist Party?

"You are a good brother," a Lebanese Arab once told me, "so I am sure you hate Jews just as much as I do." "I do not hate Jews," I clarified, as this was tantamount to racism, "I hate Zionist invaders, occupiers, and oppressors." "There are Jewish reverts to Islam," I observed. "I would never trust a Jewish convert to Islam," he said, "they are evil; it runs in their blood." This demented loon started ranting about how much he would love to kill Jews. "If you brought me a Jewish baby, I would kill it," he proudly professed. I knew, at that moment, that the man in front of me was the very manifestation of evil. In fact, this maniac wanted Muslims and neo-Nazis to join forces in their opposition to Israel. I objected, pointing out that neo-Nazis would target Muslim women for sexual assault in Germany. "They probably mistook them for Jews," he rationalized. For me, the Israeli-Palestinian conflict was primarily political in nature. For some "Muslims," however, it was racial and racist. I had no interest whatsoever in any strategic alliance between fascists and so-called Islamists. As a Canadian, as a French Canadian, as a Québécois, and as a Métis Person, I was incensed at the level of racism and bigotry that I found among these self-professed Islamists. Since there was nothing but hate in their hearts, there was no place for God and goodness.

This burly Lebanese lunatic, who dreamed of killing Jewish babies, had lived a life of complete and total decadence and debauchery. As part of some sort of middle-age or identity crisis, he had "rediscovered Islam," and now hated the West with a passion after having worshipped it like a pagan goddess for most of his life. Part of his jihad consisted of living on welfare as a means of weakening the infidel country of Canada. "God-willing," he said, "If we get enough Muslims on social assistance, we will bankrupt this *kafir* country!" I noted, in horror, that his young sons would spend an inordinate amount of time playing the most violent and bloody of video games in which they mercilessly killed people in a virtual world. "I am training them to be terrorists," he explained, as he broke out in maniacal laughter. As can be imagined, I soon became highly critical of the Canadian government's lax screening process for immigrants and refugees. Why on earth was the government allowing terrorists and terrorist supporters to enter our country?

For a time, a very short time, I associated with the Tablighi Jamaat.

These big-bearded brothers were kind, peaceful, and welcoming. They had many good qualities, no doubt, the foremost of which were piety and hospitality. They had, however, their fair share of faults and no shortage of foolishness. When asked how many children he had, a man proudly responded that he had four girls. "We are so sorry," the uncles responded with dismay and distress, "We will ask Allah to give you a boy." In contrast, the Prophet had assured that any man who raised three daughters would go to Paradise. The Messenger of Allah viewed girls as blessings; not curses.

I remember sitting in a Tablighi Jamaat gathering in Brampton, Ontario, were devotees were piously reading from their sacred scripture, the *Tablighi Nisab*. These God-fearing nincompoops had reached the section concerning the consequences of missing an obligatory prayer. In the first hadith or tradition that was read, the Prophet supposedly stated that anyone who misses an obligatory prayer, regardless of the reason, would go to Hell. They shook their heads in reverential fear, imploring that God would protect them from such a sin. The second hadith or tradition narrated that the Prophet and the Companions overslept so much one morning that they were awoken by the sun shining on their heads. There was pin-drop silence in the mosque and, then, suddenly, and simultaneously, all of the Tablighis broke out in loud cries and tears: they had come to the realization that even the Prophet would have to burn in Hell! I shook my head, walked out of the room, and never returned to their study circle again. I had no regrets, except perhaps one: I should have grabbed some samosas before I left.

I recall another memorable incident that took place at another religious gathering. Their so-called spiritual leader was recounting the story of the cave in which the Prophet and Abu Bakr sought refuge while they were being hunted down by their polytheistic enemies. This is the famous story of the spider that spun a web and the dove that built its nest to give the impression that the cave was unoccupied. Apparently, there was much more to the story than that and this is what the *shaykh* was expounding upon in imaginative and provocative detail.

Prior to the arrival of the infidel search party, Abu Bakr insisted that he secure the cave from scorpions or snakes. He started to tear off parts of his clothing in order to stuff any suspicious holes in the rocks. Soon, Abu Bakr was butt-naked in the presence of the Prophet. He proceeded to plug one hole with his foot, another with his other foot, still another with his hand, and yet another with his other hand, leaving all but one hole unsecured. Abu Bakr then proceeded to plug that hole with his penis and, to his shock and surprise, was bitten by a venomous snake! The brothers broke out in tears, crying and wailing at the courage, bravery, and piety of Abu Bakr. When I heard this pious tale, I could hardly contain my laughter. How, I wondered, could people willingly suspend their faculty of reason? I knew this story, of course, and was well-aware that it was the toe of Abu Bakr that had reportedly been bitten and that the Prophet had allegedly healed it with is blessed saliva. Either the preacher was exaggerating or he was making a mockery of his gullible audience.

On another occasion, destiny, in all of its didactic cruelty, brought me in contact with a Guyanese Indian family that lived in a cockroach infested hell-hole in Downsview, Ontario, Canada, and whose rug-rats used to literally swing on the curtains and toboggan down stairs with newborns. The brother, whom I shall call Kabir or Big, was actually a tiny man with a long beard that appeared to weigh down his bony, emaciated, frame. "The first time I saw Kabir," explained his lovely wife, "was at our wedding;" "I almost dropped dead he was so ugly." "I was ecstatic," interjected Kabir, "had it not been for an arranged marriage, how on earth could I have landed such a gorgeous woman!"

Kabir was a warm and welcoming man so long as one was not an infidel. If you were a non-Muslim, he would probably stab you in the back. However, if you were a Shiite, he would likely dispense with formalities and stab you in the front. "Killing people is a mercy," this man once told me, "You do them a favor by preventing them from committing more sins." Unfortunately, despite Kabir's conditional hospitality, the hadith that "Purity is part of faith" or the saying that "Cleanliness is godliness" never reached him. I remember sitting with this miniature man, and pointing out, "Brother, there is a roach on your beard," to which he responded with a smile, "Ah, this little thing… That's nothing… You should see the size of the insects in South America!" Violating every rule of reason, sanitation, and hygiene, I was foolish enough to share a meal with this man and his filth-infested family. In retrospect, the risks to my health were well worth it, as the story that I learned was priceless. Plus, the potato-stuffed roti was absolutely delicious!

Expounding upon the virtues of *tawhid* or divine unity, this monotheistic madman explained to me that any man-made image or shape of any creature amounted to *shirk* or polytheism. (To my Western intellect, or to any intellect for that matter, this made no sense at all: polytheism was the worship of more than one god. Unless adored, in the literal sense of the word, no object could, in and of itself, be inherently polytheistic). "Even teddy bears are *shirk*," said this sage and insectophile. "The jinn," he warned me, as he referenced some Saudi Wahhabi treatise on *tawhid*, "can possess stuffed animals." "However, there is a solution," he said confidently, to my great relief. "Rip out their eyes at night," he declared. "Otherwise, the *jinn* will possess them," he claimed, as I looked in terror at his children's eyeless teddy-bears. "In the morning, you can always plug them back in," he reassured me, as I tried to assess the level of permanent psychological damage he had caused to his small kids. Of course, this was the same man who would call the *'adhan* for *fajr* or morning prayers and then beat his kids senseless with shoes in order to force them to pray. What a lovely association they would have between prayer and punishment and between religion and violence. As adults, they probably developed a sado-masochistic shoe fetish.

When this monotheistic madman paid an uninvited and unwelcomed visit to my humble home, he noticed that the names "Allah" and "Muhammad" were displayed in my foyer. "*Shirk!*" he shouted. "How dare you place Muhammad at the same level as Allah?" "Allah Himself did so," I responded, "when he asked us to say 'There is no god but Allah and Muhammad is His Messenger.'" Compared to other Salafis, however, this man was a moderate. The contempt the Wahhabis had for the Prophet was blasphemous: "Muhammad was just a normal man, like any man. He was nothing special. God could have given the revelation to anyone." One convert I knew, a white Russian rapper from the East Coast, objected to sending salutations and blessings upon Muhammad in his daily ritual prayers. He refused, on religious grounds, to recite the second segment of the *shahadah*. (It came as no surprise to me when I learned, years later, that this man had become a beer-drinking Buddhist). Ommmm… pass the Budweiser!

Although I was only sixteen years of age when I embraced Islam, my Muslim mentors insisted that it was obligatory for me to get married. This seems odd to me now as most of them were in their thirties and forties and were still unmarried. It makes me wonder if there was something more behind their brotherly physical embraces and invitations to spend the night at their homes. Perhaps they were grooming me both spiritually and sexually. After all, fornication and adultery is frowned upon in many Arab and Asian cultures while homosexuality is generally tolerated. My fears were confirmed when one supposedly pious brother, who was married with children, invited me to watch hard-core pornographic movies with him (an offer I roundly rejected). He had also confided in me that he planned to finger his nine-year old daughter while she slept in order to test her virginity. "Are you nuts?" I protested, "You are going to break her hymen to test her hymen?!" "No, brother," he tried to reassure me, "I will only use one finger." "What if she wakes up?" I retorted, "How do you think she will react?" "If you have concerns she was abused," I stated, "have her examined by a physician." The situation was reported to a leading Imam who, to no surprise, ended up siding with the father. Fortunately, the mother of the girl put this sicko in his place. Unfortunately, this was not the only case of corruption that I came across.

One Maulana revealed to me that a girl in his congregation came to him for counseling because her father had raped her. "It is your decision whether you wish to forgive him or not," he responded, in what was a very progressive answer coming from an East Indian cleric. "Did you report the case to the authorities?" I inquired. Pin-drop silence. I met another young Pakistani brother who surprised the community by marrying a middle-aged, morbidly obese, unemployed white woman… who happened to have a beautiful, blue-eyed, blonde teenage daughter. Within months the man was in prison: charged with drugging and sexually-abusing his step-daughter, a girl who had embraced Islam, and had proudly worn the headscarf. Did she remain in the Muslim faith after being deflowered by a devil? I certainly doubt it. How did the community deal with the scandal? They chose not to. Nobody admonished the aggressor. Nobody extended a helping hand to the victim. However, when it came to money, the militant pseudo-Muslims I knew would not hesitate to send out thugs to collect any debt.

Speaking of sexual deviants, I came across my fair share of pious pedophiles who finally felt they had found a welcoming home in Islam where they could openly express their dark, twisted, desire to marry little prepubescent girls. While most Muslims were trying to come up with clever counter-arguments to contest the claim that the Prophet wed a pre-pubescent girl, these Lolita lovers proudly pointed to Muhammad's marriage with 'A'ishah as justification for their devious desires: "If the Prophet can marry a 7 or 9-year old girl, why can't we?" In the mind of some of the primitive predators that passed my way, women who did not wear hijab deserved to be raped. As I was told, "Women who do not wear hijab are whores." They were guilty of provoking men and sexual assault was a suitable punishment. Just like inquisitors, they could take pleasure out of inflicting pain. Masturbation was forbidden; however, in the minds of these maniacs, rape was a reasonable alternative. These are the very teachings of Takfirism, a mental illness that reduces women to booty: prizes of war, property that can be bought and sold, exploited and discarded. Fornication is prohibited, but forced prostitution is permissible.

There were, of course, the African Americans who married two, three, and four wives at a time or the serial monogamists, who divorced and married in regular succession. Strangely, as much as they hated Shiites, the Salafis had adopted temporary marriage, "Sunni *Mut'ah*," while violating all of its injunctions, obligations, and protections. Rather than provide for any of their "permanent" or "temporary" wives, these brothers simply called upon social services to foot the bill. Others did not even bother with such formalities as marriage. Some of the so-called black Muslims that I met viewed all white Christian women as potential sex slaves. One such character had his Caucasian "bondmaids" share a single room and bed. I personally knew one character, who pretended to be a mystic, who allowed his temporary wife to court other men while she was married to him as he was not interested in a long term relationship. How liberal of him! What was he? A spiritual swinger? This perplexing character used to encourage his teenage daughter to wear a headscarf while simultaneously allowing her to have non-Muslim boyfriends. Therapy, anyone?

There was even one prominent Muslim cleric of East Indian origin who would offer his teenage daughter in temporary marriage to his male guests from overseas, with the blessing of his wife (and the guest no doubt!), since she wanted to avoid wearing hijab at home, something unnecessary if the visiting scholar suddenly became her son-in-law. The fact that the "temporary husband" was a middle-aged man, and their daughter was a minor, apparently did not pose any problems to these people. Whether they actually allowed their daughter to have sex with these male visitors, I cannot say. However, they certainly set up a dangerous situation filled with legal and moral perils.

As seems quite evident to everyone, some of these sanctimonious womanizers, the converts at least, had been players and pimps prior to professing Islam. Taking the *shahadah* had not changed their characters. The only difference was that they presented their philandering as piety. They just rebranded the brothel as a harem and referred to their hoes as concubines. Others pretended to be pious Muslims while continuing to earn their living as drug dealers. Some of these people, however, were so self-righteous that they insisted upon marrying virgin girls from the Muslim world, promising them paradise while providing them with hell, in the hood, and the shock of learning that they had a dozen children out-of-wedlock. Others were not so chivalrous and lured naïve Muslim girls from abroad only to turn them into strippers and sex slaves.

The problem was not just with the cultural Muslims. There were just as many players who were Muslim immigrants. While some Muslim girls were pretty much prisoners in their own homes, some Muslim boys had absolute freedom and spent much of their time clubbing, partying, drinking, doing drugs, and fornicating with non-Muslim girls. Of course, when it came time to get married, the families of these "fine young Muslim men" would find them a nice virgin, typically a cousin, from

Lebanon, Pakistan, Iran or elsewhere, since Western women were unworthy of marriage: they were only good for cheap sex. As for Muslim girls, God have mercy on them if they ever succumbed to sin. While their brothers were encouraged to fornicate, "to gain experience," a single slip on the part of one of these sisters and they were disowned by their families. In their countries of origin, their own parents would turn them over to the local whorehouse. Islam, however, taught the very opposite: fornication and adultery is prohibited for both parties, male and female. Although there was plenty of mercy for young men in these cultural Muslim communities, there was none reserved for young women.

Within a few years, I had heard it all and seen it all: fathers threatening to kill their sons unless they accepted the arranged marriages that were planned for them; young women who discovered, to their dread, that the "prince charming" they were forced to marry was a wife beater or a heroin addict; families destroyed because married men felt that it was their right to take as many wives and concubines as they wished; domineering married men who brought "temporary wives" to their homes, and made no secret of sleeping with them, just to assert their power over their permanent wives; not to mention an East Indian Muslim scholar who asked me to help find him a young white woman for a temporary marriage. We, converts, were commanded to marry "pious women;" however, that apparently did not apply to some of the ulama. One Somali *shaykh* told me straight out: "I want a white woman." Not a pious woman; not an educated woman; no, just a white woman: a prize.

During these dark but illuminating days, I met plenty of promiscuous women who sincerely believed that they had gone from being sluts to saints simply by uttering the testimony of faith. One African American Imam learned this lesson the hard way when he discovered that his wife, a Puerto Rican convert, had been prostituting herself orally to help pay for bills. One sister, who was a former biker with the Hell's Angels, thought she had suddenly become the Virgin Mary. She belonged to God now (after having belonged to the whole gang). While it is true that Allah is the Most Merciful, and that He forgives the sins of people who sincerely embrace Islam while being remorseful and repentant of their past sinful actions, social, moral, ethical, and spiritual growth takes time, effort, and discipline. The sins of new or new-born Muslims may have been washed away but their sexual transmitted diseases have not. Unfortunately, far too many Muslims have picked up STDs from their spouses, male and female.

Befriending ex-cons who "discovered Islam" in prison, where they were serving sentences for drug dealing, armed robbery, sexual assault, and murder, is not necessarily advisable. And still, I met delusional men who opened their doors wide open to such con-artists, exposing their wives and children to potential harm. It is not enough to embrace Islam: one needs to live Islam. Some people need to prove that they are practicing Muslims prior to earning one's trust and confidence. How many Muslim women from overseas have married men from North America and Europe, who claimed to be committed Muslim converts, only to discover that they were dogs? Far too many for my taste. But, as the Qur'an says: "corrupt women are for corrupt men, and corrupt men, for corrupt women--just as good women are for good men, and good men, for good women" (24:26). So if materialistic green card chasers ended up with compulsive liars and hypocrites with more baggage than the airport lost-and-found, I shall not shed tears. What goes around comes around. It is all *kif kif.*

As I came to learn from experience, many so-called Muslim converts never truly change. If they were criminals before Islam, they persisted in their criminality after Islam. Only now, they called it jihad! They were at war against the infidels. They robbed, mugged, and murdered people in the path of Allah. They argued that the wealth of the unbelievers belonged to the believers. They were just reappropriating it. Criminals with a cause! What a concept! Of course, they only kept the money for themselves as opposed to redistributing it to the poor and needy. These thugs were no Robin Hoods: they were simply robbing in the hood. Let all be warned: simply because a person takes the *shahadah* does not make them good. If there were some reverts who never changed, there were others who tried too hard, and soon suffered from spiritual burnout. When several scholarly studies were released, showing that as many as 80% of converts stopped practicing Islam or left the religion altogether within years of embracing it, these verifiable findings simply served to confirm what I had observed all along. This is not to say that there are no good Muslim converts or reverts. On the contrary, many of them are outstanding and exemplary Muslims. However, just like panning for gold, one needs to separate the gold dust from the worthless minerals.

Although, like many Muslims, I associated the hijab with modesty and chastity, I gradually overcame my idealistic stereotypes. An East Indian friend of mine, who happened to be in his mid-thirties, had recently married a fifteen or sixteen-year old girl from Pakistan through an arranged married. How on earth he got her through immigration is beyond me. I assume birth certificates were forged or deliberately mistranslated. In any event, one day, I decided to drop by to see my Muslim brother, whose name I have modified in comic irony, and rang the doorbell. "Salaamu 'alaykum," I saluted, "Is brother Dayyus home?" "Wa 'alaykum salaam," the pretty teenager replied, "Come on in." Since she had not answered my question, I repeated it: "Is your husband home?" "No," she said with a smile, as she grabbed my hand, and started to pull me into the house. For some, this may suggest that she was simply being hospitable. However, the look in her eyes, the seductive smile on her face, the joy at her husband's absence, and the manner in which she held my hand and invited me into her home, suggested otherwise. This was not the first nor the last time that I averted seduction at the hand of Muslim girls or women. As confusing as it may be to most men, who tend to judge books by their covers, there are harlots who wear hijab and virgins who wear mini-skirts and bikinis. I would see some supposedly pious sisters in the mosque with full hijab, only to see them in sexy bathing suits at the pool right after congregational prayers. Others would walk a block from the mosque, take off their chador, and return to their regular routine in little black dresses and stiletto heels.

If this behavior was extreme, it was nothing compared to what was witnessed at women-only swimming sessions organized for Muslims where it was not unusual to see fully clothed women take a jump in the pool. Sure, some younger sisters wore bathing suits. There were only women there after all. Some were more modest and wore t-shirts or shorts on top of their swimwear. Some went further and swam in yoga pants or tights. However, there were always women who would go swimming while wearing chadors, abayas or cloaks, with full hijab on their heads, niqab over their faces, and socks on their feet! This was quite a contrast to the hammam or Turkish bath culture in Iran and the Arab world. If Arab women would wander around topless in such settings, Persian women would also walk around bottomless.

By the time I was eighteen or nineteen, I was eager to get married, and approached some Muslim elders concerning what was lawful and prohibited in marital relations. "It is *haram* or forbidden to see your wife naked," I learned with disappointment and comic disbelief. "If you must have sex with your wife," I was told, "you must approach her in the dark, through a sheet with a strategically placed hole." "Condoms are prohibited in Islam," a Somali sage said to me, "otherwise, you deprive the woman of her pleasure." "And what pleasure is that?" I inquired. "Getting filled with ejaculate," he explained." "If you were really concerned about the pleasure of women," I interjected, "perhaps you should stop cutting off their clitorises and sowing together their labia." He stormed out of the room. End of conversation.

When I inquired about oral sex with one's spouse, I was told that it was prohibited. One Salafi scolded me, saying: "How can you put your penis in a mouth that recites the Qur'an?" "What about cunninlingus?" I pried, pushing a fundamentalist to the point of stroke. "Why on earth would you want to lick a woman's vagina?" asked one of my pseudo-Muslim mentors, "Don't you know that they pee from that hole?" I could imagine all of the sexual frustration that these rules must cause among Salafis and Wahhabis. No wonder they were so violent. "Now I get it," I thought, "this explains why all those Gulf Arabs spend their time with prostitutes in Dubai, London, and Las Vegas." When there is no food at home, you go buy some at a restaurant. Or, as some of these sexual perverts used to explain to their wives: "I cheat on you because I respect you. I do with those women what I cannot do with you."

Perhaps marrying a Muslim girl from the old country was not such a good idea after all. Even if I wanted to, there was no Muslim family at the time who would ever have given their daughter to a Canadian convert. God forbid. If they were Indo-Pakistani Muslims, they would have preferred to give their daughter to a Hindu polytheist than to a pious, educated, Muslim convert from a good family. Unlike many other converts, who fetishized foreign girls in colonial fashion, I had received a cold shower at the "New Muslim Class" put on once a month at a downtown mosque. "Muslim men must shave their armpits," said the Imam. That made sense to me. "Muslim men must remove the hair from their private parts." "Isn't that kind of kinky?" I asked a French Canadian convert who turned tomato red. Still, I had no problem there. "What about the legs?" asked a Moroccan immigrant who wanted to learn more about his religion and help guide his French Canadian convert wife. "Does she have to shave her legs?" "No," said the Imam; "we like our women natural." (Speak for yourself, *shaykh*: I like legs that are long, sexy, and smooth. You can keep the short, stubby, hairy legs for yourself.) "What about the eyebrows," he continued, "can women pluck them?" "No," said the *shaykh*, "that is *haram*." At this point, things were getting scary for me: hairy-legged women with unibrows. After all, maybe a Western girl was more suitable. I would pass on these followers of Frida Kahlo.

Although the "New Muslim Class" was taught by a Western convert who had completed a Bachelor's degree in Islamic Studies at the University of Medina in Saudi Arabia, he addressed the most unusual of issues. In our class on *taharah* or ritual purity, he tackled the topic of *mani*, the Arabic term for semen or sperm. To my dismay, I learned that some Muslims jurists believed that both men and women produced sperm and that it was the mixture of male and female semen that created the child. How such idiotic, outdated, unscientific nonsense could be taught to anyone in the twentieth century was beyond me. While I hate to be the bearer of bad news, if these Muslim authorities were intimately familiar with women who ejaculated semen, then they were most certainly sleeping with transsexuals. I suppose that such things can happen when one has sex in the dark through a holey sheet. If you turn on the light and tear off the sheet, you might just well scream: "holy shit!"

What stunned me the most, however, was the theory of "suspended sperm" in which the semen of the man and the "semen" of the woman remained in suspended animation, potentially for years! For the Hanafis, the maximum gestation period was of two years. It was four for the Shafiis and the Hanbalis while it ranged from five to seven for the Malikis. In other words, any child born to a woman two, four, five, or even seven years after sexual intercourse with her husband is considered legitimate. This is the case even if the woman was divorced or widowed during all the years in question.

Considering that they were issued in the 8th and 9th century, when scholars and scientists had a very rudimentary understanding of the birds and the bees, these rulings were reasonable and erred on the side of caution. What I found most shocking was that such edicts were being treated as fact and a fundamental part of Islamic law in the 20th century. In fact, they continue to form part of the legal system in many Muslim nations to this very day. Imagine the following scenario. A Muslim man divorces his wife. The divorced woman does not remarry. Two years later she gives birth. According to archaic Muslim courts of law, the former husband of the woman would be treated as the father of the child with all the financial responsibilities that such a status entails. This would also be the case with a married man who was traveling or living abroad for a few years and never had sex with his wife during that period.

On a similar note, I remember another case that defies logic. The wife of a Muslim man gave birth. The father had a paternity test conducted on the child. The result was negative. The man was not the father of the child. Understandably, the man wanted a divorce. His request, however, was denied by a Muslim jurist on the grounds that "Paternity tests are not proof of adultery in Islamic law. Adultery is only proven by the presence of four witnesses to the act." So, not only was the cuckold stuck with his adulterous wife, he was stuck with a bastard son as a bonus: a constant reminder of her infidelity. Who says that "Islam" oppresses women? On the contrary, some of its schools of jurisprudence give them the green light to get inseminated by men other than their husbands.

Yes, the mosque was a great place, a place devoid of logic and reason, a place where we were taught about *taharah* or ritual purity while the washrooms were dirty, disgusting, devoid of toilet paper, and, of course, lacking soap or sanitizer. The principles of purity we were taught stood in sharp contrast to the filthy condition of the restrooms I found in most of the mosques that I attended at the time. In fact, it was virtually impossible not to become contaminated with a ritual impurity in such settings. I remember a time when a small child was caught playing in the toilet. His mother said: "I need to give him *ghusl*," namely, a ritual bath. The Imam inquired: "Was there any urine or feces in the toilet?" The Muslim sister responded that there was not. "In that case," clarified the Maulana, "the water was not ritually impure." Ah, what exacting standards of hygiene!

"It is *haram* to urinate while standing up" we were taught in our *taharah* class. We were commanded to sit, even on filthy public toilets. Believe it or not, it was prohibited, and a sin, to stand while urinating. Even in downtown Toronto, in the middle of the night, one was expected to take off one's pants, crouch down, and do one's duty in a sitting position. Relieving oneself against a wall or a tree was not within the realm of the permissible even if this caused some unfortunate and embarrassing accidents from time to time. Not only could one get arrested for urinating in public, one could get charged with indecent exposure for inadvertently flashing one's posterior to passers-by. Pants have zippers. They were made for a purpose. It is plenty for men to face a wall. Please do not give us a moony in the process.

One Trinidadian brother took these totalitarian toilet teachings a tad bit too far during Eid prayers in Brampton, Ontario, when he attempted to act as the potty police. While in the washroom doing *wudhu* or ritual ablutions, he noticed a young boy, around ten years of age, take a stand at the urinal. Motivated by his desire to teach proper Islamic practice, he told the boy: "Brother, brother... We are Muslims... This is not how we urinate... Let me explain to you..." By God, the kid ran out of the bathroom, remembering the lessons that he learned from his parents about dirty old men in public bathrooms, and fled for safety from this bearded nutcase who wanted to teach him how to pee properly.

Speaking of *wudhu*, it was essentially impossible to keep it as everything appeared to break it. While urinating, defecating, passing wind, or sleeping, were reasonable causes to nullify the state of minor ritual purity, my fundamentalist friends taught me that it was also broken by touching one's private parts, by touching a woman, by having impure thoughts or by getting sexually excited. No wonder I met a Palestinian man who had only started to pray at the age of thirty-five: "Brother," he confessed, "I simply could not keep my *wudhu*. As a teenager, and a young man, I would drip like a leaky faucet. Once, a sexy woman sat next to me in cab. Not only did I lose *wudhu*, I lost my *ghusl*!"

Not only were some of the pseudo-Muslims I met completely and totally insane from a psychological standpoint, they competed with each other in religious extremism. One Jordanian-Palestinian insisted on wearing cotton robes, a fez, and sandals in Canadian winters. Apparently, so-called Islamic dress was obligatory even on the snow-covered streets of Toronto. I came across many cultural Muslims and converts who believed that it was obligatory to wear pseudo-Islamic clothing, namely, Saudi or Pakistani style garb, none of which the Prophet himself had ever worn. Eat only with your hands, we were instructed (even among non-Muslims and even in public restaurants). What scenes my friends must have made.

One French Canadian convert was such a fanatical literalist that he insisted that the Arabic word used in a hadith was not "shave" the armpits, but "pluck" them. (Since he spoke no Arabic, I wonder how he came to this conclusion). I once went to visit him and found him, with pious tears in his eyes, zealously plucking his underarm hair with tweezers. I met one brother who insisted that it was *haram* or prohibited to trim one's beard. "The Prophet said, 'Grow your beard, and trim your mustache'" he pontificated, with his ragged, crazy beard, reaching down to his groin. "He never said to trim the beard," he insisted. "Yes," I responded, "but the Companions of the Prophet used to grab their beards with their hands, and trim the excess." This merely infuriated him: "That is the *Sunnah* or practice of the *Sahabas* or Companions! Not the *Sunnah* of *Rasul Allah*, the Messenger of God!" he responded, implying that even the Companions had failed to follow the example of the Prophet.

Yes, we were taught some *'aqidah* or beliefs. However, I eventually realized that our Imams were not teaching any of the traditional creeds of the Sunnis. They were teaching the *Tawhid* of Muhammad ibn 'Abd al-Wahhab, the founder of Wahhabism, and one of the greatest innovator in the history of Islam. They claimed that they were teaching us "true Islam" and "pure Islam" and that the Islam practiced by Muslims around the world was filled with falsehood, innovations, superstition, and polytheism. Consequently, we were not permitted to follow schools of jurisprudence; rather, we were only allowed to directly follow the Qur'an and Sunnah, namely, the deviant, literal, interpretations of the Wahhabis. This, in reality, was also a form of following. While they objected to *taqlid* or following jurists, they themselves were doing the *taqlid* of Muhammad ibn 'Abd al-Wahhab.

When I showed the Imam a copy of the Qur'an that I was reading, he objected, claiming that the translator was a Shiite. He was not. However, since Hashim Amir Ali was Iranian, he was duly dismissed as a religious deviant. The Imam perused the Qur'an and exclaimed: "Ha! This is a Shiite Quran. It is missing *Surah al-Khilafah* in which God appoints Abu

Bakr as the Caliph." The Imam was not an idiot; he was telling a bold-face lie in his paranoid fear that I might stray into Shiism. It was people like him, who alleged that the Shiites had a different Quran, who were ascribing lies to Allah. Although I have heard many ignorant Sunni Muslims make this claim, the appointment of Abu Bakr, 'Umar, 'Uthman, and 'Ali, as the four-rightly guided successors, is not found anywhere in the Qur'an.

Rather than teach proper beliefs, etiquette, morals, and ethics, as well as supplications and spirituality, my Muslim mentors focused on the most bizarre of things. "Farting pleases the devil," taught the Prophet. Following this prohibition could lead to death by intestinal explosion (and it almost did). I was quite literally relieved to violate this idiotic injunction after a week of rectal repression. Understandably, I have feared praying behind lines of menacing Wahhabi buttocks ever since. At times, I suspect that such gas is the source of many suicide bombings. I can imagine taco-eating terrorists stuffing themselves with refried beans and heading off on martyrdom operations: armed only with a lighter and twisted intestines overloaded with methane. Wahhabis have no need for dirty bombs or chemical weapons: they can basically blow away any infidels by simply bending over. How could I ever have imagined that the freedom to flatulate, a liberty that most take for granted (at least in private), was an act of defiance against Wahhabi extremism?

My Salafi-Jihadi friends also taught me that "Yawning pleases Satan." While I briefly and stupidly tried to suppress my yawns in their presence, since they would scold me for doing so, I soon learned from a psychology textbook that the only people who do not yawn are those who are mentally ill as these brothers most certainly were. I once took a drive with a Latin American convert and my heart skipped a beat when he ran a red light. When he did it a second time, I knew this was not an accident. "What the hell are you doing?" I shouted, fearing for my life. "Only Allah has the right to make laws," he replied. This man was on a mission: a mission to break all man-made laws. He was a Salafi scofflaw!

I was once in downtown Toronto when a man ran through the mosque. He had attempted to run away from a taxi without paying the fare and had tragically sought refuge in what he thought was a church. Unfortunately for him, the church had actually been converted into a mosque and was filled with other Somali taxi-drivers who proceeded to give the man a beat-down on grounds that he had entered without taking off his shoes. What image of Islam did these Salafis portray? It reminded me of the time when a man entered the mosque of the Prophet and urinated on the ground. Some Companions got up, sword in hand, with the intention of killing him. The Prophet grabbed one of them by the arm and said "Get a bucket of water, clean it, and ask the man to come see me." The Arabs were stunned. They did as they were instructed, cleaned the spot, and then asked the man to speak with the Prophet. The Messenger of Allah explained to him that this was a place of prayer and that it was not proper to urinate in it. This was the method of the Prophet.

The mosques I used to attend where patrolled by Salafi S.S. officers always on the lookout for any *haram*, *bid'ah* or *shirk* [prohibition, innovation or polytheism]. I was walking in the mosque when I was surrounded by three Somali thugs saying "*Haram*! *Haram*! *Haram*!" while pointing to the hole in my jeans. "*Haram*! You cannot show you knee!" By his tone, it was clear that I had deeply offended this vigilante of virtue. God forbid that the thought of my knee had aroused him. I lifted my leg, pulled apart the hole, and showed the Wahhabi Gestapo that I was wearing long-johns underneath. It was Canada and it was winter after all. They smiled, nodded their heads, and went on their merry way to "promote the good and forbid the wrong" or, to be precise, to harass and intimidate others "in the path of Allah."

I was also confronted with religious extortionists who were always out to scam people and take advantage of them. One asked me for a drive to a certain part of town. I politely declined explaining that I lived in the other direction and that it would make my return trip two hours long rather than one. "I am sorry," he snarled, "I thought you were a Muslim." Such cases of "religious blackmail" were quite common. I succumbed a few times to their scams, but soon steered clear from these con-artists. I found the same sort of dishonesty among some cultural Muslim vendors: people who would set aside the freshest meat for their friends, relatives, and countrymen, while selling putrid poultry to some poor African immigrants.

Once, I had the misfortune of being in the mosque when some *mujahidin* from Afghanistan, you know, those CIA agents who spawned al-Qaedah, were visiting Toronto in order to collect funds for their fake jihad. All of a sudden, I was surrounded by four angry Afghans, who pointed at my fuzzy and furry hat, saying "Russian?!" By the look in their evil eyes, they were ready to kill me on the spot and ask questions later. "Canadian," I affirmed, "This is a Canadian hat." By then, of course, I had long lost any "romantic" notion of the jihad in Afghanistan. I had learned from actual Afghans that these so-called *mujahidin* would rob, steal, extort, rape, and traffic in opium. Last time I checked, none of these actions were virtues. What is more, I could not help but notice that these foreign jihadists were able to travel and circulate freely in the Western world. Not only were their activities facilitated by secret service agents from the CIA and CSIS, these terrorists were protected by the RCMP and the FBI. These people were not fighting for Islam and Muslims. They were serving Western interests.

Violence was not only being exported, it was also being imported. When one brother was accused by his nieces of fondling them, I was told to keep quiet about it. As the Imam explained, the punishment the man merited was a beating; however, the Somalis and the Arabs, he warned, did not beat people up: they killed people. When this Imam was terminated by the Saudis, a gathering was held in the house of an influential Arab elder who acted like a mob boss. "Just give me the names of the people who did this to you," offered this burly, middle-aged Arab, "and I will kill them for you." The Imam tactfully declined the offer as he eyed me with unease. As he told me, in confidence, afterwards, he did not want to have anyone's death on his conscience. Offers of mafia-style hits, family feuds, ethnic and religious conflict... Sometimes I wondered whether I was really in Canada. This felt like Afghanistan or the Lebanese Civil War.

So-called jihadists attempted to recruit me. Some of my so-called Muslim brothers enlisted and went off to wage "holy" war in Afghanistan. Some returned, and others, did not. As for those who remained behind, I received word that they had met in secret to discuss targeting the publisher of the infamous Salman Rushdie book in Canada. Within a question of years, I had witnessed first-hand how certain foreign leaders used converts as a cover to raise funds for armed jihadist groups abroad. I was astounded to see that there was never more than two degrees of separation between me and a terrorist operative. All I had to do was mention to one brother that I was interested in joining the jihad, be it in Afghanistan, Bosnia, the Philippines, or elsewhere, and I would be contacted by a facilitator who would take care of everything. At the time I had been musing about studying Islam in Arabia, Malaysia, or elsewhere, and found that it was easier to become a jihadist than to get a scholarship to study abroad. Although it was kept under the radar, many mosques were actually operated by the Muslim Brotherhood. A large number were also under the direct or indirect influence of Saudi Arabia. The United States, Saudi Arabia, and foreign Islamist groups were all fueling the mosque to jihad pipeline, recruiting cultural Muslims and converts to serve their geopolitical agenda.

As much as I stood by the oppressed of the earth in their struggle against tyranny, and as socially committed and conscious as I may have been, I was sickened to see that so many "Muslims" supported suicide bombings aimed at civilians and the slaughter of non-combatants. At the time, I was very active with solidarity groups that supported Latin American liberation struggles. Whether they were Cubans, Nicaraguans, Guatemalans or Salvadorians, the freedom fighters I frequented, many of whom were Socialists and Communists, seemed to have superior ethics and morals than any of the Islamist-Jihadists that I had encountered. For these guerrilla groups, killing civilians, and sexually assaulting women, were crimes punishable by death. For Islamist terrorists, there was no limit to the evil and atrocities they would commit. I knew it then and I know it now. And there was not limit to their sheer stupidity. I once had a conversation about suicide bombings or "martyrdom operations" with an educated middle-aged Muslim convert who reasoned that it was perfectly Islamic to drive a dynamite-laden bus into a civilian target or even to crash planes into office buildings as was done on September 11th, 2001. "It is a war crime to target civilians," I explained, "the only legitimate target is a military one." "What?" he objected, "Do you expect us to attack a military base? That would be suicide!" Let the reader ponder upon that irony. Killing oneself to kill civilians was rational; however, killing oneself to kill combatants was irrational.

As a result of attending mosques and Islamic events, I came to realize that certain so-called Muslim charities were simply fronts for terrorist rackets. "Help a poor Muslim family buy a lamb for Eid" really meant "Help us buy some AK-47s so we can kill that very family" while "Charity for Palestine" translated into suicide bombings aimed at civilian targets. I myself was personally involved in raising funds for "humanitarian aid" to Bosnia. The event ended in an arms auction with the speaker, a local dentist, calling out: "Who will donate five hundred dollars for an Uzi? Six hundred? Can I get six hundred?" I had met the Turkish terrorist who acted as a sub-commander in the Bosnian army. "The only language that the Serbs understand," he yelled in his speech, "is the language of slaughter!" While many concerned Muslims of the world supported the jihad in Bosnia, few of them knew that the combatants they were supporting were little better than the Serbian chetniks. They were jihadists who raped women, sold them into sexual slavery, and who slaughtered civilians. They were people who funded their global jihad by means of the drug trade. "Anything that harms your enemy," explained a Lebanese lunatic, "is permissible in jihad." I had no problem, in theory or law, with soldiers killing soldiers. I had a grave and serious problem, however, with calls to massacre civilian populations. It was unconscionable. If this international Turkish terrorist and jihadist wanted to fill mass graves with Serbian Christian civilians, how were we, as Muslims, any better than the war criminals who filled mass graves with

Bosnian Muslim civilians? I did what I could only do: I walked out of that fundraiser and refused to return to that Islamic center ever again. In fact, I broke all ties with the parties involved in organizing the event.

While I met with real terrorists, was given tapes of lectures by Abdullah Azzam, the ideological mentor of Osama bin Laden, who visited mosques in over fifty cities in the US and Canada, and watched videos produced by the murderous *mujahidin* of Afghanistan, in which they executed their own combatants on allegations of espionage, without any proof or witnesses being produced, I also came across some comic-book jihadists.

For a time, I attended an infamous *halaqah* or study circle which should really have been called the *hala*-cult. These brothers used to gather in the forests of northern Ontario to train for holy war. There, in the backwoods of Canada, they would learn to ride horses, fight with swords, and use bows and arrows. When asked why they did not learn how to handle guns, and drive tanks, they responded with pious disdain: "They are prohibited innovations." These brain-damaged religious lunatics believed that Almighty Allah would miraculously grant them victory over their infidel enemies in battle. If only they had faith, they fervently believed, their arrows would turn into bombs and they would defeat the most advanced military technology. Rather than oppose extremism, perhaps we should promote such fanaticism, defusing the danger posed by such "radical Islamists." We could even rename them "ridiculous Islamists."

Although these intellectually-impaired Islamists were not particularly violent, they were subversives with a grandiose scheme to Islamize Canada. The leaders of the *hala*-cult pressured their followers to abandon their worldly affairs, and relocate to a small-town in rural Ontario. Gradually, thanks to *hijrah* or migration, and ample procreation (you need to do something while on welfare), they would become the majority in the small town. They would then run for all political positions, take over city hall, and impose sharia law on the infidel minority. Eventually, if they were patient, and their child-bearing women produced children on a regular basis, they would spread from town to town, city to city, and province to province, finally attaining their glorious goal of turning Canada into a Caliphate. If these people were so eager to live under "Islamic" law, why did they not just move to some terrorist hell-hole? Leave Canada for the Canadians. And by that, I include Canadian Muslims. Canada may be the second largest country in the world, but we have no place for violent fanatics and fundamentalists of any ilk.

It was only by miracle that I escaped these green-necks in their derelict cult compound in Canada where one false step would send you plunging through the floor and into the dark basement of doom. For some reason, the transmission on my vehicle sustained damage and I could no longer reverse. The mini-van could only move forward. (Suddenly, I suspect that it may have been sabotage. Maybe it was. Maybe it was not. However, who could blame me for being paranoid at this point?). As can be imagined, being stranded on a homestead surrounded by forests was not an ideal situation. I asked one of the leaders of this "new religious movement" (the politically-correct term for "cult") if he could help me out as I knew there was a mechanic among their members. "Now, brother," he grinned, "you should know that our mechanic only fixes the cars of those who are members of the *halaqah*." In other words, "unless you join our cult, you can count on remaining stranded in the boonies more than three and a half hours away from the city." I jumped in my van, and managed to make it out of the abandoned homestead, even though I could only drive directly and had to make some mad manoeuvers. With friends like these pseudo-Muslim brothers, who needs enemies? Hey, man, nobody ever threatened to kill me in church. Only Muslims have issued death threats.

There was no limit to the madness I encountered. I knew one young woman, who had left Islam, and then returned to Islam again, and asked her what had caused her to abandon the Muslim faith. She confided in me that the first thing that she was taught by some bald-headed Imam in California was that toilet paper was *haram*. Yes, toilet paper was *haram* and *bid'ah*. It was both a prohibition and an innovation. "You must clean yourself with your left hand and water," he explained, ignoring, obviously, that the Arabs used to wipe themselves with leaves, sand, or smooth stones, prior to rinsing themselves with water, the logical equivalent of toilet paper. Apparently, even soap was a sin. This poor sister attempted for a time to wipe the feces off her backside with her hand but quickly came to the conclusion that "Islam" was a really ridiculous religion. She was quite literally sick of all the crap. Eventually, she found her way back to Islam, and away from Islam, once again, due to a whole host of reasons. Like many, she was attracted to the theory of Islam. However, she could not deal with the reality of Islam. "If this is Islam," many have concluded, "then we do not want to have anything to do with it." Others, however, remained devoted Muslims, understanding that the problem was not Islam as a whole but merely a small set of psychotic pseudo-Muslims who were in dire need of some serious psychiatric treatment, if not straight-jackets and padded walls.

Continuing with my crazy but entirely accurate accounts, I once found myself in a mosque, where I was focusing attentively on my ritual prayer.

Suddenly, and unexpectedly, I felt a tap on my head, which startled and distracted me. I did not, however, break my prayer. I felt my head, and found that someone had plopped a kufi on it. After I completed my prayer, I looked behind me and saw on old man. He waved his finger and said: "It is *wajib* to cover your head in *salat*;" in plain English, "It is a religious obligation to cover your head during the five daily ritual prayers." In actuality, it is sunnah or *mustahab* according to some schools of jurisprudence; namely, it is a recommended practice of the Prophet; but it is certainly not advisable to slap a hat on a person's head while in prayer.

On another occasion, I came across a fellow convert who reeked of body odor with a hint of cheap perfume. "Deodorant is *haram*," he said proudly, "The Prophet never wore deodorant." "Yes," I responded, "but his sweat used to smell like musk and you smell like a horse." Perhaps it was a sin to say this. Hence, I ask all horses for forgiveness. I have met many a horse, but none that smelled as foul as this Afro-Canadian convert. Ah, but who am I to judge? This young hustler was always surrounded by sexy white temporary wives. Perhaps his stench was magnetic to women of loose morals or, should I say, women who were open to learning about Islam.

As for my French Canadian friend, who had ironically lost his French, making him a former French Canadian or a new Anglo Canadian, I once saw him wearing a white abaya with a thick layer of eye-liner. "*Kuhl* is *Sunnah*," he said. With his beautiful blonde hair, his green eyes, and his white dress, he looked like a pretty girl (had it not been for that beard!). "Brother," I told him, "you look like a transvestite." I suppose I understand why I lost so many of my Muslim friends. It seems that I may have offended a few of them. Ah, well, what can I say? Perhaps, good-bye and good riddance.

Yes, these were the type of people that I used to frequent. "According to Islam," I asked a Jordanian-Palestinian engineer, "how should one discipline children." "Beat them," he stated. "And how should one handle problems with one's wife," I inquired. "Slap her across the face," he sternly responded. "Women often need to be hit," he reasoned. It was bad enough that domestic violence posed a problem in the Muslim community, as in all other communities, it was another thing altogether to see that it was justified culturally, religiously, and theologically. "Canada is a multicultural country," said one misogynistic Somali Salafi, "We have the right to keep our culture and in our culture we beat women." I thought of the Prophet's words, "I wonder about a man who beats his wife, while he himself deserves to be beaten more." The Imams were no better. In most cases, when a woman had the courage to come forward and complain that her husband was beating her, the cultural Muslim clerics would say one of two things: "It is his right;" or "Be patient, sister." Some even went so far as to say that "a man may only beat his wife with a small stick." Some consolation. Others were not so apologetic. When a brother I knew asked a Maulana what to do about his unfaithful wife, he reportedly responded: "Beat her up and divorce her!" "Why not just divorce her?" I thought to myself. Was I the only sane person in these surroundings?

I was once invited to speak with a Latina who was interested in Islam. The young woman in question was a single mother. She was renting a room in the home of an East Indian family and they had been introducing her to Islam. I arrived at her home and we discussed religion for quite some time. I figured we were making progress. However, one of her questions stopped me dead in my tracks: "What does Islam say about domestic violence?" "Why?" I asked, fearing what was to follow. "Well, brother so-and-so beats his wife. He beats her bad. He even slapped me once because of something I said." When she approached the Pakistani wife in private, trying to offer her support, she scorned her. "What? Did you leave the father of your child simply because he hit you? All men hit their wives. It's their right." How, on earth, could I try to bring this Hispanic sister into Islam when Muslims like this were the example. From a social stand-point, these cultural communities were generations behind the Western world. Women's rights, human rights, civil rights, workers' rights… you name it: these are problems we addressed and resolved decades ago and sometimes centuries ago. Bringing cultural Muslims from Medieval times to Modernity was not my battle.

Women were always a problem with the people I dealt with. While many mosques would not even allow women to enter, or granted them a dirty closet in the basement, one of the mosques I attended had a small, second floor section for women, a type of balcony at the back, where women could pray. While I was sitting in the Imam's office one day, a furious man entered fuming, crying *"Fitnah!"* a term that means temptation, trial, sedition and strife. *"Fitnah,"* he said, "this is *fitnah!"* "What's the problem?" asked the Imam who attempted to appease him. "I can see women," the man answered with anguish and despair. "I see women…" It reminds me of *The Sixth Sense* (1999), that film with Bruce Willis: "I see dead people." This man from the Maghreb saw a woman in full *hijab* performing prayers at a mosque. Can you imagine the horror? How did this man cope in everyday life? I suppose it was the fault of the wicked women who should really be at home, barefoot and pregnant, as it was *haram* for women to go to school, to go to work, or to leave their household without a male guardian. I even heard one Algerian Islamist assert that women could only leave their homes three times: the day of their birth, the day of their marriage, and the day of their burial. These people were not just at war with the West: they were at war with women. Misogyny was a fundamental part of their ideology.

When the French were attempting to ban *hijab* in schools, I approached a Lebanese *shaykh* in an attempt to organize Muslims. In my mind, we had to stand up for our Muslim sisters and pressure the French government to respect basic human rights. "What's the point?" said the scholar, "Education is not important for women." For him, wearing hijab was more important than education. His solution? Have Muslim girls drop-out of school and stay at home. Far too many grown women, educated women, are subjected to being minors for life in a free, Western country. I even knew one African American brother who refused to allow his wife to answer the phone as her voice was *awrah*, namely, a pudendum. (If anything, he was the private part). He would not even allow her to greet guests. She had to remain confined. Such women were better off outside of Islam or, to be more accurate, outside of this mockery of Islam.

Time and again, I witnessed women being mistreated, scolded, and shunned both in public and private. Far too often did I bite my tongue and fail to stand up for my Muslim sisters. I was at a man's home when he gave his children their allowance. The boys, who were around ten years of age, received twenty dollars while the only daughter, who was about fifteen, only received ten. "And if there be only one daughter, her share shall be half" (4:11), recited the sexist Arab, as his sons mocked and teased their older sister. I knew full well that the verse applied to inheritance and that it was limited to a certain time and a certain place. It certainly did not apply to allowance and it certainly was not an all-encompassing injunction. It was certainly not binding nor did it have any bearing in 20th century Canada. Like many, the man used and abused Qur'anic verses and Hadith to dominate and humiliate the women in his domestic domain. I was outraged and appalled at this exploitation of Islam.

On a similar note, I once met a Muslim man from Morocco while I was in Barcelona, Spain, in the late 1980s. We met at the mosque. He invited me for lunch after which we went for a walk. Block after block, I could not help but notice that a woman was following us at a distance. I said, "Brother, I think we are being followed." "Ah, that's just my wife," he said, "She always follows ten paces behind me." And she was a Catalan convert to Islam; a Western, formerly liberated woman, who had fallen to such a level of dehumanization. I could not comprehend how a woman could go from being a first class to a second class person. This was like an

African American accepting to go back to segregation or a South African black rushing back to apartheid.

I know many women, both Muslim and non-Muslim, who were prohibited access to places of prayer or physically expelled from them. I entered a mosque once, in the company of a young Muslim woman, to cries of *"Haram! Haram!* No women are allowed!" Wild-eyed, bearded men in robes may have intimidated others; however, I stood my ground:

> This is Canada and what you are doing is against the law. It's a violation of the Canadian Charter of Rights and Freedoms. Furthermore, what you are doing is *haram*. The Prophet said: 'Do not forbid the female servants of Allah from praying in mosques.'

They ceded their ground. I had made my point. Either that or they were intimidated by my imposing stature. Sometimes one needs to look crazier than the crazies and one needs to "out-terrorize" the terrorists. I led *salat* or ritual prayers with the young Muslim woman behind me. If African Americans had sit-ins to demand their civil rights, Muslims need to organize pray-ins to demand the religious rights of women. This problem of sexual segregation and gender-based exclusion, which has no basis in Islam, is far from solved and continues to pester in both East and West. If women are denied their rights by certain ignorant or extremist Muslims, it not because of Islam, it is in spite of it.

If the lay Muslims left much to be desired, the Imams were not much better. One of my teachers, an American *shaykh*, left a female Canadian convert stranded in downtown Toronto at midnight. She had asked for a ride home from the mosque, for safety's sake. The wise Imam, however, told her that it was *haram* for a man to be alone with a non-*mahram* woman, namely a woman who did not belong to the category of unmarriageable kin, and that the sharia was the sharia. Yes, and I am sure that it was Islamic, and chivalrous, to abandon a young woman in an urban center late at night without even the availability of public transportation or a taxi. That was not your finest moment, *shaykh*; I hope you have repented. On another occasion, a French Canadian brother took the Muslim woman he we courting to an Islamic lecture at York University. He refused to sit beside her because it was *haram*. She shook her head, in dismay, and reasoned with him: "If you do not sit next to me, another man will do so." Even adult Muslim women could not have a private conversation with an Imam in his office. "When a man and a woman are alone together," said the Prophet, "Satan is the third." These people could not reason. The tradition clearly cautioned against the dangers of fornication and adultery. The prohibition logically applies to situations in which there is a real risk of sin. As if the Imam was going to commit adultery in the mosque office with a veiled woman!

I myself was stranded by another teacher of mine. I had made an appointment to ask him questions about creed and jurisprudence. It took me several hours by city bus to reach his office in an isolated industrial area in a neighboring town. When I arrived, he only spent five minutes with me. I asked him about slavery in Islam. He asserted that slavery was permissible and that nobody had the right to prohibit it. I asked him whether it was acceptable for a man to have sex with a slave girl. He insisted that it was. I asked him whether her consent was required. He said that it was not. "She is your property," he said with a grin, "you can do with her as you please." The meeting coincided with the First Gulf War, in which an American woman soldier had fallen into Iraqi hands. Nodding his head with a sly smile, he asserted that the Iraqi soldiers were entitled to use her for sexual satisfaction. Here was a man, who claimed to be a *shaykh*, and who had delusions of spiritual grandeur, claiming that Islam permitted sexual assault and gang rapes of prisoners. I was sick to my stomach. My soul was in open revolt. I had met pimps with higher ethical standards than this man.

After my five minutes were up, the Imam explained that he needed to drive his wife home because the baby was cold. He gave the front seat to a goofy Indian brother and a back-seat to his wife, where she sat holding her baby. Although there was a seat next to her, the *shaykh* refused to allow me to sit next to her, as that would have been *haram*. He left me stranded, late at night, in an industrial area, in a freezing cold and dark Canadian winter. (To think about it, there was a simple solution: he could have let me drive, and sat next to his wife in the back seat). God have mercy on the Imam's soul who abandoned me at the mercy of the elements. If this is the *adab* and the *akhlaq* of the so-called Sunni ulama, if these are the manners and ethics of Sunni scholars, then this explains the sad state of the Muslim Ummah or World Community. Such scholars, however, speak not for Islam. If anything, they dishonor it.

As much as I was inspired by the universality of Islam, having been moved to the core by the spiritual journey of Malcolm X, I was deeply disappointed to find a chasm between Islamic teachings on race and its practice. I soon saw and felt the enduring legacy of Arab arrogance, chauvinism, and tribalism, the conflict between Arabs and Persians, and the paternalistic attitude taken toward African Muslims. It seemed like every Indo-Pakistani mosque I visited had a black brother named Bilal who worked as a janitor. Whenever work needed to be done, such as staking chairs, mosque leaders would never ask their own people: they would invariably call upon my black convert friends. It was not even conscious. It appears to have been subconscious. Some of these wealthy Indians who had lived in Africa were so used to having black servants that they always saw blacks as subservient.

Not only did prejudice prevail among immigrants from the East, it was also dominant among converts from the West. Time and again, I witnessed the naked racism and discrimination of Afro-American, Afro-Caribbean, and Afro-Canadians towards Caucasian converts who were subjected to social segregation. Many of these blacks from the Americas were adamant that blacks should only marry blacks. So much for the "brotherhood" of Islam. One such character, who eventually became an Imam, told me straight out: "I want to establish a mosque for blacks." Where did that leave the rest of reverts? What is more, I also noted that some cultural Muslims marginalized converts and treated them as second-class citizens in the Ummah of Islam.

Yes, I met some really neat people, on my journey into Islam, brothers who insisted that "If you see a black dog, you must kill it." "That's against the law," I said, and "Islam says we have to obey the law." "You are right brother... We cannot kill it... but we can pick it up, bring it to the animal shelter, and if nobody adopts it, they will kill it! That way, we follow the Prophet and get the *barakah* or blessing for killing the *najis* or impure beast." I was also taught that demon possession was a reality and that people could vomit black puppies, marry demons, and unwittingly have semi-demonic half-breed children. How quaint! But Halloween, Easter, and Christmas were all *haram* as they were filled with pagan superstitions (which Westerners do not actually believe in). It was the cultural Muslims and the "radical Islamists," not the Westerners, who believed in magic, sorcery, and demonology. In fact, anyone who denied the reality of witchcraft and genies was considered an apostate.

According to any criteria, the award for the craziest Wahhabi I ever met goes to a Guyanese Muslim who was revered for having spent a whole two years of study at the Islamic University of Medina. "You must meet this brother," I was told, "he is so pious." Although his apartment was on the second floor, I could already smell something fishy: a faint odor of urine. The smell increased as we approached his apartment. By the time the door opened, the stench was overwhelming. The entire apartment was permeated with the smell of urine and feces. Compared to this domestic domain, an uncleaned chicken-coop smelled like the finest French perfume. As I saw this holy man's toddler, I realized that I had found the source of this foul stench: the child was diaperless! "Diapers are *haram* and *bid'ah*," the Wahhabi university drop-out decreed. Yes, even diapers were forbidden and a prohibited innovation.

The Arab Bedouins, and some Africans, did indeed allow their children to walk around without diapers. However, they live in dry, arid, sandy, and extremely hot regions, were urine is immediately absorbed into the earth or evaporates and where feces dry up and solidify in short order, only to be swept outside of the tent or hut with a broom. How a family could attempt to emulate such an example in an apartment in Canada was incomprehensible. I soon came to realize that there are some people who are criminally insane and that there are people who are religiously insane. The actions of this man were not philosophical; they were pathological. This man was so fanatical in his fundamentalism that I fear that even Muhammad ibn 'Abd al-Wahhab would have denounced him as a dangerous extremist.

Noticing that there was a huge void in the area of Islamic literature and music for children, I decided to address the issue. I received push back from people who insisted that drawing was prohibited in Islam. The greatest backlash came when I recorded a CD of Islamic songs for children. In order to satisfy my Wahhabi patrons, I had limited the soundtrack to drums and other percussion instruments. However, even this concession was insufficient as I soon started to receive ritualized curses sent by Salafi zealots. "Read the Qur'an, and you will find, Allah wants you to be kind, be kind..." Yes, recording such songs certainly deserved damnation and maledictions. The same happened to other brothers who produced Islamic videos for children. They suffered from a smear campaign that alleged that their products were part of a conspiracy to destroy Islam that was sponsored by Salman Rushdie himself!

It was my faith in Islam that led me to endure the torture and torment that I describe for cathartic purposes. It is not an experience I would ever repeat. That is not to say that I would not have embraced Islam. I had embraced Islam, well before meeting any so-called Muslims. I had learned Islam from God, via the Qur'an, and from the Prophet, via the Sunnah. I learned Islam from both primary and secondary sources. What I would never have done is make my Islam public. I would have kept it in my heart until I eventually found like-minded people. I would never have mingled with any of the mental-case pseudo-Muslims that I met. What I would have liked, what I would have loved, would have been to find some true, traditional Muslims, whether they were Sunnis, Shiis, or Sufis. I would have openly shared my Islam with them. I would have befriended them. I would have walked the spiritual path with them. Alas, Toronto, in the mid-1980s was devoid of traditional guides. My experience, however, was like baptism by fire and it still burns to this day.

Eventually, and in spite of the agony I endured, it took but a straw to break my back. Told over and over again that Shiites were *kafirs* or unbelievers, I actually went to a Shiite mosque and consulted with Shiite scholars in an attempt to acquire a correct comprehension of Shiism. I wanted a clear conscience. I wanted to know what they believed. I had not embraced Shiism; I was simply seeking answers. No sooner had the word spread in Sunni circles that I associated with Shiites that I was accused of being a Shiite myself. "I hear you have become a Shiite," claimed one of my so-called Muslim convert friends, "you know your blood is now *halal*." These were the last words or threats that I heard from anyone who claimed to be a Sunni.

As a result of rumors of my Shiism, I was warned not to return to the mosque I frequented as there were people intent on assassinating me. I broke all ties with so-called Sunnis and soon purchased two huge guard dogs for personal protection. "If we can't reach you," I was told through a second party, "rest assured that we can reach your family." Such were the Salafi-Wahhabi-Takfiri psychopaths with whom I had once socialized. It would take decades for me to set foot in a so-called Sunni mosque ever again and, only then, with utmost suspicion, and a fist of fury ready to knock the teeth out of any Takfiri terrorist.

I take Allah as my witness; I take Muhammad as my witness; I take the Qur'an as my witness: I came into Islam seeking Heaven and found nothing but Hell. And I am not alone. How many Muslim converts did I meet, who entered Islam, only to leave Islam as a result of the traumatizing experiences they had with Takfiri-Wahhabis who pretended to be Sunni Muslims. By the grace of God, I soon escaped from this house of horrors that was falsely presented as Islam and entered into true, traditional, Islam were I met many marvelous men and women. If only I could say the same for the rest of Muslim reverts...

Far too many people have fallen under the spell of the Salafis who employ sophisticated techniques to brainwash them, turning ordinary human beings, who sought to quench their spiritual thirst, into hate-filled bigots, rapists, and sadistic mass murderers. The enemy is not at the gate. The enemy has broken into the citadel. They have breached the barrier of true Islam. While these religious fundamentalists only represent a minute fraction of the Muslim community, most of whom are moderates, they pose a clear and present danger to Islam and humanity as a whole. Although people have no need to fear Islam and Muslims in general, as traditional Islam is tolerant and most Muslims are wonderful human beings who are worthy of respect and admiration, there are some so-called Muslims that they should fear. When it comes to Salafi-Wahhabi-Takfiris, hear my words and hear them well: be afraid, be very afraid.

As morose and gloomy as my recollections may be, they are totally truthful. I may have modified names, merged characters, and modified the chronology; however, the facts are entirely accurate. Such changes were required to protect all parties: both innocent and guilty. However, before hurling epithets and casting imprecations at me for my honesty, let me reiterate, once again, that the target of my condemnation is not the Islamic community as a whole but merely a small fraction of mendacious Muslims who ascribe to extremist ideology.

For the record, the evil I faced among this fringe group of pseudo-Muslim zealots was nothing compared to the moral depravity I witnessed among the so-called Christians, Jews, and secular liberals that I came across during my teenage years. To a large extent, it was the immorality that saturates Western society that helped propel me into the orbit of Islam. By the time I was sixteen, I had been exposed to every evil imaginable. From alcohol and drug abuse to fornication and adultery, I saw it all and rejected it all. It was only by the mercy of the Most Merciful that I was protected from major sins. I credit the Roman Catholic Church and the Bible for cultivating my faith and providing me with a sound moral and ethical foundation.

Unfortunately for me, many of the first quasi-Muslims that I met were actually morally corrupt militants who belonged in mental institutions for the criminally and morally insane. Compare it to converting to Christianity only to be targeted for indoctrination and brainwashing by white-supremacist, fundamentalist, militias. Compare it to a peaceful Californian hippy converting to Hinduism only to fall into the hands of extremist organizations like RSS, BJP and VHP. Compare it to embracing Judaism only to fall into the grip of the Stern Gang, the Haganah, the Irgun or the Jewish Defense League. Compare it to seeking solace in Buddhism, only to be surrounded by the murderers from the 969 movement. I was attracted to the beauty of Islam and came full face with the most gruesome of imposters. I sought the scent of a rose and sniffed nothing but the most nauseating, vomit-inducing, stench imaginable.

Some may say that these memoirs will do more harm than good. Some may say that they will only fuel Islamophobia. However, such people are short of understanding. They have no experiential knowledge. They lack empathy and vision. They have never stared evil in the face. I love Islam and I love Muslims. However, I hate Takfiri-Wahhabi terrorists, along with all other extremists. There are religious extremists in any community. There are Shiite Takfiris just as there are Sunni Takfiris. There are Christian extremists just like there are Jewish extremists. There are Hindu extremists just like there are Buddhist extremists. Terrorism knows no religion. Ultimately, whether it is Islam, Christianity, Judaism, Hinduism or Buddhism, religious fundamentalism is the real enemy of people of faith. They take something that is inherently good, religion, and turn it into something utterly evil.

Since the mid-1980s, much water has passed beneath the bridge. I have met, mingled with, and befriended, Muslims all over the world. I have visited Muslim communities in Canada, the United States, Morocco, Spain, France, Belgium, The Netherlands, the United Kingdom, Ghana, South Africa, Mauritius, India, Malaysia, Japan, and the United Arab Emirates. While I did have some negative experiences during my journeys, as is inevitable when dealing with human beings, my dealings with the Muslims of the world have been predominantly positive. Muslims may face difficult challenges. They may have shortcomings. However, there is an overwhelming amount of good that emanates from Islam and Muslims.

I may have met some moderate people during the first few years after I embraced Islam; however, the negative elements ruined the experience for me. As studies have shown, Muslim converts are prime targets for terrorists. Had it not been for God, I could have ended up as a jihadist somewhere. After I embraced Islam, my sister asked me: "Have you joined a cult?" I said that I had not. However, this was a half-truth. Some so-called Muslims were attempting to radicalize me. Although they succeeded in damaging me to various degrees, I resisted their indoctrination and repudiated them vehemently. In the tragic case of many confused converts, however, they do indeed join a cult, a Takfiri-Jihadi-Salafi cult.

For those who call upon Muslims to clean up their mosques, let them know that the soul-sucking cannibals in question rarely, if ever, attend mosques in Canada and the United States; they left after 9/11. They were no longer tolerated by the moderate majority. Now, they recruit mostly on the internet. They do not meet in mosques as they did before. They gather in secret and in private. However, they are still out there, and continue to pose a grave danger. I wish to warn Muslims and non-Muslims of a very real peril. There is a mortal disease in the Muslim community and it needs to be diagnosed. The epicenter of the pandemic has already been identified: it is Saudi Arabia. The Saudis are responsible for the spread of Wahhabi extremism. Even the moderate Salafism that is taught in some mosques is just a gate-way drug. It eventually leads some susceptible subjects to become hard-core Takfiri terrorists. Murder and mayhem simply represent the lethal stage of the extremist disease. If we have diagnosed the disease, we need to administer its antidote. We need to inoculate our children against the ravages of religious or, better yet, irreligious fundamentalism. The only cure to "Radical Islam" is Traditional Islam. The only cure to an "Islam of Hatred" is an Islam of Love. I call upon all concerned parties to join us in our struggle to save the heart of Islam. If we fail to act, the immune system of the Ummah may become overwhelmed in which case, not only Muslims, but Islam itself may succumb to the Salafi-Jihadi scourge.

Chapter Thirty-Seven

Hope?

When I embraced Islam in the mid-80s, I came across some seriously shady characters. Many of the mosques that I attended at the time were under the overt influence of Salafi and Wahhabi extremists and jihadists, a situation I found deeply disturbing and disconcerting. Although they professed to follow *Ahl al-Sunnah*, I soon came to realize that the people I frequented were Takfiris, modern-day Kharijites and Nasibis, who spewed hatred like active volcanoes spew lava. I do not, however, wish to give the impression that my experiences were entirely negative. I did meet some decent human beings and I did learn a great deal during those early days. Invariably, it takes only a drop of vinegar to make milk go sour. In my case, I was essentially doused in vinegar, leaving me with a bitter taste that continues to linger decades after the fact.

Like many Western Muslims, I gradually extricated myself from the Muslim community which reminded me more of the *dar al-fitnah*, the House of Discord, than *dar al-islam*, the House of Peace, Submission, and Surrender. While it may surprise many people, there are, I would estimate, hundreds, thousands, and even tens of thousands of Western Muslim intellectuals who are devout, practicing Muslims, and scholars of Islam, but who rarely, if ever, attend mosques. On the contrary, they prefer to maintain a low profile and avoid soiling their souls with all the political and cultural problems that suck the spirituality out of many mosques. For about fifteen to twenty years, I lived in virtual isolation, making rare appearances at unexpected locations around the word: giving sporadic *khutbahs* or sermons at mosques in Minneapolis, Toronto, Cape Town, and Chennai. Otherwise, I immersed myself in study, scholarship, research, writing, and communion with Allah and His Creation.

It was in 2013 that I received an email from Nazim Baksh, a producer from the CBC, asking me to be a guest of honor at a dinner celebrating scholars of Islam at the Reviving the Islamic Spirit Conference in Toronto, Canada, and where arrangements had been met for me to meet with other scholars, such as Shaykh Hamza Yusuf, Shaykh Zaid Shakir, Dr. John Esposito, Dr. Jamal Badawi, Shaykh Abdalla Idris, Seyyed Hossein Nasr,

Shaykh Abdul-Karim Yahya and, most notably, al-Shaykh al-Habib 'Ali al-Jifri. Although time had stood still for the past fifteen to twenty years since I left the Muslim community in Toronto, the terrible experiences I endured remained vivid in my imagination; hence, it was with some reticence, and no shortage of anxiety, that I made it to the conference. To be succinct, I was simply dazzled, dazed, and amazed.

Muslims, unfortunately, are infamous for being poorly organized. The RIS conference operated smoothly and efficiently. The conference, which is attended by tens of thousands of people, had hundreds of volunteers all meticulously dressed in suits. The professionalism was unparalleled. The technology was cutting edge. And the speakers were awe-inspiring. What had happened? Twenty years had happened. A new generation of Muslims, those who were born or raised in the West, were now running the show and taking control of their communities. These young people, as it appeared to me, had embraced what was best from their cultures, and rejected what was unbefitting of Islam. Likewise, they had embraced what was positive from Western culture, and had rejected what was objectionable. For the first time in decades, I felt renewed hope for the future of the Muslim community in the West.

As a result of my networking at the Reviving the Islamic Spirit conference in Toronto, I soon received an invitation to speak at the 40th Annual ISNA Convention in Canada. To accept or not to accept that was the question. "It's a set-up," warned a political advisor. "If you go, whatever you do, do not drink or eat anything they give you. They might give you some plutonium to kill you like the CIA did with Chávez in Venezuela." "It's a double-standard," said a spiritual advisor, "these are the same people who support Takfiri terrorists in Syria and Iraq." After a great deal of debate, discussion, and dialogue, it was concluded that I should attend but remain vigilant and alert.

I arrived in Toronto as apprehensive as ever. I was picked up by a charming young brother, all professionally attired, at the Lester B. Pearson International Airport. I was taken to my hotel and learned that, not only did I have a driver, I also had a bodyguard, and a personal assistant, available to me 24 hours per day. They were all impeccably dressed and groomed not to mention polite and perfectly professional.

What I saw at the ISNA convention truly opened my eyes. The conference was green. Imagine! Muslims who care about the environment? They had a "take back the tap" campaign to cut down on the quantity of plastic bottles that ended up in landfills. My gift bag, which included a prayer rug and chocolate, also contained a metal drinking bottle. Everything at the convention was recycled. One young speaker,

Ustadh Amjad Tarsin, lectured about Islam and the environment and encouraged Muslims to eat organic *halal* meat. When the convention came to a close, hundreds of brothers and sisters spontaneously started to stack chairs, sweep the floor, and clean up the convention center, something that would have been unthinkable in the past. The Tablighi Jamaat, for example, could never hold their conventions in the same place twice. They left the premises so filthy that they were always banned from ever returning. Having seen the state of the Muslim world, where decent toilets are virtually non-existent, sewage systems are lacking, and entire countries are treated as garbage dumps, I was positively impressed at how Canadian these Muslims had become. I was even inspired.

Unlike the 1980s and 1990s, most of the speakers were, dare I say it, moderate, a term I dislike as I myself am extremely Muslim. After all, why content oneself with a moderate amount of love and kindness? We should do good deeds in abundance. Over the past decades, the discourse had undeniably moved towards the middle-ground. Out of the dozens of speakers who lectured at the convention, every single one denounced extremism in one mode or another. Shaykh Ahmad Saad Al-Azhari provided an intellectual exposition on the blessings of *ikhtilaf* or difference of opinion in matters of Islam. Dr. Altaf Husain, and others, spoke openly about sensitive subjects such as mental illness, sexual abuse, racism, and sexism, topics that Muslims would not touch in decades past on the pretext that they "presented Muslims in a poor light." In the past, I myself had been shunned for merely bringing up such subjects.

I asked a young brother whether there were still crazy fanatics who wandered around mosques. "There are a few," he acknowledged, "but they are very careful about what they say." September 11th may have been a curse, increasing animosity towards Islam and Muslims; however, it was also a blessing in disguise. On the one hand, many non-Muslims became interested in learning what Islam was really about while, on the other hand, it slammed the doors shut on violent fundamentalists and die-hard fanatics. Sick of being associated with terrorists, most mosques cleaned up shop and sent the extremists packing.

The presence of women at the conference provided a great deal of hope. "You have no idea how good you have it," I told the audience. "Twenty years ago… even ten years ago, women would never have been allowed at such a convention. Had they been allowed, they would have been confined to a dirty closet." At his convention, however, half the hall was reserved for women, the other half was reserved for men, and there was even a section for families and mixed gender groups. If marrying a Muslim girl had been as unlikely as finding a Tasmanian tiger, I got the distinct impression that I could have easily married a beautiful, intelligent, Muslim woman without any of the problems I would have confronted a decade or two before when racist and tribalist Muslim clerics gave speeches telling Muslim women not to marry converts. Many Muslims appeared to have overcome their obsession with endogamy.

When I had embraced Islam in the mid-80s, I, like many, if not most, converts, lost my family and my friends. The Muslim community, however, had nothing to offer me in return: there was no support structure whatsoever. They would convert Canadian women to Islam and then tell them they had to wear hijab. The hijab inevitably led to loss of employment which, Muslims leaders explained, was not a problem because women were prohibited from working according to Islam. Professional Muslim converts were condemned to become housewives for cultural Muslim husbands or enduring the humiliation of living off of social assistance. Now, I was excited to learn, the community offered a buddy system. They had prepared a curriculum to teach new Muslims about their new faith and they paired them up with practicing Muslims who could help them integrate into the community.

If the first wave of Muslim immigrants who came to Canada in the 1970s and 1980s came with an immigrant agenda, namely, a desire to get rich quick and return to their country of origin, their children, who were born and raised in Canada, had no interest whatsoever in such plans as Canada was their country and their homeland. I had always found it profoundly offensive to meet immigrants, who were Canadian citizens, but who refused to identify as Canadians, and who insisted that they were Lebanese, Pakistanis, or Somalis. I met many of them who devoted themselves to scamming the system shamelessly, fraudulently collecting welfare under various names, and bringing over non-Canadian relatives so that they could exploit the Canadian healthcare system. I warned these misguided Muslims on many occasions: "you may wish to return to your country; however, your children will refuse to do so. For them, Canada will be their country."

As I interacted with young Muslims in 2014, this was made perfectly clear to me again and again. The young people I met identified as Canadians first and foremost. Many even played hockey! They all insisted on speaking English stating that this was the language of the land. This did not mean that they did not maintain their heritage languages at home; however, they understood that they had to operate in one of the official languages of the country: English or French. In the 1980s and 1990s, it was infuriating, as a Canadian, to attend mosques where the Imams arrogantly and defiantly insisted on preaching in Arabic, Urdu or Farsi, effectively excluding English and French-speaking Canadian Muslims. This is not to say that there are no problems in the Canadian Muslim community. There are. However, compared to the 1980s and 1990s, Muslims in Canada had come a long way and made a notable degree of progress.

By June of 2014, I was in the Netherlands, France, Belgium, Wales, and the United Kingdom, as part of the Covenants Tour organized by Radical Middle Way. I would meet hundreds of Muslims from all walks of life, many of them converts, and many of them children of Muslim parents who were born in the West, and found that we all shared a great deal in common. For starters, we all rejected extremism in all of its manifestations. We were also deeply committed to the future of Islam in the West and to the cause of social justice, tolerance, and co-existence. We also shared the same love for traditional Islam.

If some Muslims were Salifized, Wahhabized, and Takfirized by Saudi propaganda during the 1970s, 1980s, and 1990s, a movement devoted to disseminating traditional Islam had emerged and had made notable advances among certain sectors of the Muslim community. In the 1980s and 1990s, there were so few traditional Muslims that we felt like the last of the Mohicans. Now, we were not only in the hundreds, we were in the hundreds of thousands. This, my fellow friends, believers, and foes, provided me with a great deal of hope for the future of Islam in the Western world. "The Sun will rise from the West," foretold the Prophet Muhammad. I am convinced that the Sun symbolizes Islam and that true Islam, original Islam, traditional Islam, and civilizational Islam will surge from the West and reconquer the lands of East, if not militarily, at least spiritually.

APPENDIX 1:
THE COVENANTS INITIATIVE

The Covenants of the Prophet Muhammad with the Christians of the World was published in October of 2013. The work brings to light a series of treaties that the Messenger of Allah concluded with the Christian communities of his time. These documents, many of which were rediscovered in obscure monasteries and collections, uniformly state that Muslims are not to attack peaceful Christian communities, rob them, stop churches from being repaired, tear down churches to build mosques, or prevent their Christian wives from going to church and taking spiritual direction from priests and elders. On the contrary, the Prophet commands Muslims to actively protect these communities "until the End of the World." Inspired by this ground-breaking book, Charles Upton conceived of the Covenants Initiative, an international movement of Muslims to protect the People of the Book, which invites Muslims to subscribe to the theory that these covenants are legally binding upon them today. The heart of the Covenants Initiative is the following Declaration:

> *We the undersigned hold ourselves bound by the spirit and the letter of the covenants of the Prophet Muhammad (peace and blessings be upon him) with the Christians of the world, in the understanding that these covenants, if accepted as genuine, have the force of law in the sharia today and that nothing in the sharia, as traditionally and correctly interpreted, has ever contradicted them. As fellow victims of the terror and godlessness, the spirit of militant secularism and false religiosity now abroad in the world, we understand your suffering as Christians through our suffering as Muslims, and gain greater insight into our own suffering through the contemplation of your suffering. May the Most Merciful of the Merciful regard the sufferings of the righteous and the innocent; may He strengthen us, in full submission to His will, to follow the spirit and the letter of the covenants of the Prophet Muhammad with the Christians of the world in all our dealings with them. In the name of Allah, Most Gracious, Most Merciful. Praise be to Allah, the Cherisher and Sustainer of the worlds.*

Any Muslim who wants to sign this Declaration or learn more should visit www.covenantsoftheprophet.com

APPENDIX 2:
THE GENOCIDE INITIATIVE

We, the undersigned, call upon all political powers: beyond all questions of political affiliation, and in the true spirit of human solidarity and decency, to categorize the crimes being committed by ISIS and other Takfiri terrorists against Christians, Twelver Shiites, Ismailis, Alawis, Sufis, traditional Sunnis, and others, as acts of religious, cultural, and ethnic genocide.

Before ISIS, all religious denominations stand in the line of fire. Christians and Muslims know only too well the bitterness and despair of a life spent under the ominous flag of Takfirism--a heretical perversion of Islam, also known as Wahhabism, which reared its hideous head a mere two centuries ago. Evil has a new face and it is Takfirism! Doing nothing while millions of lives are at risk is tantamount to murder. We owe it to our children to carry on this fight so as to prevent the shadow of our shameful inaction from falling on future generations.

Before the threat of Wahhabi-inspired radicalism the world can no longer afford to stand on the sidelines--the enemy needs to be engaged on all fronts: ideologically, through the denunciation of its nefarious dogma; religiously, through the coming together of people of all faiths; politically, militarily, financially ... everything conceivable must be done and no effort should be spared.

We demand that local, regional, and international powers act decisively to neutralize ISIS and other Takfiri terrorists by cutting off their legs from under them--systematically dismantling their networks, whether financial, political or religious.

While we remain committed to peace, local populations have the right to defend themselves; and we have a duty of care towards them. Therefore, concerted efforts, in keeping with international and territorial sovereignty, should be made to combat this evil by all means necessary.

We urge political and economic powers to freeze all bank accounts of ISIS and other Takfiri terrorists; to seize their assets; and to prosecute any and all who provide material support to genocidalist war criminals.

We further urge these powers to do all they can to determine how the black market trade in oil, drugs, arms, art treasures and enslaved human beings that ISIS and other Takfiri groups rely upon to fund their efforts can be interrupted and brought to a halt, and how anyone involved in any aspect of this trade, as either seller or buyer, can be prosecuted under existing laws.

We challenge all international organizations, human rights groups, intelligence agencies, national security agencies, law enforcement agencies, and military forces to coordinate their efforts to locate, arrest, indict, try, and convict any and all parties responsible for supporting ISIS and other Takfiri terrorists in any form or fashion, including, but not limited to, financial, military, strategic, political or ideological assistance. We call upon members of the legal profession to determine how the perpetrators of these crimes can be indicted under existing laws, including but not limited to those against criminal conspiracy, hate speech, and providing aid to the enemy in time of war.

Finally, we demand that any and all parties who have supported ISIS and other Takfiri groups, in any form or fashion, be labeled as war criminals guilty of genocide.

Any Muslim or non-Muslim who wants to sign this statement should visit https://www.change.org/p/all-political-players-the-genocide-initiative

APPENDIX 3:
EDICT AGAINST ISIS

"My Mercy prevails over My Wrath," says Almighty Allah in a sacred saying (narrated by Bukhari, Muslim, Nasa'i and Ibn Majah). For Takfiri terrorists like IS, the so-called "Islamic" State, it is wrath that prevails over mercy. When asked to curse the polytheists, the Messenger of Allah, peace and blessings be upon him, responded that "I was sent as a mercy" (Muslim). If anything, the rapists, torturers, and mass murderers who have infiltrated Syria, Iraq, Libya, Egypt, Pakistan, Afghanistan, Somalia, Nigeria, and other parts of the world, can only be seen as a curse, the likes of which have not been seen since the Mongol invasion of Genghis Khan in the 13th century.

While Islam does indeed permit jihad, in the form of armed struggle, to combat certain oppressive conditions, it is highly regulated by a detailed code of norms and conduct. The killing of non-combatants, civilians, women, children, imams, priests, monks, nuns, and other members of religious orders, is categorically prohibited in Islam. Torture, rape, and the trafficking of women are all crimes which merit capital punishment under Islamic law. The Prophet Muhammad, peace and blessings be upon him, forbade Muslims from sacking sacred sites and places of worship, stating that anyone who destroyed a church or a monastery would receive the curse of Almighty Allah.

IS, ISIS, ISIL or Daesh is a terrorist, mercenary, army at the service of imperial forces. They do not speak for Islam or represent Islam in any shape or form. To describe such psychopaths as Sunnis is to insult the Sunnah. To describe Daesh as "Islamic" is an insult to Islam. The only terms that adequately describes the ideology of these demons is Takfiri, Wahhabi, Khariji, and Nasibi, Excommunicators, Wahhabis, Separatists, and Haters of the Household of the Prophet. While they call themselves jihadists, they pervert the term jihad or sacred struggle. While they call themselves Salafi, followers of the pious predecessors, they are an offense to the true Salaf, the righteous Companions and their Followers.

As Almighty Allah, glorified and exalted be He, warns in the Holy Qur'an, "Do not exaggerate in your religion" (4:171), a verse that can also be translated as "Do not be fanatical in your faith." The Qur'an also warns believers to "Beware of extremism in your religion" (5:77). In short,

Muslims are supposed to be "a justly balanced nation" (2:143). Although some scholars may argue that the reproach against extremism contained in the Qur'an applies only to the People of Book, the Prophet, peace and blessings be upon him, explained that it was equally applicable to Muslims. In fact, he warned his followers to "Beware of extremism in your religion for it is that which destroyed the nations which came before you" (Nasai and Ibn Majah). In another tradition, he stated that "The religious extremists are destroyed" (Muslim and Abu Dawud). The Messenger of Allah, may Allah bless him and grant him peace, also warned: "There are two groups of people from my Ummah who will not receive my intercession: oppressive rulers, and religious extremists" (Tabarani).

The Messenger of Allah, peace and blessings be upon him, was confronted with extremists during his lifetime, fanatics that he himself rejected and excommunicated saying that they did not belong to his Ummah or Community. As the Prophet Muhammad, may Allah bless him and grant him peace, said, "The Kharijites are the dogs of Hell" (Ahmad, Ibn Majah, and al-Hakim). He also warned his future followers that the Horn of Satan would rise in the Najd, the very region in Arabia where the Wahhabi heresy took hold a mere two hundred years ago (Bukhari). As Imam 'Ali, may Allah be pleased with him, advised in Nu'aym ibn Hammad's *Kitab al-Fitan* or *Book of Tribulations*,

> When you see the black flags, remain where you are and do not move your hands or your feet [namely, "Stay put and do not get involved in the fighting"]. Thereafter there shall appear a feeble folk to whom no concern is given. Their hearts will be like fragments of iron. They are the representatives of the State (*Ashab al-Dawlah*). They will fulfill neither covenant nor agreement. They will invite to the truth, though they are not from its people. Their names will be agnomens [i.e., Abu So-and-so], and their ascriptions will be to villages. Their hair will be long like that of women. [They shall remain so] till they differ among themselves, and then Allah will bring forth the truth from whomever He wills.

It should be noted, however, that Takfiri combatants are not committed Muslims. In reality, they are all mercenaries. Large numbers of them are non-Muslim soldiers of fortune and guns-for-hire, and many are drawn from the criminal class. "Allah is Beautiful and loves beauty," says the Prophet Muhammad, may God bless him and grant him peace (Muslim). Takfiri terrorists, however, are hideously ugly. "Allah is good and only accepts that which is good," said the Messenger of Allah, peace and blessings be upon him (Muslim). Takfiri terrorists, however, are devoid of good. Since "Allah is Just and loves justice," and "Allah is Loving and loves love," the true representatives of Islam are *Ahl al-Hub* and *Ahl al-'Adl*, the People of Love and the People of Justice. As Almighty Allah warns in the Holy Qur'an: "Do not commit evil in the land for God does not love the evil-doers" (28:77).

Takfiri terrorists, such as ISIS/ISIL/IS, as well as al-Qaedah, al-Shabab, the Taliban, al-Nusrah, Boko Haram, and other criminal organizations, do not speak for Islam or represent Islam. Not only are they not *Ahl al-Sunnah* (Sunnis), they are not members of the Ummah (Community) of Muhammad, peace and blessings be upon him, as a result of their own beliefs and actions. The Takfiriyyin, (those who believe that all Muslims, save themselves, are infidels), the Khawarij (those who broke away from the community in the early days of Islam, accusing both the Sunnis and the Shiites of apostasy) and the Nawasib (those who hate the Household of the Prophet and their followers) are agents of the enemies of Islam.

We do not condemn the Takfiris as "infidels who may be legally killed" as they do in the case of traditional Sunnis, Shiites, and Sufis. The traditional Muslim sharia does not grant *carte blanche* to kill someone simply because he or she is an atheist, an agnostic, a Jew, a Christian, a Hindu, a Bahai or a Salafi-Jihadi. As Almighty Allah warns in the Qur'an: "Whosoever kills a human being unless it be for manslaughter or for mischief in the land, it shall be as if he had killed all of humanity" (5:32).

Although people cannot be condemned to death on the basis of their beliefs, they can be killed in combat or receive the death penalty on the basis of their actions. Consequently, any and all terrorists who have committed crimes against humanity and the Divinity should be brought to justice. And while Shimr may have murdered Imam Husayn, the grandson of the Prophet, peace and blessings be upon him, the true culprit was Yazid, his Commander in Chief, may the curse of God be upon him. Likewise, while Takfiri terrorists should be held accountable for their crimes, those who founded them, funded them, armed them, trained them, and supported them, in any form or fashion, should be exposed and face the sword of justice.

The so-called "Islamic State" should be known as the "Satanic State" as it does nothing but spread corruption on earth (*fasad fi al-ard*). Territory under the control of Takfiri terrorists is the abode of unbelief (*kufr*), falsehood (*ifk*), heresy (*ilhad*), and immorality (*fawahish*). They represent the path of error (*sirat al-d, alala*), the pulpit of discord (*minbar al-khilaf*), the den of iniquity (*'arin al-ghawayyah*), and the land of criminals (*dawlat al-mujrimin*). The Takfiris are the enemies of Allah and

His Messenger (*'adu Allah wa rasulihi*). As such, it is categorically prohibited to support them in any form or fashion. Moreover, it is the obligation of all Muslims from *Ahl al-Sunnah*, *Ahl al-Tasawwuf*, and *Ahl al-Bayt* (the Sunnis, the Sufis, and the Shiites), to oppose the polytheism (*shirk*), hypocrisy (*nifaq*), apostasy (*irtidad*), and schism (*shiqaq*) that the Takfiris are spreading throughout the lands of Islam.

The only people authorized to establish the Government of God on Earth are the Mahdi and Jesus, the Son of Mary, peace be upon them both. As we anxiously await their rise, we must stand for peace and justice, uphold Islamic ethical values, defend human dignity, and respect and preserve human life. Do not be deceived during these times of trials and tribulations (*fitan*). People who rape, torture, mutilate and murder civilians, non-combatants, hostages and prisoners of war are not Friends of Allah (*'awliyya' Allah*). People who destroy places of worship and sacred sites, who burn churches and blow up mosques with copies of the Holy Qur'an still in them, are not Friends of Allah. People who violate the teachings of the Qur'an, the Sunnah, the sharia, and the Covenants of the Prophet Muhammad, peace and blessings be upon him, are not the Friends of Allah. If anything, they are the Friends of Satan (*'awliyya' al-Shaytan*). As Muslims, our response towards terrorists can only be one: "Fight the friends of Satan" (Qur'an 4:76); "And slay them wherever you may come upon them, and drive them away from wherever they drove you away for tumult and oppression is even worse than slaughter" (Qur'an 2:191).

In light of the non-Islamic character of the Takfiris and their role as agents of western and globalist imperialism against Islam, Muslims should find it easy to see through their absurd claim to be "defenders of Islam!" In light of the great deceptions of these times, lets us pray--in the words of the Prophet Muhammad, peace and blessings be upon him--"O Lord, show me things as they really are."

APPENDIX 4:
WHAT SHOULD MUSLIMS SAY TO DONALD TRUMP?

Introduction

Since some of you attending this conference today clearly belong to the Muslim faith, I feel it is appropriate for me to compare and contrast Donald Trump, who has called on his followers to take an oath of allegiance to him personally, with the Prophet Muhammad, who received the Pledge of Allegiance from his followers under the Tree at Hudaybiyyah. I beg the believers in both the Messenger of Money and the Messenger of God to bear with me with patience and forbearance as I expound upon the radical differences between the respective ideologies and personal qualities of these two messengers.

Language

The Prophet Muhammad preached to the people in the language of the people, in Classical Arabic, and presented to the people, the Qur'an, a masterpiece of eloquence, unparalleled and unsurpassed, that set the standard for Arabic grammar. Donald Trump also speaks in the language of the people, at about the level of a fourth-grader, though he does indeed have a very good brain. When it comes to vocabulary, he has been well-advised by paleo-conservatives and closet Klansmen. He has attentively watched, read, and studied the speeches of such masters of semantic simplicity as Adolf Hitler, Benito Mussolini, and Francisco Franco. When appealing to angry, frightened people without the background or the resources to understand exactly who or what is destroying them, 20th century history has proved that radical simplifications and recognizable scapegoats are definitely the way to go.

Wealth and Wisdom

As the Prophet Muhammad taught Imam 'Ali: "There is no greater wealth than wisdom." But all the wisdom in the world cannot buy you the Trump Tower—or even a cup of coffee for that matter. Donald Trump seems to believe that his billions are proof that he is a wise man, but he can only make the equation between wisdom and money by reducing wisdom to "the art of the deal," to something that requires only insight into human greed and fear. But there is a lot more to wisdom than that. Specifically, in terms of what it takes to be President of the United States, wisdom includes a knowledge of history, an understanding of different human cultures and psychologies, and a willingness to make hard and painful decisions tempered by enough human compassion to prevent the holder of that office from turning into a mad dog. Can anyone here imagine Donald Trump as a person capable of conducting the kind of "delicate diplomatic negotiations" that JKF did during the Cuban Missile Crisis?

Wisdom is also inseparable from human dignity because it is based on a true understanding of what a human being is. The Prophet Muhammad, his wives and his companions—unlike Donald M. Trump and some of those closest to him—were models of modesty and self-respect. The leader who has no interest in maintaining his own dignity can never respect or protect the dignity of the people he leads. Power without dignity has a fatal flaw in it; it will either crack under pressure or go to work destroying everything it sees.

Humility

The Prophet Muhammad taught that "Humility increases dignity… Be humble and Allah will exalt you." He said: "Indeed, the most beloved of you to me and the nearest of you to my position on the Day of Judgment are the best of you in nature and in humility; and the furthest of you from me are the vainglorious, that is the arrogant." He also warned that "Most of those who go to hell are the arrogant." Donald Trump, however, is proud, haughty, and arrogant: qualities that are unfortunately admired by many Americans whose pride in their nation has been betrayed by the globalists, whose future has been stolen by the super-rich, whose human rights have been liquidated by the national security state, and who have been told by the regime of "political correctness" that they have no right to exist. But the arrogance of the self-styled billionaire will never translate into the well-earned self-respect of a hard-working American husband or wife or parent. Self-respect comes from the love of family, the love of community, the love of country, the love of justice and the love of God, not the arrogance of the hate-monger or the threats of the bully.

Non-Violence and Just War

The Prophet Muhammad was persecuted for professing that God was one and that people should be good. Although he was oppressed, exiled and physically wounded by his enemies, and his followers assaulted, tortured, raped, starved, and murdered, he taught them to turn the other cheek. He said that: "The strong man is not the one who is the best at fighting; the strong man is the one who can control his anger." And when the time came to fight to throw off oppression and establish justice, that battle was not to be carried on in a state of anger, or simply as a way of relieving one's feelings, but according to the strict standards of just war. On the other hand, Donald Trump said (and I quote): "If we're attacked, we'll beat the shit out of them... We have to beat the savages." And given his often-expressed views on Blacks, Mexicans and Muslims, I think I have a pretty good idea who these "savages" are.

Civil Society

The Servant of Allah, Muhammad the son of 'Abd Allah, immigrated to Medina, as a refugee, with many of his followers. The people of Medina, a town that was roughly half Jewish and half pagan, accepted him as their leader. Muslims, at that time, numbered in the hundreds. The non-Muslims were probably in the tens of thousands. The first thing that the Prophet Muhammad did in Medina was prepare the *Covenant of Medina*, known also as the *Charter* or *Constitution of Medina*. He created an Ummah, a Motherland, or a State. Identity was no longer based on tribe or kinship. It was based on citizenship. "They are one community" said the Prophet Muhammad. "To the Jew who follows us belong help and equality," he wrote, "He shall not be wronged nor shall his enemies be aided." As the Prophet said, "The Jews...are one community with the believers." Jews, Muslims, and even polytheists, were one: so long as they were members of the Ummah. Some scholars view Muhammad as the founder of secularism. Others, like myself, stress that he created a Confederation of Believers, a pluralistic and inclusive society under the cover of the Creator. He granted citizens all the rights and freedoms that we enjoy in Western, secular, democracies, with one fundamental difference: that these rights were bestowed, not by Man, with a capital M, but by God, with a capital G.

But Donald Trump, as he has repeatedly expressed, does not believe in civil society. He does not believe in diversity and multiculturalism. He wants to make America great again which means he wants to make America white again. But America was never "lily white" as Trump likes to believe. There were millions of Black slaves before the Civil War, and—before the white race came—millions of Native Americans, as there are again today. But Blacks will never again be reduced to slavery, nor will Native Americans ever again submit to genocide. And we must never forget that the Prophet Muhammad accepted people of all races into his Ummah; Bilal, one of his closest companions and the first muezzin, was a freed Black slave. As the Prophet expressed so eloquently:

> All humankind is from Adam and Eve, an Arab has no superiority over a non-Arab nor a non-Arab has any superiority over an Arab; also a white has no superiority over a black nor does a black have any superiority over white except by piety and good action.

For Donald Trump, however, there is no room for Muslims in America. According to his supremely uneducated opinion we are a source of insecurity, we have never contributed anything to the building of this country. However, maybe 10% of the Black slaves imported into North America, who built much of the economic power of the nation, were Muslims. Some sources suggest that as many as 20 to 30% were Muslims. (We must be careful never to let Trump find this out, however, or he might decide to start *exporting* their descendants.)

Setting aside the pseudo-scholarly fantasies of people who believe that my people, Native American people, were actually *Arab Muslims*—they insult us, and themselves too, with their condescending, paternalistic, fairy tales—Muslims have helped build and shape this nation from the 1800s to the present, starting with the Syrian-Lebanese settlers and homesteaders who settled in North and South Dakota. Traveling Muslim traders were also an important presence in the newly-settled West. There are nearly 3 million Muslims in the United States. Some sources say 5 million. Some even claim 7 million. One quarter of them are African Americans. How can less than 1% of the population pose such a threat in the eyes of the majority? They themselves are under a much greater threat from hate speech and hate crimes. Muslims are among the most highly educated Americans. Muslims are some of the most entrepreneurial people in this country. We do not take jobs. We create jobs. We start businesses.

We have excelled in every imaginable field. Is this any reason to boycott Muslims and ban them from entering the United States?

"If you cannot guarantee that there is no terrorist among them, then none of them should be allowed entry" says Trump. Really, now? In that case, we should ban men from entering America. Yes, ban men. The last time I checked most rapists were men. 18% of women are sexually assaulted, at some point in their lives, by men. Hence, following Trump logic, we should ban men. After all, how can be guaranteed that no man who immigrates to the United States will sexually assault a woman. We cannot. So, ban them all.

Freedom of Religion

The Prophet Muhammad protected and defended religious liberty: "To you your religion and to me mine" (109:6). In the proverbial words of the Holy Qur'an: "Let there be no compulsion in religion" (2:256). He granted Covenants of Protection, and Charters of Rights and Freedoms, to Jewish, Christian, and Zoroastrian communities. He personally protected the Christians of Najran, the Monastery of St. Catherine in the Sinai, the Monastery of St. Macarius in Egypt, and the Monastery of St. George al-Humayrah in Syria. He protected the holy sites in Jerusalem and placed them under the guardianship of the Armenian Orthodox Church. He protected the Christians of Persia. He protected the Zoroastrians. And he protected the Jews in northwestern Arabia. In the *Covenant of the Prophet Muhammad with the Christians of Najran*, the Messenger of Allah says:

> I commit myself to support them, to place their persons under my protection, as well as their churches, chapels, oratories, the monasteries of their monks, the residences of their anchorites, wherever they are found.

He also adds:

> It is not permitted to remove a bishop from his bishopric, a monk from his monastic life, or an anchorite from his vocation as a hermit.

Donald Trump, however, is committed to closing mosques, in clear violation of the *American Constitution* and the *Universal Charter of Human Rights*, both of which grant freedom of religion.

I have no objection to closing Salafi/Wahhabi/Jihadi/Takfiri mosques, though only if sedition and conspiracy and incitement to terror can be proved against them by due process of law. Mr. Trump, however, should beware of sweeping generalizations.

According to the FBI, only 0.001% of self-professed Muslims are terrorists. They have the passive support of maybe 7% of Muslims. So for Trump to deliberately alienate and potentially radicalize the moderate Muslim majority of the United States is a policy of sheer madness—unless it is his real plan to incite civil conflict in order to build his power, at which point we are no longer in the field of madness but in the field of evil.

Some Trump supporters have openly voiced their support for placing American Muslims in internment camps, as they did with Japanese Americans, for "reasons of national security." This would not be anything new to us Muslims. After all, we suffered a boycott and were placed in what was effectively a concentration camp outside of Mecca for three years where we stood steadfast alongside our beloved Prophet. These were the Years of Sorrow. We remember them, and, if Trump has his wicked way, we are soon to relive them.

Torture

The Prophet Muhammad, may God grant him prosperity in the Hereafter, prohibited torture. The Christian world kept torturing people until recent centuries. Drowning witches. Burning people at the stake. Quartering them with horses. Who am I kidding? The Western world still tortures people today. It is called "extraordinary rendition." It is called Abu Ghraib. It is called Guantanamo Bay. It is called state and federal prison. Muhammad, however, said that: "He who tortures in this life will be tortured in the hereafter."

Trump however, may God grant him prosperity in this life and poverty in the Hereafter, has declared: "Torture works"—an idea which has been discredited as a method of gaining reliable intelligence by many studies—though if Trump's real goal is to destroy civil and human rights and replace them with collective terror, then he is certainly right: *torture works*. Speaking of torture, he callously stated that: "Waterboarding is fine with me." Well, if that is the case, then may he be waterboarded for eternity in the next world. Amen.

God is watching, Mr. Trump. God is listening. And, if you do not believe in God, there is something called in the International War Crimes Tribunal in The Hague. Your statements concerning torture can and will be used in a court of law in the event you are accused of committing war crimes.

Retaliatory Assassinations

The Messenger of Allah, Muhammad, the son of 'Abdullah, forbade the killing of non-combatants. Apparently ISIS terrorists missed that class—but little can be expected from a group that is home to so many drug-addicted drop-outs, mercenaries and criminals. As you have heard, over and over again, the Qur'an is clear on the subject: "Whosoever kills a human being for other than murder or corruption on earth, it shall be as if he had killed all of humankind" (5:32). In the instructions given by the Prophet; in the instructions given by Abu Bakr; in the instructions given by 'Ali, Muslim soldiers were formally and categorically prohibited from killing non-combatants.

Trump, however, has come with a new Talmud, a new Gospel, and a new Qur'an... Yes, he has come with a new Halakhah, a New Canon Law, and a New Sharia: "I would intentionally kill families to defeat ISIS." Retaliatory killings. A crime against humanity. A war crime. Islamic law and international law both allow the killing of combatants. They do not, however, permit the targeting of non-combatants. "No bearer of burdens will bear the burden of another" (35:18), says the Qur'an.

We cannot punish Trump for the fact that his father was reportedly a Klansman. If U.S. law followed Trump's principles, which we do not, then he most certainly would be. Trump believes in pre-emptive strikes for reasons of national security—and many Americans fear that he is making himself the potential target of a pre-emptive strike.

Trump knows perfectly well that he cannot deliver on 99% of his promises, which means that he is going to make some of his supporters very, very, angry when they realize he has sold them out, as he already has done at the recent AIPAC convention where he pandered to the Zionists. So we have to be extremely careful to preserve the life of this reckless and dangerous man; his assassination could have dire consequences for the whole nation. Muslims definitely do not want Trump dead—though some of them would apparently like to see him in an institution for the mentally, morally, and ethically insane.

Oath of Allegiance

Last, but not least, the "Prophet" Trump proposes that all American Muslims should be entered into a registry. And not only that, the Messenger of Materialism proposes that all American Muslims be made to take a loyalty oath to the United States of America. However, no government, no candidate for office, no non-Muslim entity or individual has the right to demand that Muslims, specifically *as* Muslims, perform this or that action, or adhere to this or that belief. U.S. Muslims are bound by the sharia, by same the civil laws that apply to all U.S. citizens, by their conscience, and by nothing else. As Muslims, as Americans, we are all bound to the American Constitution.

As immigrants, millions of Muslims have pledged allegiance to the United States to become citizens. Our children, on a daily basis, pledge allegiance to this country. No way, no how, are we going to be forced to pledge allegiance specifically as Muslims to prove that we are loyal to this country. We refused to be targeted in such discriminatory fashion. We refuse to be scapegoated. We reject the implication that we are not faithful Americans. We refuse to apologize for crimes that we have not committed. We refuse to be forced to prove our loyalty when we prove our loyalty already on a daily basis, living in this country, developing this country, contributing to this country, and taking up arms to defend this country. There are 5000 Muslims bearing arms for the United States. Tens of thousands of Muslims have served in the US military. Show them some respect whether or not you agree with US foreign policy.

I propose that we respond to Donald Trump's call for a loyalty oath to the U.S. Government with a loyalty oath to the Prophet Muhammad, in the form of the Covenants Initiative, where Muslims swear to obey Muhammad's command not to rob or vandalize peaceful Christian communities or kill peaceful Christians. We agree that there are scattered ISIS supporters among U.S. Muslims and that they need to be identified— but since we do not have the resources of the FBI, our contribution to this effort is the Covenants Initiative. After all, Muslims are much more likely to tell the truth when swearing allegiance to the Prophet on the Qur'an than when pledging loyalty to the Federal Government on the Bible. Here is our oath:

> *We the undersigned hold ourselves bound by the spirit and the letter of the covenants of the Prophet Muhammad (peace and blessings be upon him) with the Christians of the world, in the understanding that these covenants, if accepted as genuine, have the force of law in the* sharia *today and that nothing in the* sharia, *as traditionally and correctly interpreted, has ever contradicted them. As fellow victims of the terror and godlessness, the spirit of militant secularism and false religiosity now abroad in the world, we understand your suffering as Christians through our suffering as Muslims, and gain greater insight into our own suffering through the contemplation of your suffering. May the Most Merciful of the Merciful regard the sufferings of the righteous and the innocent; may He strengthen us, in full submission to His will, to follow the spirit and the letter of the covenants of the Prophet Muhammad with*

the Christians of the world in all our dealings with them. In the name of Allah, Most Gracious, Most Merciful. Praise be to Allah, the Cherisher and Sustainer of the worlds.

Any Muslim who wants to sign this oath or learn more about the Covenants Initiative may go to www.covenantsoftheprophet.com. We urge all U.S. Muslims to sign, in the few remaining months before the general election, though we pass no judgment on those who do not; acts are judged by their intent, and we have no special insight into the reasons people make the choices they do. We only wish to emphasize that the opportunity to choose has arrived. Besides being eminently newsworthy as a bold Muslim challenge to Donald Trump, this loyalty oath to the Prophet Muhammad will have three visible effects:

1) The Covenants Initiative Oath resoundingly declares our unbending opposition, as Muslims, to ISIS and other Takfiri terrorists, but does so without committing us—as Muslims—to any specific U.S. government policy, or asking us to bow to the demands, or the threats, of any popular leader, or expecting us to surrender our freedom of religion to any government on earth. Like all other American citizens, Muslim Americans have the right to exercise individual freedom of choice as to which policies we will support, which leaders we will follow, and which candidates we will vote for.

2) The Covenants Initiative Oath opens the door not simply to ceremonious expressions of mutual amity between Muslims and Christians, expressions with no teeth in them and little relevance to conditions on the ground, but to the possibility of real, working alliances between the religions in the face of a common enemy. This enemy has many faces: ISIS and other terrorists, who are happy to kill Muslims as well as Christians; Islamophobia; Christophobia; the slander of Christ in the media; the slander of Muhammad in the media; the burning of mosques; the burning of churches. When a mosque is burned, why can't Christians come out in support of Muslims? When a church is burned, why can't Muslims come out in support of Christians?

3) The Covenants Initiative Oath is the best way we can think of to respond to whatever good there may be in Donald Trump's proposals, while uncompromisingly discrediting his unconscionable attacks on freedom of religion, his irresponsible statements that have gone a long way toward legitimizing hate crimes against Muslims in this country.

We Muslims have all we need from our own religion and tradition to brand ISIS and the other Takfiris as the devil-worshippers they are. Instead of trying to meet some mark that secular culture sets for us—a culture that can only play the less-than-convincing role of guardian of human rights and civic virtue when matched against the worst criminals on earth—we need to recover, hopefully with the help an interested and open-minded media, our own supremely humane and civilized standard of what it is to be a human being. All we need to do then is act on it.

Muslims are coming out against ISIS all over the world. 70,000 Muslim clerics signed a mass fatwa against the "Islamic State" in India. 1.5 million Muslims have endorsed it. In Morocco, leaders and delegates from many Muslim nations have recently met to issue the Marrakesh Declaration, reaffirming the rights of non-Muslim religious minorities. In the United States, Daisy Khan of Wise Muslim Women is producing an anti-ISIS community guide for mosques, and working with Google to interrupt ISIS recruiting in cyberspace.

Will Donald Trump credit any of these efforts? Is he even aware of them? Or would he rather see U.S. Muslims with no alternatives but to descend into terrified silence or drift into an equally terrified sympathy with the "Islamic State"? If he pleads ignorance of these efforts, we would be happy to educate him; the same offer goes for all the presidential candidates, Democratic, Republican or Independent.

If any candidate is foolish and short-sighted enough to reject the growing opposition to ISIS coming from Muslims themselves, then such a person does not deserve to be President of the United States. But if the candidates are willing to learn about our efforts and accept our help against ISIS and their ilk, who represent the worst threat to global civilization since the Nazis, the Stalinists and the Khmer Rouge, then we are more than willing to give it. But whatever decision they may make regarding us, we of the Covenants Initiative and its allies have already made *our* decision: ISIS must be stopped—and so must Trump.

In Closing

The times of trials and tribulations have fallen upon us in the midst of the Great Apostasy of the Western world. During these dark days, a "prophet" has arisen, a "prophet" by the name of Donald Trump. And he is a false prophet. He is a false messiah. He will not lead the people to the Promised Land. Nay! He will lead them to death and destruction in the desert, while he retreats into his personal empire of properties and holdings and acquisitions.

Donald Trump is simply the face of a new fascist movement in the United States. In the 1960s this country was a primarily white, Anglo-Saxon, Christian nation. By 2016, a seismic shift had occurred, with minorities gradually becoming the majority and Christianity being replaced with secular liberalism. The silent majority, namely, white conservatives, who represent half of this nation, have been marginalized. They were convinced, for generations, to support country-club Republicans, people from Old Money, in the hope that wealth would trickle down. It did not and it will not. The wealthier they become the greedier they become.

Over the past decades, the one-percenters have seen their wealth increase exponentially while the income of white Americans has stagnated. The middle class, a status of stability, has disappeared. The so-called middle class is now no better off than the lower class. They live from paycheck to paycheck on the verge of homelessness. The Republicans, who were supposed to represent them, sold the country out to the obscenely rich, destroyed communities, and the country itself, through so-called Free Trade deals that only benefit multinational corporations. White, working-class, Americans are angry. We understand that. We need to understand that. They are angry for economic reasons and they are angry for religious reasons. This country, for good or bad, depending on how you view it, has undergone a shift in values that is staggering. The US is not the country that it used to be.

Noam Chomsky recently said this about the growing percentage of White Americans who are staring at the specter of poverty:

> [they are facing] the dissolution of their lives and world.... [They] are sinking into hopelessness, despair and anger—not directed so much against the institutions that are the agents of the dissolution of their lives and world, but against those who are even more harshly victimized. Signs are familiar, and here it does evoke some memories of the rise of European Fascism.

But does Donald Trump direct their anger against the system that is impoverishing them? No. He directs their anger against their fellow victims, turning White against Black, Christian against Muslim, making sure that those whose economic security and civil rights are being stolen by the global elites can never see clearly enough to unite against them. "I love the under-educated" says Trump. Why? Because he knows that the poorly-informed are easier to fool, nor does he show the slightest sign of wanting to better inform them. Tyranny loves to patronize ignorance because—like George Orwell said in his novel *1984*—ignorance is its strength.

Donald Trump nonetheless is right about a number of things. He is right when he says that the U.S. invasion of Iraq was a disaster that destabilized the entire Middle East. He is right when he says that the U.S.

was partly responsible for creating ISIS. And he is right that the U.S. immigration system needs to be overhauled to cut down on the chances of ISIS agents entering the U.S. If certain forms of immigration are now acceptable *even if they are illegal*, something is terribly wrong with immigration policy, since it creates an "official" underclass of persons who can be arrested at any time and who can be used to further erode the power of the unions, as well as providing a ready commodity for the human traffickers; anyone who wants to economically exploit or sexually abuse his or her servants or employees will find things much easier if there is a large pool of illegal immigrants available for these purposes.

BUT: When Trump proposes excluding every member of a particular religious group from the U.S.—Muslim in this case—he is dead wrong, unconstitutional, un-American, and playing with fire.

When Dalia Mogahed recently told MSNBC's Chuck Todd that Muslims should not continually be challenged to condemn terrorism—especially in light of recent statements by Trump and others—she was right. No government, no president and no presidential candidate has the right to demand that Muslims—*as* Muslims—condemn terrorism; if the federal government or any agency thereof were to make such a demand, a demand based entirely on religious affiliation, that would be a great blow to freedom of religion in this country—and anyone who thinks that such a precedent would not be turned against other religions, probably beginning with Christianity, is politically naïve and has not been paying attention. If the U.S. government can demand that Muslims take what amounts to a loyalty oath, such as Donald Trump has proposed, it can certainly demand that Christian churches support this or that social agenda or lose their non-profit status.

But there is one group who has not only the right but the duty to denounce terrorism, and that group is—Muslims themselves. The Holy Qur'an, through many *ayat*; the Prophet Muhammad, peace and blessings be upon him, in many hadiths and through his covenants with the Christians and Jews of his time; and the holy sharia well, absolutely prohibit terrorist actions against any group, just as they prohibit making any sort of war against, or misappropriating the property of, peaceful Christians, peaceful Jews, and law-abiding Muslims.

Groups such as ISIS have violated every one of these laws, rulings and commands, slaughtering Muslims as heartlessly as they have killed Christians, Yazidis and members of other religions, and in doing so have put themselves outside the Muslim fold. Consequently it is the duty of Muslims not only to renounce the methods of these bands of terrorist mad dogs who have falsely appropriated and viciously soiled the name of Islam and the reputation of our Prophet Muhammad, but to actively oppose them by any means necessary, doing all we can to see that they are exposed, defeated, and brought to justice—as if merely *making excuses* for ourselves, tremulously protesting that "we are not all terrorists," were in any way an adequate or an honorable response.

Donald Trump or Barack Hussein Obama may accuse us or defend us, may flatter us or slander us, but to us their words mean nothing; they are dust in the wind. As Americans we are bound by the civil laws of the nation in which we live, but as *Muslims*, the words of presidents and presidential hopefuls can in no way bind us: our loyalty is pledged to the Prophet, to the Holy Qur'an, to Almighty and All-Just Allah, and to no-one else. Bear witness Almighty Allah, bear witness! And bear witness Donald Trump and al-Masih al-Dajjal! I pledge my allegiance to the Prophet Muhammad. I leave you in peace at this dawn of war.

[Written by Dr. John Andrew Morrow and Charles Upton. Delivered by Professor Morrow at Rutgers University on Sunday, March 27, 2016, as part of the 9th Annual Prophet Muhammad Day Interfaith Conference organized by Muslims for Peace, Inc.]

Permissions

Morrow, John Andrew Morrow. "The Covenants of the Prophet Muhammad: A Revolutionary Revelation." Angelico Press (July 28, 2014). Copyright © 2014 by Angelico Press and John Andrew Morrow. Reproduced with permission of John Riess.

Morrow, John Andrew. "How Has a Religion of Beauty Been Presented as Ugly by ISIL?" *The National* (March 8, 2015). Copyright © 2015 by *The National* and John Andrew Morrow. Reproduced with permission of Laura Koot, Managing Editor of *The National*.

Morrow, John Andrew and Charles Upton. "Muslim Leaders Ask God to Waterboard Trump for Eternity." *Veterans Today* (March 30, 2016). Copyright © 2016 by *Veterans Today*, John Andrew Morrow, and Charles Upton. Reproduced with permission of Dr. Kevin Barrett, Editor of *Veterans Today*.

INDEX

A
Aaron: 152
'Abbasids: 52-53
Abbot: 118-119, 136
Abboud, Joseph: 57
Abboud, Peter: 66
Abdul, Paula: 57
'Abd al-Wahhab, Muhammad ibn: 71, 141, 172, 185
Abdallah, Hassan: 57
Aberdeen: 59-61, 114
Abraham: 3, 8, 16, 54, 138, 140, 142, 148
Abu Bakr: 18, 126, 138, 161-162, 172-173, 209
Abu Dawud: 13, 37, 38, 44, 80, 114, 124, 126, 132, 200
Abu al-Fida': 132
Abu Ghraib: 207
Abu Hanifah: 54-55
Abu 'Ubaydah: 132
Abu Yusuf: 126-127, 132
Academia: 147
Achtiname / ashtinameh: 108, 113, 117, 119, 152
Adab: 32, 183
Adam: 2, 3, 7-16, 23, 30, 48, 54, 80, 142
'Adhan: 163
Adultery: 10, 126-127, 160, 166, 170, 182-183, 187
Afghanistan / Afghans: 5, 73, 102, 108, 174-177, 199
Africa / Africans: 6-10, 14-24, 104, 122, 174, 181-185
African Americans: 10, 17, 20, 23-24, 48, 77, 80-81, 88-89, 122, 164, 182
Afrocentrists: 7, 14, 17, 19
Aghtamar: 138

Agnomens: 140-141, 200
Agnosticism / Agnostic: 201
Ahl al-'Adl: 201
Ahl Allah: 150
Ahl al-Bayt: 2, 31, 33, 35, 61, 85, 114, 142, 150-151, 202
Ahl al-Dhikr: 151
Ahl al-Hub: 201
Ahl al-Kitab: 120, 139
Ahl al-Shakk: 145
Ahl al-Sunnah: 71-72, 114-115, 129, 142, 150, 190, 201-202
Ahl al-Tasawwuf: 72, 142, 202
Ahmad: 10, 13, 37, 80, 105, 118, 124, 126, 200
Ahmadis: 79, 108
AIPAC: 209
'A'ishah: 18, 54, 164
Akhbaris: 42
Akhlaq: 183
Alamut: 53
Alawis: 33, 197
Albinos: 14
Algeria / Algerians: 57, 108, 115, 180
'Ali, Abdullah Yusuf: 12
Ali, Hadji: 58
'Ali, Hashim Amir: 172
'Ali, Imam: 2, 14, 18, 44, 54, 85, 87, 140-141, 200, 203, 209
'Ali, Maulana Muhammad: 12
Ali, Noble Drew: 7
Alosh, Mahdi: 66
American-Arab Anti-Discrimination Committee: 60
Amharic: 17
Amin, Muhsin al-: 26, 33, 40
'Amiyyah: 65
Amrus: 132
Andalus: 18, 20-21, 53, 104

Angels: 1, 2, 68
Anka, Paul: 57
Antidote: 103, 188
Anti-Semitism: 71, 89, 160
Apostasy / apostates: 102, 114, 128-129, 201-202
'Aqidah: 172
Arabic: 1, 12-13, 18-19, 42, 48-50
Arabs: 5, 9, 16-20, 22-23, 42, 57-61, 64-65, 67, 74-75, 84, 89, 93, 109, 169, 174-175, 183
Aramaic: 84
'Askari, Imam Hasan al-: 39
Arberry, AJ: 12
Ardabili, Ahmad ibn Muhammad: 31
Ark of the Covenant: 10
Armageddon: 115
Armenia / Armenians: 17, 42, 103, 117-118, 131-132, 149
Arranged marriages: 162, 166-167
Asad, Muhammad: 12
Ashura: 31, 33-35, 38-41, 43, 45, 54
Assemani: 132
Assimilation: 65
Assyria / Assyrians: 103, 120, 129, 131-132
Atheism / atheists: 145, 150, 201
Attrition: 65
Australia: 49
Austria: 50
Awrah: 181
Aylah: 120
Azadari: 40, 43, 45
Azerbaijan: 31-32, 37, 42
Azeris: 5, 56
Azhari, Ahmad Saad al-: 192
Aztecs: 68
Azzam, 'Abdullah: 124, 126, 177

B
Badawi, Abduh: 19
Badawi, Jamal: 190
Baghdad: 37, 40
Baghdadi, Abu Bakr al-: 141, 150

Bahai: 201
Bahira the Monk: 136, 145
Baker, Peter: 59
Baku: 32
Baladhuri: 132
Baqir, Muhammad al-: 2, 21, 44
Bar Hebraeus: 132
Barcelona: 181
Batin: 72
Bayhaqi: 3, 38, 44, 49, 124
Beards: 172
Beheadings: 97, 108
Belgium: 188, 194
Berbers: 9, 16-17, 19-22
Bible: 2, 8, 11, 15, 77, 79, 123, 187
Bid'ah: 32, 40, 71, 156, 174, 178, 185
Bikinis: 168
Bilal: 24, 183, 206
Bill of Rights: 139
Bin Laden, Osama: 124, 150, 177
Birth control: 158
Biruni: 11
Bishops: 109-110, 118, 128
Black Shiism: 43
Black flags: 140-141, 200
Black market: 197
Blacks: 9-11, 16, 18-19, 23-24, 81, 184, 205
Blatty, William: 57
Boko Haram: 102, 108, 140, 201
Book of Revelations: 19
Bosnia / Bosnians: 175-177
Brainwashing: 187
Brampton: 161, 171
Britain / British: 37, 58, 73
Brothel: 165
Buddha / Buddhism / Buddhists: 92, 123, 128, 163, 188
Bukhari: 11, 13, 44, 86, 106, 110, 114, 126, 199, 200
Burma / Burmese: 123
Burstad, Kristen: 66
Byzantine Empire: 137

C

CIA: 38, 45, 156, 175, 191
CSIS: 175
Canada: 49, 82, 84, 88, 99, 104, 106, 160, 162, 174-182, 185, 188, 190-194
Cannibalism: 127
Canon Law: 97
Carter, Jimmy: 143
Catalan: 181
Catechism: 97
Catholic Church: 142, 187
Catholics: 97, 122
Caucasians: 14, 16-18, 22, 88-89, 165, 184
Cave of Moses and Muhammad: 152
Cedar Rapids: 59
Celts: 17
Centennial Exhibition: 58
Chador: 75, 168
Change.Org: 133, 198
Charter of Rights and Freedoms: 139, 182
Chaucer: 64
China / Chinese: 49, 53-56
Christ: 115, 202
Christophobia: 211
Christmas: 108, 151, 157, 184
Church of Nubia: 22
Churches: 108, 110-111, 115, 118, 120, 127, 131, 138-139, 142, 195, 202, 211
Chávez, Hugo: 191
Chomsky, Noam: 212
Civil War: 206
Civilians: 47, 99, 115, 123-124, 140, 175-177, 199, 202
Clay: 11-14
Clitoridectomy: 168
Clubbing: 165
Cole, Juan: 31
Colonialism / Colonialists: 98, 106, 120, 122, 138
Communism / Communists: 38, 56, 112, 176
Compulsion: 111, 120, 139
Condoms: 168
Confederation of Believers: 119, 154
Constitution of Medina: 101, 117, 119, 136, 139, 154, 205
Converts / Reverts: 9, 19, 20, 24, 75, 83, 88-90, 156, 158, 160, 165-167, 169, 172, 175, 184, 186, 188, 193-194
Cook, Michael: 148
Coptic Church / Copts: 22, 131
Corporatocracy: 143
Cortés, Julio: 12
Covenants Initiative: 130, 133, 195, 210-211
Covenants Tour: 194
Cree: 104
Crimes against humanity: 133-134, 201
Critical thinking: 51-52, 70, 72, 76, 92, 121
Crone, Patricia: 148
Crucifixion: 111, 115, 125, 127
Crusades / Crusaders: 120, 125, 138
Cuban Missile Crisis: 204
Cubans: 176
Cuckolds: 165, 167, 170

D

DNA: 16-19, 22
Daesh: see IS
Dajjal: 215
Dan Fodio, Usman: 23
Dar al-Fitnah: 189
Dar al-Islam: 189
Darijah: 67
Darimi: 51, 80
Daschle, Tom: 61
Da'wah: 53, 88
Dawlah: 140-141, 200
Defense Language Institute: 97
Democracy: 137, 143, 205
Deobandi: 97
Deodorant: 179
Devil-worshippers : 211

Dhikr: 72, 151, 157
Dhimmi: 126
Dialogue: 93, 132, 142, 191
Diapers: 184-185
Dictators: 90, 95
Diplomacy: 43, 134
Discrimination: 7, 19, 184
Dogs: 83, 141, 147, 167, 186, 200
Domestic violence: 179-180
Dominionists: 122
Drugs: 165, 197
Dubai: 169

E
Eagle: 118, 136
Earth: 1-3, 13
Egypt / Egyptians: 16, 22, 40, 58, 66, 93, 103, 108, 118, 149, 157, 199
Elijah: 152
Endogamy: 193
English: 48-50
Environment: 24, 65, 191-192
Eritrea / Eritreans: 17
Esau: 11
Esposito, John: 190
Ethics: 54, 76, 92, 143, 159, 173, 176, 183
Ethiopia / Ethiopians: 10, 17-18
Ethnicity: 5, 6, 23, 61, 123
Etiquette: 76, 173
Eurocentrists: 8
European Parliament: 134
Europeans: 16-18, 88, 120
Excommunication: 71, 112, 114, 140, 156, 199
Extraterrestrials: 1-4
Extremism / extremists: 31, 33, 44-46, 99, 103, 112, 135, 143, 153, 158, 172-173, 177, 188, 192, 194, 199-200
Eye for an eye: 130

F
FBI: 108, 112, 175
Fadlullah, Muhammad Husayn: 6, 27-30, 35, 39-40, 70
Fahd, King: 90
Fard, W.D.: 7, 9-11, 24, 79-81
Farr, Jamie: 57
Farrakhan, Louis: 7, 24, 77, 79, 81
Fascism / fascists: 131, 148, 154, 160, 212
Fatimah: 54
Female genital mutilation: 168
Final Sermon: 6
First Nations: 68, 104-105
Fitnah: 150, 180
Flatulence: 173
Flutie, Doug: 57
Forensic linguistics: 63
Forgeries: 139
Fornication: 128, 164, 166, 182, 187
Founding Fathers: 143
France: 83, 90, 138, 188, 194
Free Syrian Army: 111
Free Trade: 212
Freedom of expression: 28, 92-94, 150
French: 48, 50, 59, 61, 65-68, 82-84, 104, 122, 160, 169, 172, 179, 181-182, 184, 193-194
Fushah: 67

G
Gabriel: 100, 118
Gandhi: 118
Garvey, Marcus: 7
Genesis: 11
Genocide Initiative: 130, 133, 197-198
Genocide: 133-134, 197-198
George, Jeff: 57
German / Germany / Germans: 48, 50, 57, 59, 65, 73, 83, 90, 123, 138, 160
Ghana: 9, 188
Ghazali: 3, 71
Ghulat: 31, 36, 42-43, 45
Ghusl: 171
Gibran, Khalil: 57
Glickman, R.J.: 68

Gnosis / Gnosticism: 28, 33, 55, 72
Goebbels, Joseph: 122
Golden Calf: 152
Golden Rule: 140
Gospel: 79, 86, 122
Great Apostasy: 212
Great Spirit: 68
Grigor: 132
Guantanamo: 207
Guatemalans: 176
Gucci: 62
Gulf War: 183
Guyana / Guyanese: 162, 184

H
HIV: 37
Hair removal: 169, 172
Hajj: 48, 88
Halakha: 97
Halal: 36, 40, 47, 71, 75, 149, 156-157, 186, 192
Halaqah / Hala-cult: 177-178
Ham: 14
Hamadani: 11
Hamidah: 20-22
Hamidullah, Muhammad: 12
Hamzah: 10
Hanbalis: 153, 170
Hanukkah: 108, 209
Hatred: 89, 111, 122, 135, 143, 157, 189-190
Hawass, Zahi: 16
Hawenneyu: 68
Hawzah: 5, 6, 7, 27, 69, 149
Hayek, Salma: 57
Hazaras: 5
Hebrew: 11, 16, 84, 85
Heinz-Ohlig, Karl: 148
Hell's Angels: 166
Heresy / heretics: 71, 125, 129, 200-201
Hijab: 29, 97, 158, 164-165, 167, 168, 180-181, 193
Hijrah: 137, 151, 177
Hilali, Muhammad al-: 12
Hinduism / Hindus: 43, 89, 92, 128, 169, 187-188, 201
Hira, Mount: 72
Hiroshima: 123
Hitler, Adolf: 71, 143, 160, 203
Hockey: 193
Homestead Act: 59, 60, 178
Homo sapiens: 2-3
Homosexuality: 123, 163
Horn of Satan: 200
Hui: 53
Hulul: 81
Human rights: 139, 180-181, 198
Husayn, Imam: 10, 32-34, 37, 39-41, 43, 54, 201
Hussein, King: 90
Hygiene: 162, 171
Hypocrisy / hypocrites: 10, 51, 62, 78, 86, 90, 134, 153, 157, 167, 202

I
Ibn 'Abbas: 3
Ibn 'Abd al-Barr: 49
Ibn Abi Waqqas, Sa'd: 53
Ibn Adam, Yahya: 132
Ibn al-'Amid: 132
Ibn 'Arabi: 71
Ibn al-'Athir: 132
Ibn Hammad, Nu'aym: 200
Ibn Hawqal: 132
Ibn Hibban: 80
Ibn Hisham: 132
Ibn Ishaq: 132
Ibn Kathir: 3, 132
Ibn Khaldun: 11
Ibn Majah: 38, 44, 80, 199-200
Ibn Manzur: 12
Ibn Qutaybah: 10-11
Ibn Taymiyyah: 71, 118
Ibn Thabit, Zayd: 85
Ibn Yusuf, Ahmad: 132
Idris, Abdalla: 190
Ihtiyat: 39, 70
Ijtihad: 6, 49
Ikhtilaf: 192
'Ilm al-rijal: 62

Immigrants: 42, 58-60, 65, 82-85, 90, 107, 160, 165, 174, 184, 193
Imperialism / imperialists: 38, 93, 98, 104-106, 120, 122, 138, 199, 202
Infidels: 28, 43-45, 71, 75, 102, 114, 120, 125, 141, 156, 160, 167, 173, 201
Innovation: 32, 35-37, 40, 71, 93, 154, 156, 172, 174, 177-178, 185
Interdimensional beings: 1
Interfaith movement: 103, 114, 130, 131, 135, 154
Internment camps: 154, 208
Intolerance: 75, 101, 110-112
Inuit: 68, 104
Ireland / Irish: 17, 57, 104, 122
'Irfan: 28, 72, 105
IS / ISIS / ISIL / Daesh: 73, 98, 108, 114-115, 122-135, 140-141, 153, 197-202, 208
Isfahan: 138
Isfahani, Abu al-Hasan al-: 33-34
Islam, American: 90
Islamic songs: 185
Islamists: 101, 107, 128, 156, 160, 175-177, 180, 184
Ismailis: 53, 55-56, 197
ISNA: 133, 191
Isidore of Seville: 14
Israel / Israelis: 11, 17, 123, 152, 160
Israeli Defense Forces: 123
Isra' and *Miraj*: 151

J
Jacob: 11
Jahiz: 11
Jami Mosque: 152
Japan / Japanese: 50, 123, 154, 188
Japheth: 14
Jesus: 3, 8-9, 16, 20, 84, 115, 122, 140, 148, 151, 202
Jifri, Habib 'Ali al-: 106, 129, 191
Jinn: 1, 3, 68, 162-163

Jizyah: 110
Johnson Reed Immigration Act: 58
Jolly, Hi: 58
Jordac, George: 87
Jordan / Jordanians: 61, 134, 159, 172, 179
Josephus: 14
Judaism: 11, 20, 123, 129, 140, 142, 150, 187, 188
Jurists: 27-28, 34, 51, 69, 79, 98, 169-170, 172

K
Kafir / *Kuffar*: 114, 120, 156, 160, 186
Kahlo, Frida: 169
Kaka'e: 133
Kalisch, Sven: 148
Karabagh: 32, 42
Kasem, Casey: 57
Kashif al-Ghita, Muhammad: 33
Kashmir: 56, 89
Kazim, Imam Musa al-: 20-22
Kennedy, John F.: 204
Khadijah: 152
Khalifa, Rashad: 12
Khamene'i, 'Ali: 5, 26-30, 34-36, 40, 70
Khan, Daisy: 212
Khan, Genghis: 199
Khan, Muhammad Muhsin: 12
Kharijism / Kharijites / Khawarij: 21, 114-115, 128, 141, 149-150, 153, 190, 199-200
Khatib: 49
Khomeini, Ruhullah: 27-28, 30, 34-36
Khu'i, Abu al-Qasim al-: 5, 26, 28, 36
King, Jr. Martin Luther: 118
Kirakos: 132
Kissinger, Katie: 15
Ku Klux Klan: 122, 128, 160, 203, 209
Kubraviya: 55
Kuhl: 179

Kurdistan / Kurds: 42, 133-134

L
Lane, Edward William: 12
Las Vegas: 169
Latinos: 19, 81, 88-89, 112
Lebanon / Lebanese: 33, 40, 43, 59
Levant: 18, 58, 103
Lewis and Clark: 61
Libya / Libyans: 73, 199
Lightner, Candy: 57
London: 169
Loyalty oaths: 209-211

M
Madrasa: 97-99
Maghreb: 21, 23, 53, 180
Mahdi, Imam: 20, 23, 78, 81, 202
Malaysia: 99, 175, 188
Malik: 12, 86
Manitou: 68
Maqnah: 120
Mardin: 138
Mari ibn Sulayman: 132
Marja: 6, 34, 70
Marrakesh Declaration: 212
Martyrdom: 39-40, 42-43, 47, 54, 151, 173, 176
Masihis: 120
Masturbation: 39, 164
Mas'udi: 11, 14, 132
Mawdudi: 72
Mayas: 68
McAuliffe, Christa: 57
McGovern, George: 61
Mecca: 8, 55, 89, 136
Melanin: 14-15
Mercenaries: 73, 97, 115, 141, 201
Messiah: 20, 78, 81, 115
Mexicans: 205
Michif: 104
Mini-skirts: 168
Misogyny: 76, 118, 181
Missionaries: 5, 21, 54, 88, 97
Mithraism: 43
Mogahed, Dalia: 214

Mohammed VI, King: 90
Mona Lisa: 76
Monasteries: 110-111, 118, 120, 127, 131, 136, 138-139, 142, 195
Mongolia / Mongols: 53, 199
Monsanto: 146
Morals: 76, 126, 143, 155, 173, 176, 179
Morocco / Moroccans: 16-18, 23, 58, 64, 67, 143, 169, 181, 188
Moses: 8-9, 11, 16, 20, 54, 84, 136, 140, 148, 152
Mosque of Fatimah: 152
Mottahedeh, Roy: 31
Motzki, Harald: 148
Mufid, Shaykh al-: 132
Muhammad, Elijah: 7, 9, 24, 79, 81
Muharram: 30-46
Mujahidin: 174, 177
Multiculturalism: 80, 84, 137, 179
Muqaddasi: 11
Music: 156-157, 185
Muslim Registry: 154
Mussolini, Benito: 203
Mustaches: 172
Mut'ah: see temporary marriages
Métis: 104

N
Nader, Ralph: 57
Nagasaki: 123
Najaf: 27, 33-34, 42
Najd: 200
Najis / Najasat: 37, 171, 184
Najmah: 21-22
Nakash, Yitzak: 33
Narjis: 24
Nasa'i: 44, 199
Nasibi / Nawasib: 128, 150, 153, 190, 199, 201
Nasr, Seyyed Hossein: 190
Nasser, Jacques: 57
Nation of Islam: 24-25, 77-81, 89
Native Americans : 206
Navar, Ramita: 38

Nazis: 154, 160
Nektarios of Sinai: 132
Nestor: 136
Netherlands, The: 188, 194
Nevo, Yehuda: 148
New Julfa: 138
Nezahualcóyotl: 68
Nicaraguans: 176
Nifaq: 202
Nigeria / Nigerians: 9, 73, 102, 110, 199
Night Journey: 151
Nimatullahi: 55
Noah: 3, 14, 54
Non-combatants: 47, 118, 124, 175, 199, 202
North Dakota: 57, 59, 60-61
Nuns: 110, 199

O

Obama, Barack: 215
Orfalea, Paul: 57
Organic: 192
Orientalism / Orientalists: 5, 12, 19, 146, 148
Orwell, George: 212
Otipemisiwak: 104
Ottomans: 31, 119

P

Pagans: 37, 92, 136-137, 150, 153
Palestine / Palestinians: 18, 58, 60-61, 118, 140, 151, 159-160, 171-172, 176, 179
Pedophilia: 117, 128, 164
Penrice, John: 12
People of the Book: 109-110, 120, 131-133, 138-139, 152, 154, 195
Philandering: 165
Philippines: 175
Philips, Bilal: 156
Picasso: 76
Pickthall, Muhammad Marmaduke: 12
Pimps: 165, 183

Pogroms: 123
Political correctness: 204
Polytheism / polytheists: 68, 71, 115, 119, 161-162, 169, 199
Pooya Yazdi, Mehdi: 3
Popul Vuh: 15
Pornography: 128, 163
Possession: 184
Prayer beads and rugs: 156
Priests: 110, 118, 124-125, 131, 136, 139, 157, 195, 199
Propaganda: 99, 122, 160, 194
Public washrooms: 159, 170-171
Puin, Gerd: 148

Q

Qaedah, al-: 97-98, 102, 108, 114, 123, 126, 128, 140, 174, 201
Qajar: 42
Qalqashandi: 132
Qama zani: 35, 45
Qaribullah, Hasan: 12
Qarni, Uways al-: 41-42
Qazwini, Muhammad Mahdi: 33
Qizilbash: 31, 42
Qum: 5, 20, 24, 26
Quota Act: 58

R

RCMP: 175
Racism: 5-6, 24, 75, 80, 84, 89-90, 122, 137, 143, 160, 184, 192
Radical Islam: 142, 177, 184, 189
Radical Middle Way: 194
Ramadan: 97, 108
Razi, Fakhr al-Din: 132
Red Shiism: 43
Reformation: 95
Religious Authority: 70
Republicans: 213
Reverse colonialism: 82
Reviving the Islamic Spirit: 106, 190-191
Reynolds, Gabriel Said: 148
Rida, Imam 'Ali al-: 20-22, 44
Rippin, Andrew: 148

Robbie, Joe: 57
Rodwell, JM: 12
Rumi: 71
Rushdie, Salman: 175, 185
Russia / Russian: 50, 131, 163, 174

S
STDs: 166
Sabbath: 128
Sabean-Mandeans: 133
Sabikah: 22
Sadiq, Imam Ja'far al-: 3, 10, 21-22, 44, 147
Sahak: 132
Said, Edward: 57
Saint Catherine's Monastery: 136-138, 152, 207
Salafism / Salafis: 71-73, 82, 89, 108, 112, 114, 126, 141, 150, 154, 156, 163-164, 168-169, 173-174, 179, 185-186, 188-189, 196, 199, 201
Salawat: 72
Sale, George: 12
Salibis: 120
Salih: 152
Salvadorians: 176
Samanah: 23
Samuel: 132
San people: 15
Sarwar, Muhammad: 12
Saudi Arabia / Saudis: 18, 71, 73, 84, 90, 156-157, 162, 169, 172, 175, 188, 194
Scaliger Pacifique de Provins, René de l'Escale: 132
Scandinavians: 17
Sebeos: 132
Secularism / Secularists: 101, 129, 145, 150, 195
Seert: 138
Segregation: 7, 80, 182, 184
Selim: 119
Seminary: 5-7, 20, 22, 26-27, 69, 87, 149
Senate: 60-61, 134

September 11th, 2001: 73, 111, 176, 192
Sergius: 145
Sex: 10, 128-129, 163-164, 166, 170, 180-183, 187
Sexism: 89-90, 137, 143, 192
Sexual abuse and assault: 115, 117, 120, 124-125, 128-129, 163-164, 176, 183, 199, 202, 206-207
Shabab, al-: 102, 201
Shakespeare: 67
Shakir, M.H.: 12
Shakir, Zaid: 190
Shakira: 57
Shalhoub, Tony: 57
Shamanism: 42
Sharia: 32, 43, 72, 97, 115, 117, 123, 127, 154, 177, 182, 195, 201-202, 209
Shariati, 'Ali: 43
Sheba, Queen of: 17
Shimr: 10, 201
Shishani, Abu 'Umar al-: 141
Siachen: 56
Sikhs: 42
Simonopetra Monastery: 138
Sinai, Mount: 136-137, 152
Sinjar, Mount: 134
Sionita, Gabriel: 132
Sioux Falls: 59-60
Sistani, 'Ali al-: 26-29, 70
Skeptics: 145, 148
Slaughterhouse: 160
Slavery: 7, 110, 126, 129, 176, 183, 206
Socialism / Socialists: 31, 176
Socrates, Spiro: 12
Solomon: 17
Somalia / Somalis: 18, 73, 90, 102, 166, 168, 173-175, 179, 193, 199
South Dakota: 59-60, 114
Soviet Union / Soviets: 37
Spanish: 48, 50, 57, 65-66, 82, 115, 131

Sperm / Semen: 10, 29, 169-170
Spiritual burnout: 167
Sudan / Sudanese: 9, 23
Sufism / Sufis: 42, 55, 71-72, 75-76, 82, 89, 108, 112, 115, 142, 144, 150, 152, 185, 197, 201-202
Suicide bombings: 47, 112, 173, 175-176
Sun will rise in the West: 194
Sunnism / Sunnis: 71-73, 76, 89, 112, 150, 154
Sununu, John: 57
Superiority: 80, 137
Supreme Court: 139
Surat, India: 138
Swimming: 168
Switzerland: 83
Synagogues: 131-132, 138-139
Syria / Syrians: 18, 58

T
Tabarani: 10, 44, 200
Tabari: 10, 14, 118, 132
Tabligh: 87
Tablighi Jamaat: 160-161, 192
Tabriz: 42
Taharah: 169-171
Tahrif: 42, 86-87
Tajiks: 5, 55-56
Takfir / Takfirism / Takfiris: 73, 111-116, 128-129, 142, 150-151, 155-156, 164, 186-187, 190, 197, 201-202
Takim, Liyakat Ali: 70
Taliban: 98, 102, 123, 128, 140, 201
Taqiyyah: 68
Taqlid: 28, 34, 69-70, 172
Tasmanian tiger: 192
Tatbir: 35, 40, 45
Tawhid: 81, 162, 172
Teddy bears: 162-163
Tehran: 37
Temporary marriages: 165-166, 179
Ten Commandments: 128, 154
Terrorism / Terrorists: 73, 96-99, 102, 108, 110-112, 115-116, 123-125, 127-130, 173, 175-182, 186-188, 191-192, 197-202, 207
Thanksgiving: 108
Thomas, Danny: 57
Thomas, Marlo: 57
Thune, John: 61
Tiffany: 57
Tirmidhi: 10, 38, 44, 86, 106, 124, 126
Toilet paper: 146, 170, 178
Tolerance: 89, 101, 103, 110, 112, 117, 120, 143, 194
Torah: 79, 86, 123
Toronto: 106, 156, 171-174, 182, 190-191
Torture: 93, 117, 159, 185, 199
Trafficking: 199
Transsexuals: 170
Translations: 12, 74
Treaty of Friendship: 58
Trump, Donald: 99, 203-215
Tuareg: 16
Turkey / Turkish / Turks: 18, 31, 42, 58, 83, 138, 176
Turkmen: 133
Tusi, Nasir al-Din al-: 11
Tutankhamen: 16
Twelve Tribes of Israel: 11, 152
Twelvers: 31, 34, 36, 42, 44-45, 53, 55-56, 69, 71, 197

U
UAE / United Arab Emirates: 188
UK / United Kingdom: 83, 90, 99, 188, 194
Ulama: 6, 32, 51-52, 105-106, 166, 183
'Umar: 126, 173
Umayyads: 10, 20, 54
UNESCO: 50, 108
UN / United Nations: 133-134
United States / US / USA: 49, 57-61, 73, 82, 88, 93, 99, 112, 130, 134, 139, 142-143, 175, 188
Uncle Tom: 51, 106

Universal Declaration of Human Rights: 139
Universe: 1, 3
University of Toronto: 68, 149, 172
Upton, Charles: 195, 215
Urdu: 82-84, 89, 193
Urination: 171, 173-174, 184-185
Usulis: 43, 149
'Uthman: 53, 115, 173
Uyghur: 53, 55

V
Vernet, Juan: 12
Vietnam / Vietnamese: 123
Virgin Mary: 166
Volker, Adam: 31-33

W
Wahhabism / Wahhabism: 89, 97, 111-112, 114, 125, 128, 141-142, 150, 154, 156, 162-163, 169, 172-174, 184-188, 190, 194, 197-200
Wahshi: 10
Wakan-Taka: 68
Wales: 194
Waqidi: 132
War crimes: 123-124, 133-134, 204
Waraqah: 145
Washington Territory: 59
Washington, George: 57-58
Waterboarding: 207
Welfare / Social Assistance: 160, 177, 193
Well of Moses: 152
West, The: 7, 9. 20, 23-24, 64-65, 73, 77, 82-85, 88-90, 105, 107, 115, 141, 160, 174, 180-181, 184, 191, 194
Whites: 6, 8-11, 13-15, 17-21, 23, 68, 75, 78, 80-81, 158, 164-166, 179, 184, 212-213
Women: 10, 17-18, 21, 28-29, 39, 47, 54-55, 75, 78, 81, 89, 97, 99, 104, 108, 115, 118, 120, 124-125, 129-131, 136, 139-141, 150, 157-160, 164-170, 176-177, 179-182, 192-193, 199-200
World Cat: 48
World heritage site: 108
Wudhu: 171

X
X, Malcolm: 8, 9, 23, 89, 183

Y
Yahya, Abdul-Karim: 191
Yakub: 10
Yawning: 173
Yazdanism: 42
Yazidis: 153, 214
Ya'qubi: 10, 132
Years of Sorrow: 207
Yohanes: 132
Yusuf, Hamza: 190

Z
Zahir: 72
Zanjir: 45
Zappa, Frank: 57
Zaydism / Zaydis: 53, 54
Zayn al-'Abidin, Imam 'Ali: 41, 55
Zaynab: 41
Zionism / Zionists: 107, 160, 209
Zogby, James: 57
Zombies: 115

Islam began in exile and will end in exile; blessed are those who are in exile.

—The Prophet Muhammad